James Halliday is A... writer. Over the pas... many hats: lawyer, ... wine judge, wine con... ..., journalist and author. He has discarded his legal hat, but actively continues in his other roles, incessantly travelling, researching and tasting wines in all the major wine-producing countries. He judges regularly at wine shows in Australia, the UK, the US, South Africa and New Zealand.

He lives in the Yarra Valley with his wife Suzanne, overlooking Coldstream Hills vineyards, and continues as an active consultant to Coldstream Hills (which he and Suzanne founded in 1985). Previously, while living in Sydney, he was co-founder with two other lawyers of Brokenwood in the Hunter Valley.

James Halliday has written or contributed to over forty books on wine since he began writing in 1979 (notable contributions include the *Oxford Companion* and *Larousse Encyclopedia of Wine*). His books have been translated into Japanese, French and German, and have been published in the UK and the US as well as Australia.

His most recent works include *Classic Wines of Australia and New Zealand; An Introduction to Australian Wine; Wine Atlas of Australia and New Zealand* and *Collecting Wine: You and Your Cellar*.

Co-founder of the wine website, www.winepros.com.au, Halliday is proving to be as popular on the World Wide Web as he is in other media.

Also by James Halliday

Wine Companion (annual publication)

Classic Wines of Australia and New Zealand

An Introduction to Australian Wine

Wine Atlas of Australia and New Zealand

Collecting Wine: You and Your Cellar

JAMES HALLIDAY'S
wine Odyssey

A year of wine, food and travel

HarperCollinsPublishers

HarperCollins*Publishers*

First published in Australia in 2003
by HarperCollins*Publishers* Pty Limited
ABN 36 009 913 517
A member of the HarperCollins*Publishers* (Australia) Pty Limited Group
www.harpercollins.com.au

Copyright © James Halliday 2003

The right of James Halliday to be identified as the moral rights author of this work has been asserted by him in accordance with the *Copyright Amendment (Moral Rights) Act 2000* (Cth).

This book is copyright.
Apart from any fair dealing for the purposes of private study, research, criticism or review, as permitted under the Copyright Act, no part may be reproduced by any process without written permission.
Inquiries should be addressed to the publishers.

HarperCollins*Publishers*
25 Ryde Road, Pymble, Sydney NSW 2073, Australia
31 View Road, Glenfield, Auckland 10, New Zealand
77–85 Fulham Palace Road, London W6 8JB, United Kingdom
2 Bloor Street East, 20th floor, Toronto, Ontario M4W 1A8, Canada
10 East 53rd Street, New York NY 10022, USA

National Library of Australia Cataloguing-in-publication data:

Halliday, James 1938-.
   James Halliday's wine odyssey: a year of wine, food and travel.
   ISBN 0 7322 7831 7.
   1. Halliday, James, 1938- – Diaries. 2. Halliday, James, 1938- – Journeys. 3. Wine writers – Australia – Diaries. 4. Wine and wine making. 5. Wine tasting. I. Title. II. Title: Wine odyssey.
641.22092

Cover design by Gayna Murphy, HarperCollins Design Studio
Cover photographs from Masterfile and Getty Images
Internal design by Judi Rowe, Agave Creative Group
Internal photography by James Halliday; except month openers from Southlight Photo Agency
Maps on page xiii by Margaret Hastie, Ikon Graphics
Film by Colorwize Studio, Adelaide, South Australia
Produced by Phoenix Offset on 115gsm Matt Art

5 4 3 2 1   03 04 05 06

There is one person beyond all others whose forbearance and support allows me to spread my wings so frequently. Suzanne, too, lives a very busy life, but is always ready and willing to support me when I need it most. To her my special thanks.

Contents

Prologue	xiv

January

Yarra Valley	2
New York	2
Tasmania	4
Tasmanian Wines Show	5
Fly Fishing, Tasmanian Lakes	8
Tasmanian Wines Show Dinner	9
The *2003 Wine Companion* Tasting Grind	10
Yarra Valley	11
The Weather Warms — Slightly	11
Grape Growing: Agonies and Ecstasies	12

February

A Day of Heat	18
A Night of Rain, the Threat of Hail	18
Escape	18
Coopers	18
Frankland Estate International Riesling Tasting, Sydney	19
Florence, Italy	22
The Shrine of Coco Lezzone, Florence	24
Chianti Classico: Old World and New World	26
New Zealand	28
Auckland's Wine Society Royal Easter Wine Show	30
Yarra Valley: Cautious Optimism	31
State of Origin Challenge: Shiraz	31
The Tasting Grind: Wines and Grapes	33
Crop Estimates: The Downward Spiral	34
Wine Australia 2002, Sydney	34
The Coldest Summer Ever	34

March

Vintage: How the Best-laid Plans are Derailed	38
The Cellar Rats	39
The Infinitely Capricious Tricks of Nature	41
Hanging Rock — and a New Melbourne Food and Wine Legend	43
Stonier International Pinot Noir Tasting	46
The First Day of Vintage 2002	46
Jacques Reymond: A Twist of Fate	47
Melbourne Food and Wine Masterclasses	48
Picking: Playing Tag with the Weather	49
Good Friday Breakfast, Coldstream Hills	50
The Picking Continues	51

April

Vintage: Tonne by Tonne	54
Robe and Mount Benson, South Australia	54
Vintage: On a Knife's Edge	56
Summerfield Winery, Pyrenees	57
Seville Estate, Yarra Valley	59
McWilliam's 125th Anniversary	61
Vintage: Starting to Count the Chickens	63
Geoff Merrill, Melbourne	63
Wine Australia, Sydney	64
Vintage: Wines in the Barrel	65
Melbourne	66
California: Lodi	66
A Day to Remember, Napa Valley	68
The Wine Appreciation Guild's Wine Literary Award	73
San Francisco Rhône Rangers	73
The Last Supper at Coldstream Hills	74

May

To France	78
Arrival in Monthelie	78
Ma Cuisine: My Favourite Beaune Restaurant	78
Market Day in Beaune	79
Simon Bize and La Bouzerotte	81
Photography in Burgundy	83
Hôtel Dieu, Beaune	83
Jardin des Remparts	85
Domaine Parent and La Ciboulette	86
Meursault	87
Hautes-Côtes de Beaune	90
Domaine Parent, Domaine Dujac and Domaine de la Vougeraie	92
Housekeeping and More Photography	97
Monthelie	98
Le Charlemagne	101
The Vineyards of Burgundy	102
Domaine de la Romanée-Conti	104
Domaine Armand Rousseau	106
Maison Champy	107
Bouchard Père et Fils	109
Heading South	110
La Pyramide, Vienne	110
Avignon, Southern Rhône Valley	114
Relais Saint Victoire, Aix-en-Provence	115
Nice to Corsica	116
Occupational Health and Safety, Corsica	116
Calvi to Porto Vecchio, Corsica	120

June

Domaine de Torraccia	124
Au Trou Gascon, Paris	126
Home Again, Yarra Valley	128
Yarra Valley: Wildlife	129
Tyrrell's Vat 47 Vertical, Sydney	132
Coldstream Hills Classification: The Crunch	133
Cloudy Bay, New Zealand	136
Marlborough Sound	140
Pruning, Coldstream Hills	141
More Pruning, Yarra Valley	143

July

Brokenwood, Sydney	148
Sydney and the Hunter Valley	150
Hunter Valley	151
Howqua-Dale, Victoria	152
Brisbane Hilton Food and Wine Masterclasses	153
Chablis: Laroche	155
Riesling: Vickery and Grosset	156
Perfect Pinot: Oregon, New Zealand and Australia	157
Moss Wood: Blue-blood Cabernet	158
Oporto, Portugal	159
A Century of Vintage Ports: 1963 to 1863	162
A Fast-changing Cork Industry	164
Oporto	168
Return to Australia	171
Scotchmans Hill by Helicopter	171
Tim Adams; Back to Melbourne	173
Shaw & Smith, Melbourne	174
Yarra Valley	175
Two Decades of Petaluma Coonawarra	175
Château Latour 1920 to 2000	177

August

Wine Australia, Sydney	192
Wine Australia — Yarra Valley Masterclasses	192
Flu, Yarra Valley	194
Mudgee Wine Show	194
Still Confined to Barracks, Yarra Valley	197
Xanadu Merlot Tasting, Margaret River	198
Clonakilla 1992–2001 Dinner	200
Seppelt Para Liqueur Tawny 1878–2002	201
Macedon Wine Show	202

September

Jasper Hill Thank You Lunch	208
Sommelier of the Year	209
The Judging	209
Arthurs Creek Vertical Tasting	210
Vancouver and The Million Dollar Chardonnay Challenge	212
University of British Columbia	212
Vancouver	214
Okanagan Valley	214
Opening of Nk'Mip Winery	216
Opening of Mission Hill Estate	218
Okanagan Valley: Departure	221
Yarra Valley	222
Great Australian Shiraz Challenge	222
Jacques Reymond	224
United States Part II	226

October

The Long Trip Home	230
Yarra Valley: Budburst	230
Qantas Western Australian Wine Show	231
Frankland River, Manjimup, Pemberton	232
The Top 100 Tasting	233
La Tâche Monday Table Dinner	234
Wallabies and Other Visitors	235

Yarra Valley: Still Green	236
Hawke's Bay Wine Show, New Zealand	237
Poronui Ranch, Hawke's Bay	239
Limestone Coast Wine Show	241

November

Outlook Conference, Adelaide	246
Yarra Valley: Wildlife	247
Qantas Western Australian Wine Show Dinner, Perth	248
Melbourne: St Vincents Institute of Medical Research	248
Yarra Valley: Hosting Harvey Steiman	249
Vintage Cellars National Wine Show, Canberra	250
Len Evans Tutorials, Hunter Valley	252
Yarra Valley: More Wine Tasting	260
Yarra Valley: 2002 Pinot Noir	261
Negociants Fellowship, Sydney	261

December

Playing Host, Yarra Valley	266
Launch of *Liquid Gold*	266
Tasting, Yarra Valley	266
Fire and Drought	266
Kangaroos	267
Sirromet, Gold Coast, Queensland	268
Albert River Winery	270
Sirromet Holden Racetrack	271
Seven Scenes Vineyard, Granite Belt	273
Ballandean Estate	274
Robert Channon Wines	274
Yarra Valley: The Drought Bites	275
Christmas Day	277
Yarra Valley: The Holiday Period	279
Year's End	279

ABOVE

Aerial shot of Coldstream Hills, showing the Hallidays' house, the blocks, the winery and cellar door.

RIGHT

The small town of Monthelie, where James Halliday spends a month of each year, is located near Beaune in the renowned wine region of Burgundy.

Prologue

There is no point in denying it: I am a workaholic. Some years ago Suzanne, my wife, caught me in the office on Christmas Day and observed, 'You do realise that this means you will have worked for 364½ days this year.' The serious negotiations which followed resulted in an agreement that we would have a week's holiday each year, away from wine.

This has taken us to places as diverse as the highlands of Bali, Prague, Kangaroo Island, South Africa (game parks), Turkey and Madagascar; another year, the wine-free week was traded in for two weeks in Italy, with some wine content allowed. An Arctic cruise and China are on the drawing board for 2003/2004, but it is true that 2002 slipped by without a formal non-wine week. I would like to argue that the month we spend each year in the house in Burgundy (which we own with others) should be taken into account, but Suzanne will not hear of it.

This should not be taken to imply that 2002 has been unusual. Yes, if you include New Zealand in the overseas trips category, I have been overseas nine times, but in 1999 (for example) I made fourteen such trips. When my interstate jaunts are added in, I am away from home two days in three. About 90 per cent of the mileage of my car is travelling to and from Tullamarine Airport.

In 2001, I toyed with the idea of writing a book about my experiences, supported by my own photography; with an appropriate acknowledgment to Stanley Kubrick, it was to be called *2001: A Wine Odyssey*. Too late, I realised that it would have to be written as a semi-daily diary, as events happened. So that is what I have done for 2002.

As I write these words in late December 2002, I am involved in various stages of the production of six books: I am hard at work on the *2004 Wine Companion*; at the end stages of a new book entitled *Varietal Wines*, which I will complete by New Year's Day; the second edition of the *Pocket Guide to the Wines of Australia* is about to hit the bookshelves (co-published by Mitchell Beazley and HarperCollins); the fourth book is this one, which — like the others — is to be published by HarperCollins.

Then there is the annual rewrite of the Australian section of Hugh Johnson's *Pocket Wine Book* (another chore for the Christmas/New Year break), and the sixth is another Mitchell Beazley book, still in its infancy, called *Global Wine Odyssey — Six Languages of Wine — A Winemaker's Phrasebook*. The author is James March; I am the general editor; and five very well-known winemakers, one each from France, Italy, Spain, Germany and Portugal, will supply the appropriate translations.

Apart from various magazines (*Australian Gourmet Traveller Wine*, *Harpers* and so forth) my weekly commitments to *The Australian* newspaper and the Winepros website are in a state of flux, *The Australian* likely to increase, Winepros in the lap of the gods.

I am still actively involved in Coldstream Hills, the winery which Suzanne and I founded in 1985 and which was acquired by Southcorp in 1996. A consultancy agreement assumes the equivalent of seventy days of work a year, which mainly comes during the lead-up to and through vintage. We own the house on the vineyard, perched high on the side of the Warramate Hills and with panoramic views of the Yarra Valley below. Returning here after a trip never fails to deeply stir my emotions, as I drink in the ever-changing beauty, and the evening peace and silence.

Why do I take on so much? Suzanne says I don't know how to say no, and in a way she is right. I am lucky enough to live in a free society, and no one forces me to do any of these things. There are times when I wonder why on earth I said yes, but I don't feel sorry for myself. The world of wine is a wonderful one: I am privileged to be part of it, and to have seen firsthand the evolution of the Australian wine industry from a quaint backwater to a world power.

Finally, there is the unseen hand of Paula Grey, my PA, who knows where I am even if I don't, and who (with part-time help from Beth Anthony) types every word I write or dictate. (Voice recognition software, Via Voice, is installed, and I am about to endeavour to train it, but we shall see.) Without Paula and Beth, none of this would happen.

On a different tack, I thank *The Australian* newspaper and *Australian Gourmet Traveller Wine Magazine* for facilitating the excerpts from articles written by me during the year, and which are set in a smaller typeface. All are from *The Australian* except for those on pages 132–33, 171–81 and 181–89.

January

Yarra Valley

New York

Tasmania

Tasmanian Wines Show

Fly Fishing, Tasmanian Lakes

Tasmanian Wines Show Dinner

The *2003 Wine Companion* Tasting Grind

Yarra Valley

The Weather Warms — Slightly

Grape Growing: Agonies and Ecstasies

JANUARY 1   Yarra Valley

The coolest December on record has been and gone, with only one day over 30°C, and the longest period (since weather records began) between the last day of 30° in autumn 2001 and the first in summer 2001/2, something in the order of 164 days versus the prior record of 154 days. Flowering has been a protracted and irregular affair, adding to the damage to the nascent bunches of grapes caused by one of the heaviest hailstorms in living memory, circa November 2001, which cut a narrow swathe across the lower Yarra Valley from Yarra Glen to the Warramate Hills, inflicting heavy damage on our Fernhill vineyard and some damage to Briarston. Even at this stage it is clear that yields will be way below normal, and bunch-thinning at veraison (the colour change from green to red, or to yellow for white grapes) will be essential if secondary bunches and those from the very end of flowering are to be excluded from the crop.

Maddens Lane, which had only Warramate Winery when we arrived, is suddenly taking on a new dimension. Dominique Portet is hard at work supervising the building of his new winery and cellar door and the overnight planting of the adjoining vineyard of viognier and merlot. It is strange to remember that he was looking at Maddens Lane way back in 1985 when we established Coldstream Hills, and now, sixteen years later, he has arrived like a whirlwind. The paint had barely dried before his cellar door was opened, and across the road Leon Tokar (who also supplies grapes to Coldstream Hills) has opened Tokar Estate.

JANUARY 9   New York

I am flying to New York for a lunch, which some may view as bizarre. The occasion is a lunchtime launch of a new super-premium Chilean wine from Montes, and I am curious to see firsthand the extent of the continuing impact of September 11 on New York, but even more curious to find out why a Chilean wine producer would assemble fifty journalists from all over North America and far outposts such as Australia to taste a new wine made in strictly limited quantities.

My piece for the *Weekend Australian* below provides some of the answers, but not all. The invitation came about in part following a visit to Montes Winery in Chile in 1985 by myself, Michael Fridjhon, John Platter and Lynn Sherriff. It seems I made some kind comments about a Montes Chardonnay, and that at a simultaneous tasting of chardonnays around the world organised by the amazing Italian Slow Food Organisation (some years later), a Montes Chardonnay had come first, and the 1998 Coldstream Hills had come second. It's a funny thing how the wine mafia connects around the world.

The launch lunch was held at Daniel's, said to be one of the three top restaurants in New York, and on the evidence of the main course in particular, I would not doubt that. A slow-braised short rib of beef sat alongside a piece of eye fillet cooked rare but conventionally, and there was not a person among the fifty present who would not have swapped their fillet for the short rib, which was without question the best piece of beef I have ever tasted, obviously slow-braised for hours with an extraordinary reduction which coated it the way an aspic surrounds a cold cut.

> Why would anyone invite me to travel to New York for a lunch launch of a new Chilean wine? Why would I accept? All pure folly, and punnily enough, that is exactly what the wine is: Montes Folly, the inaugural 2000 vintage selling (on strict allocation) in the United States for US$70 a bottle, and here for A$110.
>
> The absolute importance of having credible flagships is critical. The mere fact that Montes was able to assemble journalists from all over North America, including three from *The Wine Spectator*, and guests from as far afield as Japan, speaks volumes. So does the price of the two top wines; so does the fact that Montes wines are featured on the wine lists of twenty-two restaurants in Bordeaux alone. I'm willing to bet no Australian wine company could claim such recognition.
>
> But there is yet another twist: Folly is 100 per cent shiraz (or syrah, as it is — correctly — known in Chile), produced from Montes' La Finca Vineyard, formerly a decrepit pear orchard, not acquired until 1990, and with an average vine age of seven years, that of the syrah even younger.

RIGHT
From our verandah:
'House Block'
chardonnay in front,
'G Block' pinot
noir behind.

JANUARY 14 TASMANIA

Notwithstanding apocalyptic disorganisation and queues stretching for over a kilometre at Bradley International terminal in Los Angeles, I somehow or other make it onto the Qantas flight and it, despite leaving forty-five minutes late, arrives on schedule in Melbourne at 9.30 a.m. At 10 a.m. I meet Suzanne on the pavement outside the terminal, give her my New York luggage and collect the luggage I have to take to Tasmania for the Tasmanian Wines Show, of which I have been chairman since the first show, in 1991. My plane for Tasmania leaves at 11.40 a.m., and I really need to have a shower and shave in the lounge to make myself feel (or appear) half-human after the thirty hours which have elapsed since I was last in a proper bed, and it will be another twelve hours till the next bed. More significantly, judging of the show has already commenced, albeit with the less important classes; I have to pick up the judging immediately after lunch.

My fellow judges are Huon Hooke (who has judged the show with me since its inception), together with this year's international judge, Larry McKenna, who made his name as long-term winemaker for Martinborough Vineyards in New Zealand but who now has his own venture in that region and also consults to a major development on the Mornington Peninsula.

We have to judge 170 wines on each of the two days, but I have organised the schedule so that the best (and most important) classes will all be done on Tuesday. Against the odds, I function normally throughout Monday afternoon, then take part in a two-hour Pinot Noir Masterclass-type event before sixty or so people looking at top New Zealand pinots from the 2000 vintage, and then some older vintages, before proceeding on to dinner and bed.

JANUARY 15   TASMANIAN WINES SHOW

This is the big day for the show, with the sparkling wine class, the riesling classes, all the serious chardonnays and then, in the afternoon, 60 pinot noirs from the much vaunted 2000 vintage.

BELOW
Early evening on a dam beside Maddens Lane, our street.

Once again, Tasmanian riesling proves to be a class act, although it is transparently obvious that the 2001 vintage is not in the same class as the 2000, or for that matter, 1999. Strangely, the 2000 vintage chardonnays are off the expected pace, lacking focus and definition, in a reverse image of the 2001 rieslings. Nonetheless, the 2000 Meadowbank Grace Elizabeth Chardonnay is a fine wine, winning not only the Best Chardonnay trophy, but also the Vineyards Association of Tasmania trophy for the Best White Wine of Show. Craigow is the star performer in the riesling classes, winning the top gold in both the 2001 and 2000 vintages, a tribute to the exceptional feel Julian Alcorso has got for this variety. Tamar Ridge duly wins two of the three gold medals in the 1999 and older riesling class, one for each of its 1999 and 1998 wines, both made by Julian Alcorso. Julian to one side, the show is yet another testimonial to Andrew Hood's skills: he made the Top White and Top Red Wine of the Show, and wins five of the nine gold medals awarded in the utterly remarkable 2000 pinot noir class.

> There are times when I wish I had kept my mouth shut, or, more precisely, my pen in my pocket. Having championed the cause of New Zealand pinot noir for over five years, I am fearful that I may be partly responsible for the near universally held belief by the up and coming sommeliers of Australia that — in Australasian terms — New Zealand makes the only pinots worth having, with Australia's about as appealing as yesterday's fish and chips. It irritates me almost as much as New Zealand's clear supremacy on the cricket field this summer, however much I admire the sheer class, style and intelligence of captain Stephen Fleming. So there had to be some divine justice when New Zealand winemaker Larry McKenna joined Huon Hooke and myself to judge the 2002 Tasmanian Wines Show.
>
> Mind you, I had some premonition that the 60 pinot noirs from 2000 entered in class 20 of the show might turn out as they did. Two years earlier the 1998 pinots had enthralled Huon and me (we are the two old war horses returning year after year to judge the Show), and we knew that 2000 was an even better vintage: both of us had written articles extolling the quality of the mainland pinots from 2000.
>
> By the time we had finished our discussion of the class, and decided which wines were worthy of golds, I felt like shouting, 'It doesn't come

better than this.' Instead I contented myself with a slightly more restrained class comment for the results catalogue: 'An awesome class, full of magnificently structured and flavoured wines. A rare, indeed unique, privilege to judge. What more can we say, except let there be more vintages like 2000.'

Why unique? Well, in well over twenty years of show judging I have never encountered a class of this size in which only ten wines did not win a medal. I have never seen a class of this size in which twelve wines won a silver medal. And I have never, ever, seen a class of any size in which eight gold medals were awarded. And just for the record, several of the silver medals would have won gold were it not for the feeling that if that happened, no one would believe that this wasn't a children's birthday party, with everyone winning a prize.

The divine justice stemmed from the fact that Larry McKenna had been a panel chairman at the New Zealand National Wine Show a few months earlier, and had half of the 2000 pinots — 50 or so — to judge. He had thus of course joined in the discussion with the second panel to sort out the gold medals for the combined class. In New Zealand shows they divide larger classes into small sub-segments, judge each, and then the panel chairs rejudge all the top wines to determine which should gain gold and which should not.

Larry may be Australian born and bred, but there is no doubt where his wine allegiances lie: New Zealand, and, more particularly, Martinborough. But he is also as honest as the day is long, and at the Tasmanian Wines Show Presentation Dinner he had no hesitation in saying that the gold medal winners here would have blown their New Zealand counterparts away.

Top place — and three trophies, including Best Wine of Show — went to No Regrets, which started life as a Siamese twin with Elsewhere Bay of Eight. The wine (made by Andrew Hood) came from the Elsewhere Vineyard. The difference was that the No Regrets was bottled several months earlier than the Elsewhere.

No regrets, indeed.

ABOVE LEFT
Huon Hooke on the poop deck. The Zodiac raft makes life much easier.

ABOVE RIGHT
Sushi by the lakeside; trout caught one hour earlier.

JANUARY 16–18   FLY FISHING, TASMANIAN LAKES

We escape to the Central Highlands for our annual fly-fishing venture with Andrew Hood as our chief organiser and chauffeur. For the second two days we are in the care of Peter Hayes (day one) and Neil Grose (day two), two of the best professional guides in Australasia. Last year we all caught trout under their direction, but this year, while the weather is good, the trout are very elusive. By one of those strange quirks, I return with eight trout weighing between 1–1.5kg (reported in the *Launceston Examiner* as *a* trout), while Huon and Larry remain fishless (although Larry did put back two small fish). Competitive I may be, but this is over the top.

At various times during the trip the discussion inevitably turns to the most unusual summer. Neil Snare of Winstead, one of the regular members of our fishing expedition, says that his pinot noir is still flowering. Larry McKenna observes that the Antarctic ice shelf is far further north than it should be, and propounds his own theory about growing season conditions which, in New Zealand, he believes are significantly affected by the behaviour of the ice shelf, although no one else seems to recognise that fact. I return to Melbourne a few days later to hear climatologists admitting that the Antarctic is indeed cooling, but denying that this contradicts the belief in global warming, contenting themselves with saying that they need to understand more about Antarctic weather. This, no doubt, is why the

JANUARY

Polar Bird ice ship has been trapped at the height of summer. What is common to much of southern Australia, Tasmania and New Zealand is the threat of a late vintage, and in the cooler parts, a small crop.

JANUARY 19 TASMANIAN WINES SHOW DINNER

The Tasmanian Wines Show Presentation Dinner takes place at Richard Matson's small Convention Centre dining room. With some unofficial help from former chef and food consultant, Graeme Phillips, the meal is brilliantly designed and executed. The menu is simplicity itself: 2001 Craigow Riesling, 2000 Craigow Riesling, 1999 Wellington Riesling, 2000 Lake Barrington Estate Chardonnay and 2000 Meadowbank Grace Elizabeth Chardonnay are served with a dish described as 'five flavours of Atlantic salmon'. It is in fact Atlantic salmon prepared in five radically different fashions and served on the one large plate, the change in texture and weight taking us through riesling and into the chardonnays.

Squab breasts on melted Huon Valley mushrooms with pink-eye potatoes and salad leaves accompany the 1999 Pipers Brook Vineyard Reserve Pinot Noir, 2000 No Regrets Pinot Noir, 2000 2 Bud Spur Pinot Noir and 2000 Providence Miguet Pinot Noir. I don't know

BELOW

Tasmanian fishing lunch — simple food, pure pleasures.

about squab breasts; they look to me suspiciously like two half squabs sitting on top of each other, cooked in the French fashion (uncompromisingly rare), which is exactly as they should be presented. The Huon Valley mushroom is very nearly as big as the plate, all in all a spectacular and rich combination for the glorious pinots. A selection of five of the best King Island cheeses, including a blue which had been aged for a disconcertingly long time, comes with the 2000 Coal Valley Cabernet Merlot and 1999 Tamar Ridge Cellar Reserve Cabernet Sauvignon.

JANUARY 21   THE *2003 WINE COMPANION* TASTING GRIND

The pace is picking up for completion of the annual *Australia and New Zealand Wine Companion*. With 150 new wineries for Australia already entered into the system since last year's book (which is still current on the shelves, and will remain so until August) it has become clear that New Zealand must go. It's a pity, but there are several excellent annual guides to New Zealand wines written by New Zealanders, and I have never been entirely convinced that the New Zealand add-on was worthwhile.

Nonetheless, there is a relentless schedule of tasting 160 to 170 wines one day, dictating the tasting notes the next day, then back to the tasting room, and so on and so forth. Sensodyne toothpaste has long proved an indispensable help to avoid problems with teeth sensitivity, but I'm finding increasing problems with my tongue — the surface is becoming extremely sensitive to acid; it seems that the surface is literally being corroded. A partial antidote comes in the form of either baking soda, which is extremely alkaline, and which really throws my mouth chemistry right out of gear, or the gentler protection of soda water, which I swill and spit frequently during the white wine section of the tastings. The other antidote is cheese, nibbled in tiny portions before the soda water wash.

Many years ago I discovered the magic that green olives work with red wine tasting, a powerful antidote to the build-up of tannins which can bedevil you with young red wines in particular. Plain green olives, still on their stones, are by far the best; the Spanish olives are the worst; the Australian are the ticket, but it's hard to find the latter on supermarket shelves. You only need to nibble a third or half an olive at a time to completely restore the pH balance and strip out the tannins.

The other consequence of an all-day tasting is that I don't look forward to wine that evening nearly so much as to a Coopers Pale Ale.

JANUARY 22   Yarra Valley

Today, as yesterday, one might either think the end of the world was at hand, or that the Yarra Valley had been picked up and transported to Scotland. A fine mist has been falling for the past two days, the clouds so low they reduce visibility to a few hundred metres at times. This after a brief two days of hot weather on the weekend, giving us our second and third day this entire summer with the temperature over 30°C. Actually, it's not so much the absence of 30° days which worries us; it's more the cloud and drizzle. We know February will be hot (or at least we assume it will be), and the real concern here is that the vines will go into February without being hardened at all, and then be subjected to weeks of warm to hot weather. This was the pattern in 1989, followed by colder weather then rain in March, by which time the vines had had enough and the grapes were all covered in a type of grey/black aspergillus mould. We haven't seen that since, praise be, and I have no desire to see it in 2002.

JANUARY 28   The Weather Warms — Slightly

We have now had almost a week of better weather. It has been far from settled, with the temperature mainly in the 20s, but with two weekends of temperatures in the mid-30s, with thundery changes following the hot days. But at last the general pattern seems to be warming, and the thunderstorms have meant the maintenance of soil moisture. Almost nowhere has the irrigation been turned on, and whatever may come in the next two to three months, we shall have sufficient water to carry us through to the very end of the growing season. (An intensive irrigation after the grapes have been picked does wonders for the vines, helping the build-up of carbohydrate reserve for the following year.) In any event, we shall be spending all day Wednesday, January 30, going around the company vineyards and contract-growing vineyards from the upper to lower Yarra, for this is a critical time of year as we approach veraison.

JANUARY 30 GRAPE GROWING: AGONIES AND ECSTASIES

BELOW

Andrew Fleming, Coldstream Hills winemaker.

Andrew Fleming, Coldstream Hills winemaker, viticulturist Anthony Jones and I have spent the day looking at vineyards, starting with the Coldstream Hills blocks around the winery and below the house, then Briarston and thereafter Fernhill, before moving to the upper Yarra and the Deer Farm and Peggies vineyards. The home vineyards at Coldstream Hills almost entirely escaped the hail, but not the effects of the miserable December weather — prolonged and very uneven flowering. Hen and chicken (or millerandage) is rife throughout the chardonnay and pinot noir: the majority of the berries are chickens, with fewer than two seeds, which reduces their size substantially. (The amount of pulp, or flesh, is in proportion to the number of seeds: unfertilised berries are the smallest, with no seeds at all.) Given half-decent weather, what is there (a tonne to the acre or less) should produce high-quality wine, and will also afford a measure of defence against poor weather, because the grapes are bound to ripen sooner or later, and the uneven set will result in straggly bunches less liable to attack by mildew or botrytis.

The Briarston and Fernhill vineyards are a tragic sight: the canopy has now entirely recovered from the hail, and it's only when you look a little closer that you realise there is next to no crop there. Because veraison has not started, it makes it even harder to see such bunches as are there, but it seems highly improbable that there will

JANUARY

ABOVE LEFT
Sauvignon blanc at Deer Farm.

ABOVE RIGHT
Pinot gris at Peggies, used to make white wine.

LEFT
The upper Yarra: Deer Farm with a flash of afternoon sun.

be sufficient crop on all but a handful of blocks to justify picking. Moreover, the pitted canes bearing the pockmarks from the hail will be very brittle and will only permit spur pruning next year.

It's a wonderful day and Deer Farm is at its extravagantly beautiful best. The steep mountains less than 2 kilometres away, with Mount Donna Buang behind, have a deep blue smoky haze, coming not from fires but from the eucalyptus oils. The vineyards themselves are a vivid lime green, with stripes of yellow daisies running down between the rows to the mirror-like dams. I thought about bringing my camera, but decided this was a working trip, and am now bitterly regretting the decision: over the last seven years I have visited these vineyards innumerable times, but I cannot remember them ever looking more beautiful.

Once again, the happiness does not extend to the size of the crop. There have been four separate hail incidents so far this year, which the Deer Farm and Peggies vineyards have almost entirely escaped. However, here, too, the crop will be very low, thanks to similarly miserable weather during flowering, even though flowering here takes place two to three weeks later than it does on the valley floor. All the varieties are affected, none more so than merlot, a variety noted for its refusal to set properly. Thus the yield off the main block of merlot is 20–25 tonnes in a 'normal' year and 8–9 tonnes in the years in which merlot has failed to set. We shall be lucky to get that amount this year.

We've been on the go since 9.30 a.m., and it's 3 p.m. before we swing back through Yarra Junction on the way down to the Yarra Valley floor, grabbing a quick roll as we do so. Our next port of call is the very large Brooklands vineyard on the Healesville to Yarra Glen Road, the majority of which is contracted to Southcorp. It overcropped wildly last year, and we are anxious to see what the situation is this year. The vineyard is on rich, semi-alluvial soils; even though it is on gentle slopes, the soils bear none of the characteristics of the decomposed sandstone of Coldstream Hills or Briarston, being rather a souped-up version of the Fernhill soils. Alas, just when we would wish to see hen and chicken as a de facto means of crop control, on this warm valley floor site flowering has presented no problems and the berries and bunches are relatively uniform. Here we are in a cleft stick: we are anxious for every tonne of good pinot noir, but it has to be good, and this means that in all but the very best and warmest vintages, the crop must be 6 tonnes to the hectare or less.

By the time we get back, at around 5 p.m., my forearms look like cooked lobster claws, and an ice-cold beer has never tasted better.

February

A Day of Heat

A Night of Rain, the Threat of Hail

Escape

Coopers

Frankland Estate International Riesling Tasting, Sydney

Florence, Italy

The Shrine of Coco Lezzone, Florence

Chianti Classico: Old World and New World

New Zealand

Auckland's Wine Society Royal Easter Wine Show

Yarra Valley: Cautious Optimism

State of Origin Challenge: Shiraz

The Tasting Grind: Wines and Grapes

Crop Estimates: The Downward Spiral

Wine Australia 2002, Sydney

The Coldest Summer Ever

FEBRUARY 1   A Day of Heat

Yesterday it was in the high 20s in the early afternoon, and today it reaches 36°C. At this temperature vines have long ceased photosynthetic activity, which means the ripening process stalls. The vines shut down their systems by closing the stomata (in lay terms, the breathing apparatus) to protect moisture reserves. This shutdown process starts when temperatures reach the high 20s, and the hotter it gets, the more effective the closedown. So days like this do very little for ripening. However, they have one advantage: they help dry up mildew activity.

FEBRUARY 2   A Night of Rain, the Threat of Hail

Last night there was torrential rain and, in many parts of Melbourne and the suburbs, hail with stones up to the size of golf balls. There wasn't any hail at Coldstream Hills' home vineyards, but I will have to wait until Monday to find out whether other parts of the valley were less fortunate. Today we are back to the Scotch mist and drizzle which was so much part of the December weather; the clouds barely got off the ground all day. In terms of the growing season as a whole, it's not important; indeed, it will rehydrate the vines after yesterday's searing heat. And we are promised a lovely day tomorrow, calm and with temperatures in the mid-20s. The last time we had a summer with the majority of days like that was 1992, and all of the wines from that vintage, white and red, are drinking superbly, the reds (including the pinot noir) with years in front of them.

FEBRUARY 3   Escape

A sigh of relief all round: no hail damage reported.

FEBRUARY 4   Coopers

The coopers are hard at work and will be here for the better part of a week. Their job is to dismantle the barrels, shave off the inner wine-impregnated surfaces, partially reassemble the barrels with one end still open and then toast (or fire) them over burning oak chips. This completed, the missing end (or head) is put back into place and the galvanised iron hoops which bind the barrel are hammered tightly into place.

This process is in fact copied from the steps taken to make the barrel in the first place, and gives what in some respects is the equivalent of a new barrel. Thus, a barrel which has been used to make red wine can be converted back to white wine use, for example.

At Coldstream Hills, we elect to sell the barrels rather than reuse them ourselves. The reality is that the barrels (usually four years old) do not give the same result as a two- or three-year-old barrel, and certainly not a brand new one. Nonetheless, the soaring cost of new French oak barrels (all ours are French, and from the best barrel-makers in France) ensures there is a ready market for the reconditioned barrels.

FEBRUARY 5   FRANKLAND ESTATE INTERNATIONAL RIESLING TASTING, SYDNEY

I'm off to Sydney for the second day of the Frankland Estate International Riesling Tasting, which has brought to Sydney riesling producers from all the German wine regions, and the top four riesling makers from the Wachau region of Austria, along with a tidy slice of the top Australian producers. The events (which started yesterday with a major international blind tasting) are open to all comers, but the majority of those attending are in the business one way or another — if not producers, then sommeliers, retailers or company reps.

There are parallel workshops in the morning and the afternoon; I have chosen the morning workshop 'Terroir on Trial', and in the afternoon, 'Beyond Dry'.

The morning session has Toni Bodenstein, from the famous Prager Winery in Wachau, who not only runs Prager but is an expert on local geology and chairman of the Viennese Bank. His co-presenter is Reinhard Lowenstein, from Heymann-Lowenstein at the southern end of the Mosel River.

The program notes indicate that Lowenstein is renowned for his hands-off approach to making riesling, saying, 'If I sing, if I dance, if I pray, they still do what they want. Maybe there are rules, but I don't know what they are.' He is committed to allowing each vintage in each vineyard total freedom of expression, refusing to intervene under any circumstances. It has to be said that the six wines he produces from the rain-affected 2000 vintage vividly demonstrate the effects of his philosophy, and fail to fire my enthusiasm.

However, the focus seems far too specifically linked to soil type, with the spoken or unspoken implication or assertion that there can be direct translocation from components of the soil into the grape which in turn affect the flavour of the grape. This is a myth not dissimilar to the indigenous yeast myth (in the latter case, that bloom yeasts on the grapes can of themselves take wine through the full process of fermentation) and has been debunked by (among others) Professor Seguin at the University of Bordeaux, who has spent a lifetime studying the soils of Bordeaux. Seguin points out that if

RIGHT
Driving the metal hoops to tighten dry empty barrels before refilling.

there were such a translocation, you would simply analyse the trace element or mineral found in the grape, match it with that found in the soil, and you could immediately have Château Latour or Romanée-Conti or whatever.

It is, of course, true that the physical properties of any given soil have a huge influence on how the vine grows, how the grapes ripen, and — in the broad sense — how they develop character. You need to look at the oft-quoted definition of terroir coined many years ago by Bruno Prats to come close to understanding the real meaning of terroir.

Between 4.30 and 6 p.m. I chair a symposium on 'Riesling.com — Riesling in the twenty-first century', which involves everyone and has no fixed format. It takes a surprisingly long time for the Stelvin cap issue to make its appearance, and not nearly so long for Jeffrey Grosset to lose his normal cool when a retailer seeks to question the wisdom of the use of the Stelvin cap. (This is the screw-cap which is fast replacing the cork for riesling, sauvignon blanc and semillon.)

That evening a splendid tasting dinner is held at Celsius restaurant, run by Peter and Beverley Doyle. The standard of the dinner is truly exceptional, with a great menu perfectly executed and some brilliant wines. When the wake-up call comes in my hotel room early the following morning (so I can catch the plane back to Melbourne, dash home to the Yarra Valley and taste another 150 wines), I realise that even riesling can be toxic if consumed in sufficient quantities.

> Over the past twenty years, the once mighty riesling has been humbled in Australia in much the same way it has been in Germany (and international markets) for thirty years or more. In the early 1980s, more bottles of riesling were sold annually in Australia than all other white wines combined. Indeed, riesling production peaked in 1985, when 46,500 tonnes were crushed, compared with a mere 11,400 tonnes of chardonnay.
>
> Fast-forward to 2001, and the riesling crush fell to 26,980 tonnes, and that of chardonnay soared to 245,000 tonnes. Small wonder, then, that the riesling producers of the world are banding together to actively promote their cause. One significant initiative has been that of Frankland

Estate, a relatively small, family-owned and run winery in the Frankland River sub-region of Western Australia's Great Southern region.

So where is riesling headed? Ironically, Germany remains one of the toughest markets. A combination of Lewis Carroll and Edward Lear-inspired bureaucracy and the reluctance of German wine drinkers to pay more than a couple of Euros per bottle mean that a top-flight producer like Dr Loosen (from the Mosel Valley) exports 80 per cent of its production. Australia is a niche market for Germany, with strong demand for small quantities of top German wine; France, Italy and New Zealand have around 90 per cent of the import market here, Germany a little over 2 per cent.

The Austrians have no such hang-ups: like the Swiss, they happily pay relatively high prices for their own wines, and Alsace is the white wine answer to Beaujolais in restaurant lists across France.

Which leaves Australia, and here the omens are more hopeful than they have been for years. Over the past three seasons, new plantings of riesling have exceeded those of all other premium white varieties (except chardonnay). Next, riesling grape prices offered in the Clare Valley for the 2002 vintage exceed those of either shiraz or cabernet sauvignon, and seem likely to exceed the weighted average price for Adelaide Hills pinot noir. Wolf Blass says it has been unable to satisfy its need for riesling from the Clare and Eden Valleys for the past three years.

Then, by chance, only a few days before the Frankland event, Yalumba and Jeffrey Grosset announced a joint venture to create a new super-premium Eden Valley Riesling. It is Grosset, of course, who has led the way in lifting the price of top-end riesling above many premium chardonnays.

Chardonnay may be the fat lady, riesling the thin, but neither has begun to sing.

FEBRUARY 9 FLORENCE, ITALY

It has to be my lucky day. First of all, my suitcase has miraculously arrived in Florence with me, after being transferred at Singapore from QF9 to QF17, and then at Charles de Gaulle from Terminal 1 to

Terminal 2D to catch an Alitalia flight operated by Air France and subcontracted to Jet Tours or some similar name. Second, although it is 9°C, there are clear skies. Third, I am ensconced in total luxury in a suite at The Grand Hotel, with a room looking out directly over the river and up to the Ponte Vecchio. Fourth, I think I have been able to replace the gold necklace that Suzanne bought here last May, and which was ripped off her neck in Madagascar last October. Fifth, and most amazing of all, I have found a restaurant close to the Ponte Vecchio which, while thickly populated with tourists, has wonderful food. I have porcini risotto to start with, followed by chinguli (wild boar) with a bottle of 1998 Castello di Ama. The most dreadful music is played throughout the restaurant, and the table service is typically Italian: many flourishes, but totally arrogant and disdainful. It is an experience I have had in Italian-style restaurants in many parts of the world; not even the most arrogant Parisians can come close to it. But the food …

The risotto is to die for; I am sure they have used lots of truffle oil, but I don't care. The aroma is first degree overpowering, the flavour third degree. Each grain of rice is in a silky vein of sauce, or is it oil? Each is still al dente, yet without any hardness at the core. The porcini are hardly likely to be fresh at this time of year, but that doesn't matter either. It is simply a mind-blowing dish, reminiscent of the risotto I had last May when in Florence with Suzanne, made with the little yellow ovuli mushrooms which come only rarely in spring and autumn.

The wild boar is as it always is: done in a casserole, and really just like a very old piece of ram that's chased one too many ewes around the paddock, but I can never resist it. The Castello di Ama is great. And then, most miraculous of all, the head waiter comes across and says, 'It is fantastic to have someone eat in the restaurant who enjoys good wine and good food.' There hasn't been any foreplay, and he actually means it.

Why am I here? Well, it's a long story, but it's thanks to Italian specialist wine writer/author Burton Anderson first up, and Len Evans second up. The Consorzio Chianti Classico is having a seminar to consider world wine trade, the interface between technology and

RIGHT

Marionettes in Florence; they hold the same fascination the world over.

terroir, and other such things. It lasts for four hours on Tuesday afternoon, and is followed by a tasting the following day, but it's really the four-hour seminar that I have been brought all this long way for.

Where does Len come in? Well, Burton phoned him to ask whether he would come from Australia, and Len was quick to say that no one would come from Australia unless they were flown first-class, and then passed the ball to me. I have to admit it hasn't been easy dealing with the Consorzio thereafter, and I actually set off from Australia without the faintest idea where I was staying once I arrived in Florence. It turned out a fax had been sent at the last moment. Suzanne forwarded it to me in transit in Singapore, and I was met by a driver who escorted me to my palace. After two quick trips around the world in the pointy end of a Qantas aircraft, I think I am doing my bit to help the consumption of Krug take a distinct upwards curve.

FEBRUARY 11 THE SHRINE OF COCO LEZZONE, FLORENCE

The weather continues to be magical, although an extraordinary number of people apparently refuse to acknowledge the fact. On entering a restaurant they remove quilted or fur overcoats, then a big scarf, then another coat, leaving them with a jumper, shirt and/or skivvy. I simply have shirt and leather jacket (the jacket purchased in Florence last year) and happily remove the jacket on entering the restaurant.

It was thus last night when I made my compulsory visit to Coco Lezzone restaurant, situated in the tiny Via Purgatorio, just down from its intersection with the Via Inferno. The two street names do indeed indicate that it was near Coco Lezzone that Dante lived.

I have made the strategic error of eating lunch, compounded by the choice of tomato soup to start with. Coco Lezzone's tomato soup is unlike any other tomato soup in the world, a meal in itself. I have been caught thus once before here, and I must make a big note to ensure that I do not fall into the trap again. This means that the vague ambition I had to tackle the restaurant's legendary bistecca (steak) fiorentina (which — theoretically at least — has to be preordered the day before and will only be served one way: rare) is abandoned. But I jump from the frying pan into the fire when I order roast beef in a piece, likewise rare, and which arrives as a 10 cm by 10 cm cube of beef so rare it is almost cold, and a plate of the

BELOW

The River Arno, crossed by the Ponte Vecchio; not always so placid.

largest and most tender asparagus spears (green, not white) you are ever likely to meet. Fortified with a bottle of 1997 Badia di Coltibuono, I mount a prolonged assault on the beef and asparagus, but concede defeat with a quarter left uneaten. Never mind, I shall return.

Coco Lezzone, incidentally, heads its one-page laminated menu with several warnings: 'We don't serve coffee. We accept foreign currency and travellers cheques. We do not accept any credit cards. Only full meals will be served.' The laminated menu has been typed on a typewriter of genuine antiquity: somewhere around the turn of the nineteenth century, I would guess. The only concession to the twenty-first century is the dual pricing in lira and Euros.

FEBRUARY 12   Chianti Classico: Old World and New World

With one hour to go, it seems highly unlikely that the conference I have come all this way to speak at will take place, but in typical Latin fashion it comes together (miraculously) at the last moment, and everyone seems quite satisfied with the outcome.

The panel of six speakers comprises Angelo Gaja (of Piedmont, with the highest profile of all Italian winemakers-cum-marketers), Ricardo Ricci Curbastro (of Lombardi, and among many other things President of Federoc, the national confederation of Wines of Origin), Paul Draper, founder of California's Ridge Vineyards, and two British Masters of Wine (MWs), Claire Gordon-Brown, who was a buyer for Sainsbury's for fifteen years before heading the team to oversee the Sainsbury's/Oddbins joint venture, and Sebastian Payne, who for twenty-five years has been the buyer for The Wine Society. I am the sixth panellist (and opening speaker), charged with the task of exploring the future of global wine trade, and Australia's part in it.

A hundred journalists have been flown in from all parts of the globe: Canada, the United States, Japan, Belgium, Germany, Sweden, Finland, Spain and (of course) Italy. The only obvious absentee is France, represented neither on the panel nor — as far as I can determine — in the audience.

Resourceful and charismatic, convenor Emanuela Prinetti, President of the Consorzio, understands very well the challenges which confront the terroir/territory-based producers of Europe. Moreover, all the Italian speakers recognise the problems, the chaos and confusion (their words) which have dogged the DOCG and DOC denominations since they were established in 1963.

After a determined attempt to commit viticultural/vinicultural suicide in the 1960s and 1970s, Chianti has slowly moved to reinvent itself, those moves gathering pace in the 1990s and continuing to the present time.

There is broad agreement between the speakers that areas such as Chianti need to continually focus on the intangible assets of culture, the territory (in the broadest sense) and history. Anyone who has visited Florence, Siena, San Gimignano and elsewhere in Tuscany will need no persuasion as to the strength of those assets.

Yet the most impassioned plea comes not from Italy or Europe, but from Paul Draper. In his view, the great danger is the levelling effect of industrial winemaking and mass marketing on wine quality. Through industrialisation, more reasonably good quality wine can be produced at lower prices. However, he continues, diversity, distinctiveness and the highest quality are sacrificed as the connection to terroir and the natural process is lost.

Other new world winemaker/observers (such as Brian Croser) have near-identical views, which means that it is a big mistake to assume that all new world wines come out of vast refineries. So what is all the fuss about? Why should there be any tension between the old world and the new?

Well, the bottom line is this. In 1988 the old world accounted for 96 per cent of global exports. According to the Centre for Economic Studies of the University of Adelaide, its share will have fallen to 64 per cent by 2005. Only the foolhardy would make predictions past 2005, but even if — improbably — the decline were to be halted at that point, 2000-plus years of wine trade history will have been turned upside down in less than twenty years.

ABOVE LEFT
The reflections of Florence can mirror those of Venice.

ABOVE RIGHT
Keyhole view of a Smart Car in Florence; makes parking possible.

FEBRUARY 13   CHIANTI CLASSICO

The morning is taken up with a massive tasting of Chianti Classico wines, 'blind' in one room, open (with the makers in attendance) at the other. I move to the 'blind' room, only to find that (first) the wines have to be ferried from the adjacent table to our table by overworked sommeliers, and (second) although they are solemnly wrapped in Alfoil, each bears a number corresponding to that on our tasting sheet — which in turn precisely names the wine! It doesn't take long to move to the open room, and — as it were — go straight to the bottom line.

It's now mid-afternoon, and I begin the long trip back, not home, but to New Zealand.

FEBRUARY 15   NEW ZEALAND

The plane arrives in Melbourne on time, at a little after 6 a.m., and my suitcase (miraculously) has not only once again accompanied me the whole way, but is one of the first off. I am through customs and outside by 6.30, and my plane for Auckland does not leave until 1.30 p.m. Ever pessimistic, I had driven to the airport with my New Zealand clothes (and social wine) packed in the car, in case I had to do a quick turnaround.

As things pan out, I have time to make the one-hour trip home, have a shower there rather than at the airport, put my Italian clothes into the washing machine, scan the mail which has arrived during the week, say hello to Suzanne, Paula and Saras, our brown Burmese cat (in that order, of course), deal with the most urgent bits and pieces, leave a *Weekend Australian* article for typing, and the now completely annotated 2002 edition of the *Wine Companion* for all the edits and changes to be made to the winery summaries for the 2003 edition, pick up typed wine entries for proofing, and head back to the airport to arrive at 12.30 p.m., an hour before departure.

The flurry of activity is rendered more difficult because this happens to be one of a handful of truly hot days this summer, the temperature peaking at 38°C.

The look on my face when I am told there will be a two-hour delay in the departure of the Air New Zealand flight leaves no doubt about my displeasure. Copious quantities of Krug, Murelax and Melatonin were certainly helpful in inducing sleep on the trip from Los Angeles, but the quality of that sleep can only be described as dubious, and it is now a full forty-eight hours since I last got out of a proper bed.

I ring up Bob Campbell, with whom I am staying, tell him to cancel any plans for dinner which involve me, and arrange to crash

BELOW
Our Burmese cat Saras, intrepid hunter of rabbits, rats and mice.

into bed when we get to his house, which I estimate to be around 10 p.m. However, we do manage to have a large glass each of 2001 Forrest Estate Sauvignon Blanc, a glorious wine (which turns out to be an extraordinary coincidence in the days ahead).

FEBRUARY 16–17 AUCKLAND'S WINE SOCIETY ROYAL EASTER WINE SHOW

I have set the alarm for what I think is half-past seven for an 8 a.m. departure from chez Campbell, but it's 7.45 a.m. when Bob knocks on the door and wakes me up, seconds before the mis-set alarm goes off. I hurl myself into the shower, throw on clothes, wolf a plate of fresh fruit and a couple of slices of toast, and we're on the way to the 2002 Auckland Wine Show.

Some years previously we set up a deal whereby I act as deputy chairman to Bob, who is 'Mr Wine' in New Zealand, an MW, and chairman of the Auckland show. He is to New Zealand what *The Wine Spectator* and Robert Parker combined are to the United States. His main business these days is running wine education classes, which are so successful that they are staged not only in New Zealand, but also in Singapore, Hong Kong and London. He has also long been the senior wine writer for *Cuisine* magazine and produces the annual *Cuisine Wine Magazine*, which I now learn is to be discontinued and replaced by another publication.

> Auckland's Wine Society Royal Easter Wine Show is a judge-friendly event, taking place over a weekend at (by Australian standards) a relatively leisurely pace. We each take care of two panels, and get to taste half the total wines entered, then join forces at the point of determining the gold medals for virtually every class, and, along with the judges, compare the top gold medals/trophy winners to determine the trophy for Champion Wine of Show.
>
> It is a great opportunity to keep one's finger on the pulse of New Zealand's industry, which is undergoing the same frantic rate of growth as Australia's. All you have to do is divide the New Zealand figures by ten, and the comparison is complete.

Well, almost: there is a blip caused by the low yield per hectare in New Zealand in 2001 compared with expectations of a normal yield in 2002. Add in all the new vineyards coming into bearing for the first time, and this year's grape harvest is likely to exceed that of last year by at least 70 per cent.

Amazingly, there is such pent-up demand that the price for Marlborough sauvignon blanc shows no sign of softening. There will be many Australian growers of newly planted cabernet sauvignon who will be nowhere near so fortunate.

But to return to the show … there were many surprises, almost all pleasant. The most outstanding — indeed spectacular — class was merlot from 2000 and older vintages. It gave rise to seven gold medals and, ultimately, the trophy for Champion Wine of Show. In a close-run contest, the 2000 Villa Maria Reserve Merlot, marvellously rich, ripe and luscious, prevailed over the passionfruit-perfumed but spotlessly clean 2001 Forrest Estate Vineyard Selection Sauvignon Blanc, with the 2000 Villa Maria Single Vineyard King Chardonnay another eyelash back in third place.

FEBRUARY 18 YARRA VALLEY: CAUTIOUS OPTIMISM

I finally return to the Yarra Valley with a degree of apprehension about the activities of the weather gods. However, the six days since I left for Italy have been (so I learn) absolutely ideal, and veraison, which had been so slow to start, went through with a rush. Cautious optimism is starting to take serious hold; we know the volume and yield will be down, but the portents for quality look increasingly good.

FEBRUARY 19 STATE OF ORIGIN CHALLENGE: SHIRAZ

Another hot day is on the way, but with a cool change forecast to arrive sometime tomorrow. The *Divine* magazine State of Origin tasting is on again, this year featuring shiraz. The format is as in previous years, with 15 wines from each of the four major states. Iain Riggs of Brokenwood is the judge representing New South Wales;

Trevor Mast of Mount Langi Ghiran represents Victoria; Andrew Hardy of Knappstein represents South Australia; and Gavin Berry of Plantagenet represents Western Australia. The 60 wines are judged in the morning session, and the points collated from all four judges and myself as chairman; the top 20 wines are then taken forward to the afternoon, where they are rearranged in random order and rejudged. As we leave, we know that the top three places have gone to shiraz from the Great Southern region of Western Australia, and that Gavin Berry was part of the discussion which — unwittingly — took Plantagenet from first to equal second place. So cruel. On the other hand, the public is still to have its say, and simply being in the top three is an achievement in itself.

The most remarkable thing, from my perspective, was how it took an hour for my palate to adjust to the amount of American oak in Australia's top shirazs. A week of Chianti and a weekend of New Zealand, plus copious quantities of Krug, had changed my perspective with frightening rapidity. It was an eerie sensation, knowing that I was not affected by a cold or other illness, and the judging conditions were as good as one could get, yet thinking I was tasting a weird form of cherry and vanilla milkshake.

One might have expected this challenge to be a cakewalk for South Australia, but on aggregate points it came third (1264.5 points) behind Victoria (second on 1286.5 points) and Western Australia (first on 1293.5 points).

In turn, one Western Australian region produced three of the four top wines: 2000 Howard Park Scotsdale (93.5/100), 1999 Plantagenet (91.5/100) and 1999 Houghton Frankland River (91/100), equal third with the top Victorian wine, 2000 Hanging Rock Heathcote.

The second and equal third positions for Victoria were 1997 Seppelt Great Western Reserve (90/100) and then a three-way tie for third, each 89/100, with 2000 Jasper Hill Georgia's Paddock, 2000 Summerfield Reserve and 2000 Dalwhinnie.

The top three wines from New South Wales (and a long way clear of the rest of the field for that state) were 2000 McGuigan Genus 4 (90/100) and on 88.5/100 each 2000 Brokenwood Graveyard and 2000 Tower Estate.

The South Australian honours went to 1999 Jim Barry The Armagh (90/100) with two excellent 1998 wines equal second half a point back: Wirra Wirra Chook Block (not Church Block, I assure you) and St Hallett Old Block.

There are then two ways of cutting the remaining cake: to focus on the wines that won, or to look at those which might have been expected to but didn't.

Looking at the top wines, almost all were primarily driven by the richness of their fruit rather than the power of their oak — and in a majority of instances, that oak was French not American.

Some certainly came from the big end of town — Jim Barry The Armagh, Hanging Rock Heathcote, Jasper Hill Georgia's Paddock, Brokenwood Graveyard to name a few — but all the components are in balance; the winemaker has done his bit, and now all that is required is a decade or so for these wines to openly display their intrinsic harmony and balance.

There is a tendency these days to become slightly apologetic about these bold, voluptuous, full-frontal red wines. But it is their quintessential point of difference: we cannot duplicate or even approximate the great syrah wines of the Northern Rhône Valley, but nor can the Rhône duplicate these wines.

Ring me in ten years, and I will cheerfully share a bottle of any of these wines, or, for that matter, any one of the top 14 wines.

FEBRUARY 20   THE TASTING GRIND: WINES AND GRAPES

Another day of tasting 160 or so wines for the 2003 *Companion*, with another scheduled for tomorrow. Another three or four days of this at the outside and I shall be able to give my palate a well-deserved rest. As promised, the day starts out hot, with a howling northerly, but by mid-afternoon the southerly change comes through, followed by a deluge which has everyone worried about hail: reports come in from Nunawading that hail is falling there. Once more we are spared, and the mood of optimism returns. Flavours in the vineyard are starting to appear in the pinot noir, and the skins of the sauvignon blanc and chardonnay are starting to show signs of softening from the hard, green stage. Now the speculation turns on the likely starting date: the consensus seems to be somewhere between March 7 and March 14, which would make the starting date 'normal', whatever that means.

FEBRUARY 21   CROP ESTIMATES: THE DOWNWARD SPIRAL

The weather this week has been kind, although thunderstorms are forecast for this evening. The real problem lies with the size of the crop. Each time estimates are redone, the likely crop is sharply reduced. By rights, this should have been a year of surplus in the Yarra Valley, but now I suspect all but the worst grapes will find a home somewhere or other, with wineries desperate to make enough money to keep the show on the road.

FEBRUARY 25   WINE AUSTRALIA 2002, SYDNEY

I spend today (and tomorrow) in Sydney wearing my Chairman of Wine Australia hat. It is to be held at Fox Studios from August 2 to August 5, and ever since the highly successful Wine Australia held in Melbourne in 2000, the wine industry has insisted that we don't fix what ain't broke.

FEBRUARY 28   THE COLDEST SUMMER EVER

It's official. This has been the coldest summer ever recorded in Melbourne. In the southern cool-climate areas from Coonawarra through Drumborg, across to the Port Phillip Zone (including, of course, the Yarra), the Mornington Peninsula, Geelong and across to Gippsland, yields are going to be pitifully low. Bunch weights of 40 grams for pinot noir and chardonnay are the norm for this vintage, compared with the usual weight of between 80 and 100 grams. Moreover, the bunches are not numerous. And this, of course, does not take into account the Yarra Valley vineyards (including two of ours) which were devastated by hail at the end of October.

However, if we get some reasonably warm and dry weather over March and April (part of the 'normal' weather pattern), the quality could turn out to be excellent. Certainly the summer has come as a huge relief after the appalling heat of the 1998, 2000 and 2001 vintages.

While I am engaged in (yet another) all-day tasting for the *Companion*, a container full of new barrels arrives for unloading; thanks to Coldstream winemaker Andrew Fleming's forethought in having barrel cradles ready and numerous people to help — and a temperature of 20° — the unloading happens with a minimum of fuss and sweat. How I remember in bygone years two or three of us toiling in blazing sun to empty containers. Still, whatever else it says, it certainly says that vintage is around the corner. At this point we are planning to start sparkling wine picking next Monday, March 4, and have tentatively scheduled the start on the Amphitheatre pinot noir in the week commencing Monday, March 11. We shall see.

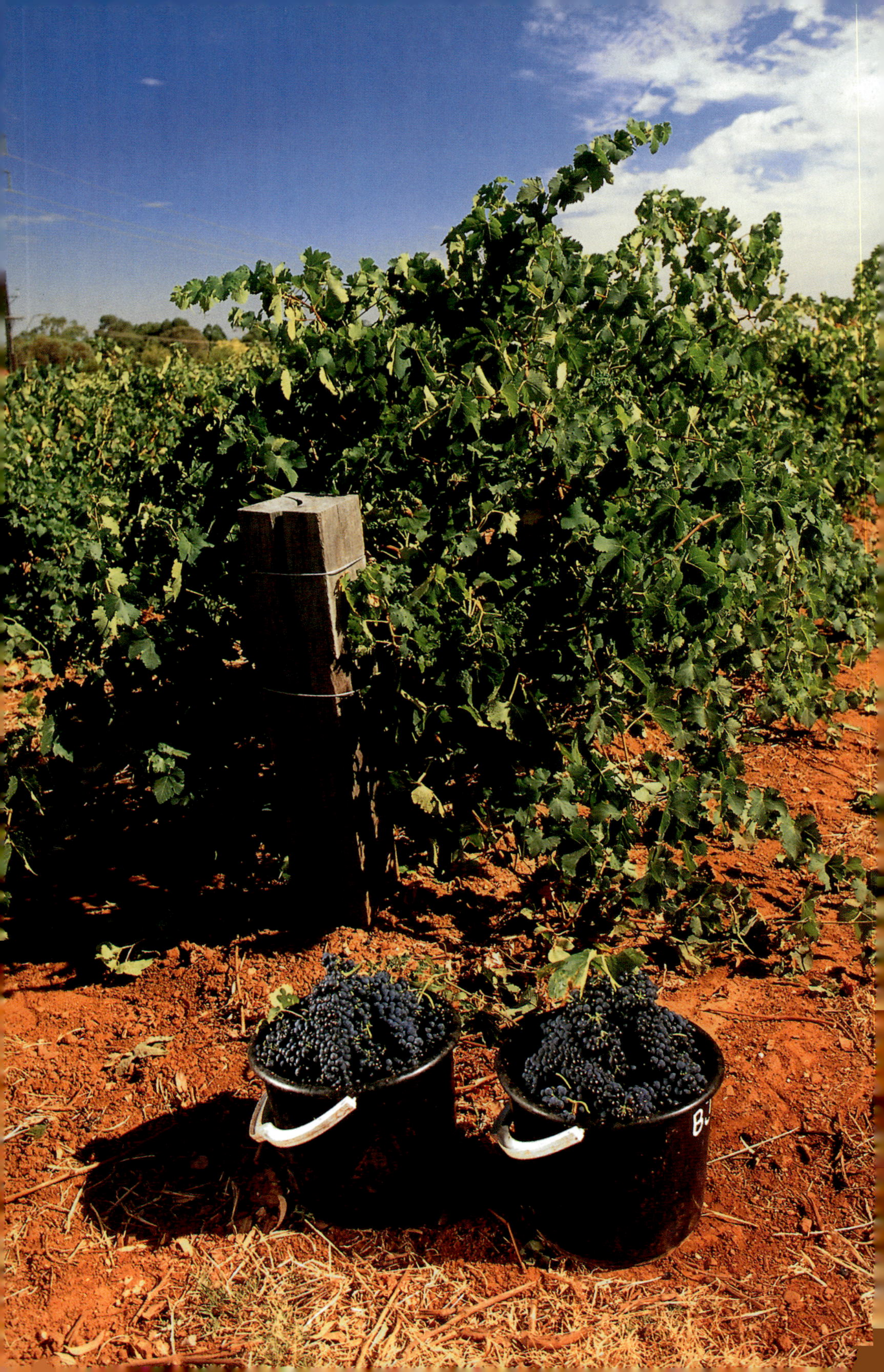

March

VINTAGE: HOW THE BEST-LAID PLANS ARE DERAILED

THE CELLAR RATS

THE INFINITELY CAPRICIOUS TRICKS OF NATURE

HANGING ROCK — AND A NEW MELBOURNE FOOD AND WINE LEGEND

STONIER INTERNATIONAL PINOT NOIR TASTING

THE FIRST DAY OF VINTAGE 2002

JACQUES REYMOND: A TWIST OF FATE

MELBOURNE FOOD AND WINE MASTERCLASSES

PICKING: PLAYING TAG WITH THE WEATHER

GOOD FRIDAY BREAKFAST, COLDSTREAM HILLS

THE PICKING CONTINUES

MARCH 8   Vintage: How the Best-laid Plans are Derailed

The pace of vintage is slowly picking up, although we are still only processing grapes for sparkling wine, with a single (albeit long) day shift. In theory, this is an easily managed stage of the vintage, as we are only involved in the production of juice, which is then shipped off to Great Western for fermentation. Only selected parcels will ultimately form the base for the Coldstream Hills sparkling wine.

So tonight we have planned a dinner to celebrate the start of vintage, with a large spit-roasted leg of pork, which I plan to take off the spit at about 6.30 p.m. All of which goes to show that vintage is never that simple, for a Booth's wine tanker, known as a B-Double, ignores the instructions as to which road it should take to get to the winery, and is completely unable to negotiate the T-intersection at the end of Medhurst Road and Maddens Lane. It becomes hopelessly stuck, blocking the traffic trying to proceed out of Medhurst Road and north into Maddens Lane. This is 100 metres from our cellar door, and 400 metres from the winery itself, but it takes two hours for the second tank to be unhitched, and for the truck driver to bring the first tank to the winery, unhitch it, and then go to retrieve his second tank.

It is but the latest of countless such events over many years — trucks and tankers have become stuck in the worst places at the worst possible time, notwithstanding the progressive upgrade of the access roads in and immediately surrounding the property. I remember only too well one weekend four or five years ago, when I was drenched with sweat and wearing only a pair of Stubby shorts, trying to build up enough earth under one of the wheels of a tanker which had misjudged the corner and was now half-suspended in air, greeting a bemused, very well-dressed carload of Americans enquiring where they might find James Halliday. The look on their faces when I told them I was indeed he was sufficient to keep me in good humour until we finally got the truck going.

But to return to the present, the weather has simply got better with each passing day, and we expect to have some glorious days coming up. A repeated cycle of three to four days gradually building the temperature from 20° to 30°C, then a weak cool change without rain, and then another four-day cycle, has now been repeated for the last few weeks, and should continue through next week. Not a breath of wind nor a cloud in the sky, with a maximum of 23° today, 25° tomorrow, then 27° then 30° and then 33° before the next cool change. But even here vintage can be a cruel mistress, because Monday is a public holiday in Victoria, and Andrew Fleming was planning on getting back to his family at Ballarat, but it now seems that pinot meunier from the Deer Farm in the upper Yarra simply has to be picked before it gets too ripe, so there will be no rest over the weekend.

MARCH 8   THE CELLAR RATS

Today also marks the arrival of the last of our vintage casuals, whom I know only as 'cellar rats', Scot Dahlstrom, from the Central Valley of California. That is a place of extreme temperatures, searingly hot by day in summer and bitterly cold in winter. If the weather continues as it is here, he will think that the Yarra Valley is paradise.

We have always tried to assemble a league of nations vintage crew, and have succeeded as well this year as ever, even with a preponderance of North American (rather than European) rats.

The first is the splendidly — if improbably — named Shiraz Mottiar, from Canada. He has no less than three university degrees, including a Bachelor of Science (Honours) in oenology and viticulture from Brock University, Ontario, and has had four years' practical winemaking experience in various Ontario wineries. (Postscript: he turns out to be one of the stars of the vintage, level-headed and conscientious, handling the night shift very well.)

Scot Dahlstrom, who is on the day shift, has worked for both the very large Bronco Wine Co and the much smaller Justin Vineyards in California. Painfully shy, despite having what most people would regard as extremely good looks, he remains quiet to the end.

Gary Thomas works the day shift. He comes from New Zealand, where he has worked at wineries such as Neudorf. His knowledge of fine wine is greater than that of anyone else on this year's roster, and

ABOVE
The eponymously named Shiraz Mottiar, one of our best cellar rats.

he does not hesitate to share his knowledge. (Postscript: he spends more time on the computer than on the winery floor, and ends up being somewhat unpopular, to put it mildly.)

Shari Merritt also comes from New Zealand and also works on the day shift. She has a diploma in viticulture and wine production, and has worked in California, McWilliams Mount Pleasant and at Montana, Lawson's Dry Hills, Huia, Allan Scott and Le Brun. (Postscript: ever cheerful and ever friendly, she is a hardworking member of the day shift, liked and respected by all.)

Kathy Nani, from San Francisco, runs the laboratory on what is meant to be the day shift, but, by her own choice, stretches from dawn to dusk. Hyper-intelligent, she is completing a research paper for UCLA Davis, and holds the American Society for Enology and Viticulture Scholarship for Scholastic Achievement. (Postscript: she, too, has a great personality, and adds very substantially to the vintage.)

Emmanuelle Bucourt, from France, has had six years of tertiary study, and has undertaken the English Wine and Spirit Education Trust diploma. She has worked at various well-known wineries in the Rhône Valley, Beaujolais and Burgundy, the latter at Meo Camuzet, one of the superstars. (Postscript: she is travelling with her boyfriend, who is a fully qualified chef and who contributes more to the success of vintage than we might ever have imagined.)

Our two intake assistants, who come from within Southcorp, are Nadia Di Blasi and Ben Langley-Jones, who establish themselves as vintage favourites, none more so than Nadia.

The crackling on the leg of pork is great, the meat horrendously overcooked because the first of us does not sit down to dinner until almost 7.30 p.m., others coming later. An array of Oregon Pinots from the great 1999 vintage, together with wines from Alsace, Italy, New Zealand and Australia, which I tasted earlier in the day, seem to make up for the pork by the time all sixteen arrive at the party.

MARCH 13 THE INFINITELY CAPRICIOUS TRICKS OF NATURE

BELOW
The cellar rats hard at work in the courtyard crushing chardonnay.

The town of Coldstream continues to make the news in the evening weather report on television with lowest minimum temperatures overnight. Not infrequently, Coldstream is extended to include the whole of the Yarra Valley. It can also claim the spotlight in winter, with temperatures at or below 0°C. The quirk is that the Coldstream weather station is situated at one of the lowest points in the entire Yarra Valley, with cold air draining into it from the surrounding slopes. Temperature inversion, with warmer air rising during the evening and colder air settling at the bottom of the slopes, plays tricks with climate figures, and it is almost invariably the case that even the slightly higher elevations have significantly higher temperatures. Suzanne's car has a gauge that reads outside temperature in half-degree increments, and it is fascinating to see the rise and fall in temperature with even the tiniest changes in elevation.

The days, however, continue to be brilliant, with early morning cloud burning off by lunchtime, and afternoon temperatures of 22–23°C, the most perfect temperature for ripening. We have had days of this, and expect days of it to come, with the temperatures rising to the high 20s/low 30s by the weekend before another weak cool change comes through — no rain is forecast.

Indeed, unless my memory is playing tricks on me, this is the most perfect weather we have had in the lead-up to vintage since 1992. Today we spend two hours walking through the very large Killara Park vineyard, which will be one of our chief external sources of pinot noir for the vintage. The samples over the last few days have confirmed frighteningly low bunch weights of 30–40 grams (normally 80–90 grams) on our own vineyards, and those of a number of other growers. We are desperate to find additional pinot noir of the quality required for Coldstream Hills, and — miraculously — there is a large block of 8 hectares (plus other blocks already contracted to us) which has 4 hectares hanging loose, as it were.

Tony Palazzo, who reminded me that we met many years ago while he was a chief executive officer of Hooper Bailey, which briefly owned Hungerford Hill, is the owner of the vineyard. After a few problems last year, he has done all the right things in terms of shoot removal, bunch thinning, and now, removal of the second crop, and the quality of the grapes on the vines looks to be excellent. It is entirely netted against birds, and — best of all — it has a reasonable crop, varying between 3.7 and 6 tonnes to the hectare on our rough calculations.

From Killara Park vineyard (over 42 hectares in all) situated on Sunnyside Road, we come back to the Lilliputian scale of Geoff Norris's vineyard, just down the road from Coldstream Hills. He doesn't count acres or hectares; he counts vines. He has 700 chardonnay vines, now thirty years old, dry-grown and shy-bearing, and is very anxious to know whether we think the grapes will be ready to pick this weekend, as he has his ten children and their families on standby. He has twice as much pinot noir, probably three or four times the 1 tonne of chardonnay, and is relieved to find that it won't be ripe at the same time as the chardonnay. Today is Wednesday, and a further sample will be taken on Friday, which will determine the picking date and the fate of his children for this weekend or next. Coldstream Hills hopes to process up to 1200 tonnes this vintage, and it's great that we can still keep up longstanding relationships with growers such as Geoff Norris.

Postscript: it turned out to be one-third of a tonne of chardonnay, or 0.0025 per cent of our crush for the vintage.

As I write these words, the sun is setting on another windless evening; the valley is at its beautiful best, and we are all holding tightly on wood in the hope that this dream run will continue through the second half of March and into April — historically, April is often a settled period of the year, with a perfect Indian summer.

MARCH 15   HANGING ROCK — AND A NEW MELBOURNE FOOD AND WINE LEGEND

An unusual day, starting with a flight in a restored DC3 from Essendon Airport taking us journalists over the new Heathcote region (new in the sense that an interim determination of its boundaries will be published any day) and, in particular, over the Mount Camel district, where many new vineyards have been established. One of those is by Hanging Rock, which has organised the trip. The proliferation of vineyards in this region is remarkable — the vivid red soil here dates back two million years, when an upthrust seabed was covered by volcanic basalt, now weathered to this rich red.

Arriving back at Essendon, we then return to Hanging Rock winery by limousine — or, in my case, chauffeured by Jeremy Oliver in the 'cockpit' of his Toyota MR2. We take the opportunity of calling in on Alec Epis's vineyard and winery (the latter under construction), having a quick taste of the high-quality wines he has made in conjunction with Stuart Anderson. Epis is a legendary figure in AFL circles, a senior mentor to the Essendon club.

At Hanging Rock we are treated first to a vertical (a multi-vintage tasting, starting with the oldest and moving to the youngest, or in the reverse order — it all depends on the wine) of all of the Heathcote Shiraz wines made by Hanging Rock to date, and then, after lunch, to a tour of the vastly expanded winery — which has finally given John Ellis all the space and equipment he could ever wish for.

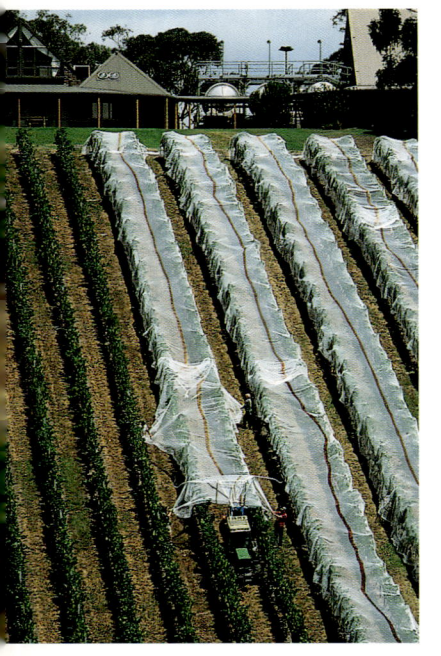

The occasion is the release of Hanging Rock's 2000 Shiraz, and the co-host (alongside John and Annie Ellis) is Athol Guy. The Seekers, it seems, produced not only great music, but some truly dedicated wine-men. Across in the Margaret River is Keith Potger; here in Victoria it is Athol Guy.

John Ellis made the first Heathcote Shiraz in 1987, sourced from a leased vineyard, and it met with immediate show success and critical acclaim. However, by 1992 increasing soil salinity made it clear that the vineyard was no longer viable — it produced less than a quarter of a tonne per acre that year.

Magically, Athol Guy had decided that he wished to establish a vineyard in Heathcote, and was referred to John Ellis as a consultant. In 1993 the first planting took place at a location 20 kilometres to the north of the original vineyard; in 1997 the plantings were increased to 10 hectares, and a joint venture was set up. Hanging Rock was to manage the vineyard, take all its grapes and make the wine.

It was also agreed that the intake from Athol's Paddock (as it is called) would be supplemented by purchases from other vineyards in the Heathcote/Mount Camel region: thus in 2000 the wine came (in order of volume) from Athol's Paddock, Colbinabbin Estate, the original leased vineyard, Joe Marton Vineyard, and a small amount from Merindoc.

The main event was the vertical tasting of all the Hanging Rock Heathcote Shirazs: 1987 to 1992 inclusive, and 1997 to 2001 inclusive (the last a barrel sample).

The first vintage (1987) is still holding sweet fruit on the palate, but definitely needs drinking. The 1988 and 1989 (both from poor vintages)

ABOVE
White netting, like a bridal veil, is the only real defence against birds.

are past their best, but the 1990, 1991 and 1992 are still purring along, rating four, four and a half and five stars respectively. There was so little of the 1992, it was all bottled in magnum — 2000 in all.

The next generation, from 1997 onwards, is remarkably even in terms of both style and quality. They all rate four and a half or five stars, the 1998 having developed very well since I first tasted it two years ago, and the 1999 showing little signs of the rain which fell at the last moment, turning a perfect vintage into a less than perfect one.

The 2000 is, as one would expect from a wine with a minimum ten years of life, nowhere near ready. It has excellent colour; the first impression on the bouquet is of high toast barrel ferment oak, followed by opulent plum and black cherry; the palate is a logical follow-on, with powerful berry fruit, equally powerful oak and fine tannins (92 points, four and a half stars; $55).

BELOW

The new winery at Hanging Rock, with John Ellis in white moleskins.

From Essendon I drive to the unit which Suzanne and I own in Melbourne, then, having climbed into my dinner suit, join Suzanne and the hundreds of guests at the Palladium Room at the Crown Casino development for a Tenth Anniversary Celebration Dinner for the Melbourne Food and Wine Festival. Five new legends are inducted this year, and Suzanne is one of them. The other four are Jacques Reymond (the celebrated restaurateur), Dominique Portet (who has just built his new winery in Maddens Lane, which means that there are three legends on Maddens Lane — I became one some years ago), Ross Campbell (a veteran radio presenter of food and wine segments), and cheese maestro Will Stud. Quite coincidentally, Coldstream Hills was the supplier of the table wines for the dinner; nothing to do with me, simply a reflection of the amount of wine Southcorp provides for the entire complex. But a nice coincidence, nonetheless.

MARCH 18   S<small>TONIER</small> I<small>NTERNATIONAL</small> P<small>INOT</small> N<small>OIR</small> T<small>ASTING</small>

More vineyard inspections in perfect weather, and grapes ripening in perfect conditions. The repeating systems of high-pressure weather cells which move across Australia from west to east are positioned so as to block any weather coming up from the lows to their south. The Southern Oscillation Index, which is more commonly referred to as the El Niño effect, also points to continuing dry weather. Nonetheless, vintage always remains a nervous time, and the decision has been taken to start picking pinot noir tomorrow and through the week, taking the Amphitheatre Block in front of the winery first up, and then the contract-grown grapes.

A rush back home to get changed and go into Melbourne for the Annual International Pinot Noir Tasting staged by Stonier Wines, with Len Evans, Brian Croser, Todd Dexter (of Stonier Estate) and myself on the panel. As ever, an interesting tasting, staged in the grand dining room of the Windsor Hotel, with well over a hundred people attending.

MARCH 19   T<small>HE</small> F<small>IRST</small> D<small>AY OF</small> V<small>INTAGE</small> 2002

The first 'real' day of vintage, the pinot noir from A block looking as good as I have ever seen it, and tasting as good as I have ever seen it. If only there were more … Our picking team this year is basically Cambodian, and has worked intermittently throughout the year on the vines. One of the women has a conical straw hat in traditional Cambodian/Asian style, but with pieces of string and corks hanging off its perimeter to keep the flies away; I am still conspiring to get a photograph.

I have already taken what may turn out to be the photograph to be used on the 2002 label, a close-up of the A Block grapes in the picking bin with two tendrils providing a minute but nonetheless striking colour contrast. Another possibility is a single vivid red leaf in the G Block pinot noir.

MARCH 21   Jacques Reymond: A Twist of Fate

A day which started, following significant overnight rain, in a blanket of fog and cloud. The pickers were told there would be no picking for the day, but fate took a hand in two ways: their van broke down, and by the time it was fixed, the sun was shining brilliantly. It continued to do so throughout the day. So picking was done, and microscopic quantities of pinot and chardonnay are now being processed, with the sun setting in crystal clear air, the temperature plummeting from the mid-20s down to 10°C.

Last night Suzanne and I went to a special banquet at Jacques Reymond's restaurant, and had one of the all-time great degustation meals. Every element of every plate was brilliant, although (with the exception of the Grosset Polish Hill Riesling) the wines in no way did justice to the food.

It's exactly twenty years since we met a much younger Jacques and his wife Kathie in their restaurant at Cuiseaux in the Jura in France, the trip to the Jura being itself unplanned, forced on us by the temporary loss of Suzanne's passport which meant that we didn't go (as planned) to the Douro Valley in Portugal. Jacques Seysses, of Domaine Dujac, suggested we fill in the time by going to the Jura, and there eat with a (relatively) young friend who had already gained a Michelin star for the restaurant owned by his parents.

We did, and were driven around the Jura for the day by Jacques, using the time to help him make up his mind to come to Australia. We also gently headed him in the direction of Mietta O'Donnell, who was so tragically killed in a car accident a few years ago. The two forged a long-term professional relationship at Mietta's restaurant, where Jacques became chef, before he decided to move out and establish his own restaurant, first in Richmond and thereafter at his present premises at 78 Williams Road, Prahran (telephone 03 9275 2178).

It is one of Australia's greatest restaurants, long the holder of three hats (the maximum) in *The Age Good Food Guide*.

WINE ODYSSEY

ABOVE LEFT
Our best pinot noir, hand-picked from the Amphitheatre.

ABOVE RIGHT
Hand-picking pinot noir; Cambodians have replaced the Vietnamese.

MARCH 23–24   MELBOURNE FOOD AND WINE MASTERCLASSES

The weekend is spent in Melbourne at the Melbourne Food and Wine Festival Masterclasses. I have a session each morning with Ann Willan, whose book *Cooking with Wine* has just been published. 'A Glass for the Pan and a Glass for the Chef' is the title, and the discussion is about wine in the food and wine with the food. Ann, who founded La Varenne Cooking School in France and the United States, makes it a challenging exercise to find suitable wines for some of the courses: mussels in a sherry marinade is easy enough (I choose Manzanilla); then warm salad of duck breast with pinot noir glaze is truly easy, pointing at a pinot noir, the final choice being 2001 Ninth Island. The next course, however, makes up for things, being oranges in red wine with olives. Ann accurately describes the flavours as acid, sweet and salt. I toss up between De Bortoli Botrytis Affected Dry Semillon and Domaine Chandon's Cuvée Riche, ultimately choosing the second, and in fact it works very well. Finally Chocolate Merlot Cake raises the question: should I respond to the chocolate or to the merlot? Being a firm opponent of the idea that you can serve red wine with chocolate, I choose the relatively safe ground of Baileys Founder Liqueur Tokay.

My task in the afternoon is to join Larry McKenna (formerly of Martinborough Vineyards) and Gary Farr (of Bannockburn and his own label, By Farr) to examine 'Life Outside Burgundy — New World Pinot Noir'. The New Zealand wines chosen are 1998 Martinborough Reserve, the last wine made by Larry before he left Martinborough, a very classic wine made with great discipline and destined to be long-lived; 2000 Cloudy Bay, complex and gamey; and 2000 Ata Rangi (one of the best ever from this vineyard), opulent yet with elegance.

Then, from the United States, 1999 Rex Hill Willamette Valley from Oregon, direct and fresh, with the promise of building complexity as it ages in bottle; and the delicious Au Bon Climat Knox Pinot Noir from Jim Clendenen's Santa Barbara winery, with all of the mouthfeel one could ever wish for, and all of the complexity, too.

The two Australian pinots are outstanding: 2000 Bannockburn and 2000 By Farr, both fragrant and beautifully proportioned and constructed, yet as different as chalk and cheese. The Bannockburn has cherry and plum fruit aromas, the By Farr a high-toned, almost citrussy aroma, with a spicy accompaniment. One was picked from one side of the hill, the other from an opposite slope; they were made identically, but the oak came from two different coopers: Damy for the Bannockburn and Reymond for the By Farr.

On Saturday night Mario Batali, from New York, and Stefano di Pieri combine their talents to produce a meal — for upwards of two hundred people — which features the true peasant cooking of Lombardy, presented without compromise.

ABOVE
Filling barrels with the new wine goes on twenty-four hours a day.

MARCH 25   PICKING: PLAYING TAG WITH THE WEATHER

Last night the idyllic weather broke with a vengeance, with wild wind storms and lashing rain, 15 mm being recorded in the rain gauge. But by 8 a.m. the clouds had been blown away, and the strong and warm winds dried the canopy very quickly, allowing hand-picking to proceed, and also denying mildew or botrytis the chance to germinate. But now, at 5 p.m., just as the Cambodian picking team is about to pick the last short row of the pinot noir under the house, the weather bureau radar screen shows heavy bands of rain in the Melbourne metropolitan region, heading our way. Luckily, all the fruit will be in before the rain arrives; with permanent access to the radar screen via our winery computers, picking decisions can be monitored to the last minute.

Earlier today, the first pinots picked finished their fermentation, having the splendid colour the small berries suggested they would. The flavour also appears to be all we could hope for, but it's still early days: the wines are taken to barrel while they still have some fermenting sugar, and the sweetness left is a great masking agent for any hidden deficiencies.

MARCH 29   GOOD FRIDAY BREAKFAST, COLDSTREAM HILLS

A large slow-moving high-pressure cell situated in the Australian Bight is directing cold moist wind in a southerly stream, bringing persistent drizzle and rain. The tiny bunches of pinot noir are holding, but only just: the very small, seedless berries are showing signs of collapse, and we really need warm days, which are forecast to arrive on Monday (April 1). The major concern is another front coming across later in the week; the picking window may prove too short, and we may have to make a very hard choice: between hoping for the best and continuing to hand-pick the pinot noir, or accepting the inevitable and machine harvesting it. I dread the loss of potentially fantastic quality if we have to adopt the latter course.

Continuing a tradition started almost fifteen years ago, we have the Good Friday breakfast at Coldstream Hills today. It is the first time the weather has been less than perfect; every other year I can remember there have been blue skies, often with mists gently rising from the dam in the bottom of the Amphitheatre. The weather doesn't stop over fifty people turning up from wineries around the valley, all telling much the same tale of tiny crops but exciting quality (still). Scrambled eggs and salmon (which I cook), involving roughly equal quantities of butter and eggs (plus salmon caviar), croissants and hot cross buns are the same as ever, but instead of the normal champagne (French, of course) I put on a selection of Domaine Chandon sparklings going back to 1986.

As someone remarks, the breakfast has been the only regular social event in the Yarra Valley involving only the winemakers, which may be why we tend to have 100 per cent acceptances. Trying to cook scrambled eggs with split-second timing while simultaneously mothering croissants and hot cross buns in the antiquated oven, finding runners to take the eggs out, then finding people to make coffee, then finding that no one has been getting replacement bottles of sparkling wine from the fridge, is a salutary reminder of why I have never been tempted to become a restaurateur.

MARCH 30   The Picking Continues

Grey skies all day, and a maximum temperature of 14°C, but no rain. Notwithstanding that it's Easter Saturday, hand-picking crews have been working flat out at Briarston, Brooklands and Killara Park, and the courtyard is filled with pinot noir from Brooklands and Killara Park, and chardonnay from Briarston. The latter is a cause for celebration: not only does the fruit look and taste great, but the amount picked actually exceeds the estimate. Killara Park continues to produce outstanding pinot noir; the Brooklands grapes taste sweet and ripe, and look good, but it's only when you taste the Killara Park grapes that you see the intensity and depth of flavour which I believe will come from this vintage. It's a ridiculous call, of course, but I feel in my bones that Killara will produce pinot with a wonderful depth of velvety, plummy flavour.

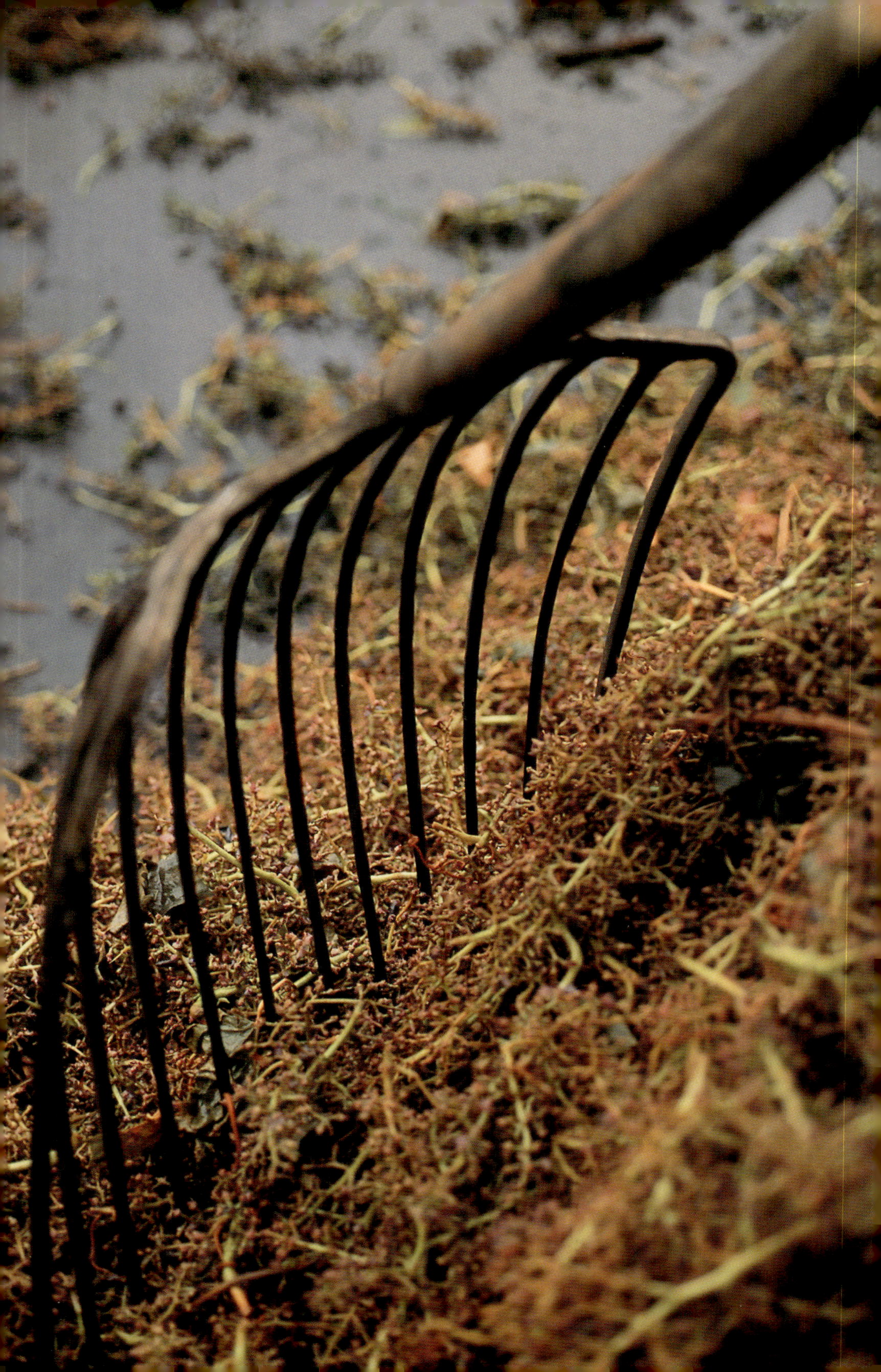

April

Vintage: Tonne by Tonne

Robe and Mount Benson, South Australia

Vintage: On a Knife's Edge

Summerfield Winery, Pyrenees

Seville Estate, Yarra Valley

McWilliam's 125th Anniversary

Vintage: Starting to Count the Chickens

Geoff Merrill, Melbourne

Wine Australia, Sydney

Vintage: Wines in the Barrel

Melbourne

California: Lodi

A Day to Remember, Napa Valley

The Wine Appreciation Guild's Wine Literary Award

San Francisco Rhône Rangers

The Last Supper at Coldstream Hills

APRIL 1   VINTAGE: TONNE BY TONNE

The sun has finally returned with a vengeance, the day becoming hotter as it progresses. Jacques Thienpont (owner of the famous Château Le Pin) and wife Fiona Morrison MW were scheduled to come for lunch, together with John Middleton of Mount Mary, Anne Willan and husband Mark. At the last moment the Thienponts had to cancel their trip to Australia, due to Fiona's sudden illness. A pity; they would have seen the valley at its best.

Hand-picking by day and machine-picking by night continue unabated. Despite the enormous teams of hand-pickers being assembled by the various vineyards, the progress of the tonnes crushed through the winery is painfully slow. At the moment only 360 tonnes have been crushed, with 240 tonnes of pinot and 50 tonnes of chardonnay making up the major part, but with a fair bit of sauvignon blanc coming through at the same time. A change is forecast for late Wednesday (April 3), and from this point on it will have to be a game of wait and see. It looks as if it may be a brief and fast-moving change, unlike the last one. If so, we may be able to continue hand-picking, rather than use machines (which would occur if there were an outbreak of botrytis or mildew).

APRIL 3–4   ROBE AND MOUNT BENSON, SOUTH AUSTRALIA

After a couple of days of warm weather in the high 20s, another cold southerly front is moving through at precisely the moment Suzanne and I board the plane to Mount Gambier, on the way to the opening of the Kreglinger winery in Mount Benson, staying at the historic seaside port of Robe tonight and tomorrow night. Initially the weather looked very threatening, but rainfall is now expected to be no more than 5 mm; we shall see.

Robe is a quite marvellous fishing port. The annual lobster season, running from October to April, is the main focus of activity — and of very substantial income. Over the past couple of years it has been possible for a boat with a commercial licence to catch half a million dollars worth of crayfish in the first two months of the season. This alone gives the town a large income, although (needless to say) not all the licence-holders actually reside there.

The town's charm comes from the fact that most of the houses built in the 1850s and 1860s were constructed from local limestone, a building material still used today, notably at the Kreglinger winery. It is cheaper to use these beautifully cut pieces of limestone than to use concrete blocks.

Robe was a major entry point for the Chinese coming to work in the Victorian goldfields from the 1860s onwards. They paid £10 for their passage, but if they disembarked in Victoria, they had to pay a £10 entry fee. There was no charge in South Australia, so they disembarked at Robe, being the nearest port to Victoria, and then simply walked to Bendigo, Great Western or northeast Victoria.

> The Belgium-based company G & C Kreglinger has been in the business since 1797, and for the last 110 years has had a base here as a buyer of Australian wool and sheepskins. It is a tightly held family business run by the de Moor family, but as well as commodity trading, the closely related (cousins) Thienpont family has two illustrious wine châteaux.
>
> The first (in terms of chronology, at least) is Vieux Château Certan, acquired by Leon Thienpont in 1924, and now owned by the Societé Civile du Vieux Château Certan. It is one of the most highly rated of all the Pomerol châteaux.
>
> In 1979 Jacques Thienpont decided he would do his own thing, becoming the first 'garagiste' and establishing the 2-hectare, 700-case Château Le Pin, the reputation of which is infinitely greater than its size, the price of its wine equalling if not exceeding that of Château Petrus.
>
> In 1999 the family's attention swung to Australia, with managing director Paul de Moor leading the way. He looked at options ranging from Henty (far southwest Victoria) through to Coonawarra, but chose the Mount Benson region. Why? 'Because we prefer to be the largest fish in a smaller pond, rather than fourth or fifth in a larger one,' he answered, referring to Coonawarra. 'Besides, the cost of land in Coonawarra far exceeds that of Mount Benson,' he continued.
>
> The project expenditure (including vineyards) was $13 million, and it has given a major boost to the economy of the region and its nearest town, Robe. Mind you, Robe already has the crayfish industry, and a

ABOVE
Young vines on Kreglinger Estate are protected by green 'grow-tubes'.

strong general tourism base. Add in the sheer beauty of the coastline and the thriving salmon farming and barramundi farming (the latter selling 10,000 fish a week raised in the warm artesian water which began its journey in the Blue Mountains 300 years ago), and you start making comparisons, as did I, with the Margaret River region.

The dinner was held in a vast barrel hall; one of these years it may be filled with barrels, but it won't be anytime soon. We couldn't drink Kreglinger wines, but did consume copious quantities of Pipers Brook, 87 per cent of which just happens to have been also acquired by Kreglinger Australia (valuing Pipers Brook at around $30 million), having passed the acid test of being the largest fish in the Tasmanian pool.

APRIL 5   VINTAGE: ON A KNIFE'S EDGE

I return from Robe around 2 p.m., and later in the afternoon we go up to the upper Yarra Deer Park and Peggies vineyards. Picking has continued apace during the week, with a hiatus on Thursday when in fact 9 mm of rain fell — twice what was forecast, but not enough to cause critical problems. The picking of pinot in the lower Yarra should be completed this week, and we will then move into the upper Yarra for both pinot and chardonnay.

Here the vineyards continue on a knife's edge. Cold nights have slowed the ripening process, and the days, while generally fine, have been cool. The net effect of this combination has been painfully slow ripening. This is particularly true of flavour: sugar is gradually accumulating, but the acids remain very high and the pH low.

We agree to pick B Block chardonnay tonight (estimated at 17–20 tonnes) and a similar amount of A Block and C Block on Sunday night. All we can pray for now is that the promised warm weather of the weekend will arrive on schedule, rather than later as has so often been the pattern this year. I still remain enthusiastic about the potential quality, but we really need to see the conclusion of both the primary fermentation and (in the case of pinot) the malolactic fermentation in barrel before forming a worthwhile opinion.

APRIL 6 Summerfield Winery, Pyrenees

I am picked up at Coldstream airport, little more than a kilometre away from home, to be flown to Summerfield Winery for its twenty-first birthday celebrations and, in particular, to do a vertical tasting of the 1979–2000 Shiraz, the 1981–2000 Cabernet Sauvignon and a handful of blends done over the years. I complete the tasting, grab a

LEFT
Mechanical harvesting: so gentle these days there's no damage to the vines.

ham sandwich and am flown back to Coldstream at half past two. The rush is not all mine: the plane is due to hop across to Essendon and pick up a Chinese couple who have flown in from China for the celebrations, and take them up to Summerfield.

Anniversaries are tricky things for wineries; do you count your first vintage through to the most recent (regardless of whether it has been released), or only to the most recently released?

In April, Summerfield celebrated its twenty-first birthday with the release of its 2000 vintage red wines. Its first vintage was 1979, and it doesn't take rocket science mathematics to work out that this makes twenty-two vintages (or birthdays). But when you do a vertical tasting — as a number of us did — you find that no wine was released from the 1985 vintage, so it turns out that the Summerfield family (father Ian and sons Craig and Mark) can indeed count.

The story starts in 1970, or perhaps even 1949. Ian Summerfield was a sheep farmer in the region, but can remember picking grapes as a teenager at Kofoed's, the last of the nineteenth-century vineyards, which was uprooted in 1949. When vine plantings at Château Remy in 1963 were followed by Taltarni in 1969, Summerfield decided to follow suit, planting 4 hectares in 1970, intending to sell the grapes to Taltarni.

Taltarni was slower to get going than Summerfield anticipated, and the grapes went to Seppelt instead, which, says Ian, provided much technical assistance at a time when viticultural knowledge was scarce. But when, in 1979, he decided to venture into winemaking, it was with the active assistance of Dominique Portet, Taltarni's winemaker/manager.

Of the oldest wines, the 1979 Shiraz (how often it is the case that the first vintage shines) and the 1983 (from a drought year, still rich in plum, prune and chocolate) are the standouts. The next highlight is the 1988 Shiraz, then the 1990 Estate Shiraz (the forerunner of the Reserve), which is even better; the first has excellent mouthfeel and a harmonious blend of gently sweet dark plum, the latter includes chocolate, mint and sustaining tannins in the mix. Both are perfect to drink now.

Since 1996 the performance has been remarkably consistent, the

Estate (or Reserve) wines offering an extra degree of richness, ripeness, extract and oak, the varietal wines easier to approach in their youth. The 2000 shirazs are among the best made to date, particularly if you like the big end of town. The varietal (89 points; $23) is highly scented, with plum, prune and oak in abundance, the Reserve (93 points; $35) with an extra layer of plush dark plum and cherry fruit, massive underlying tannins and oak. It will still be powering along in 2015.

The real question is whether the makers of the most highly prized shiraz from regions such as Heathcote (Jasper Hill, Wild Duck Creek, Hanging Rock, etc), the Pyrenees (not so much Dalwhinnie), McLaren Vale (too numerous to mention), Barossa Valley (Two Rivers, Greenock Creek) and Clare Valley have been seduced by size, and the adulation of the United States importers, critics and consumers.

Only time will tell whether the pendulum has swung too far, and whether the awesomely alcoholic super-shirazs of today will stand tall, or be regarded, like the first heavily skin-contacted and oaked chardonnays of a decade ago, as the darlings of their time.

Back here at Coldstream Hills, the D Block Peggies chardonnay came in: not 20 tonnes, not 17 tonnes, but 12 tonnes. How could it be anything else? It's just the story of the vintage, repeated again and again. The juice looks very good: while the baume is not high (12.7°), the acid is in balance at 7.5 g/l, the pH 3.3. It has a mix of citrus and more tropical flavours, and on this score everyone is happy.

APRIL 8 SEVILLE ESTATE, YARRA VALLEY

Notwithstanding a flu injection a couple of weeks ago, I have crashed with the flu. However, with my last remnants of taste and smell rapidly disappearing, I go to the thirtieth anniversary tasting at Seville Estate today, which includes a vertical tasting of selected vintages of Seville Estate Shiraz from 1976 to 2000. The weather is perfect, and this red soil-side of the valley is as beautiful as ever.

Seville Estate was one of the founding fathers, along with Wantirna Estate (in 1963) then Fergussons (1968), Yarra Yering and Yeringberg (1969), Mount Mary (1971) and Château Yarrinya (now De Bortoli), also in 1971.

Peter McMahon, who with wife Margaret established Seville Estate, was a local GP in partnership with John Middleton (of Mount Mary). Both grew wine grapes in their backyards in the 1960s, practising winemaking, and leading to intermittent claims by one or the other to having pre-empted Dr Max Lake, generally regarded as the first weekend winemaker. McMahon and Middleton also played endless practical jokes on each other, with McMahon usually, but not always, ending up on top.

Pete McMahon (as he is universally known) retired from his medical practice in 1982 to expand the vineyard and the small on-site winery (built in 1975). The following year (1983) I retired from Brokenwood in the Hunter, and moved to Melbourne for my law firm, but with the intention of starting another vineyard in the Yarra Valley. I had fallen in love with the place at the end of the 1970s, and from that point on, the only question was when, not if.

In 1985 my wife and I established Coldstream Hills, never imagining that in 1997 Brokenwood would acquire a majority interest in Seville Estate, bringing the wheel full circle. When it did so, it further extended the plantings with shiraz, pinot noir and chardonnay.

There is a view held by some critics, and one notable producer, that the Yarra Valley as a whole is unsuited to shiraz. I, for one, do not agree with that view, but think that the degree of difficulty is increased on the southern red soil side of the valley. Here a north or northeast-facing slope and canopy management which maximises sunlight interception onto the grapes are essential prerequisites; thereafter the weather gods must be in a good mood.

This came through clearly in a vertical tasting covering 12 vintages of Seville Estate Shiraz falling between 1976 (the first vintage) and 2000 (just released). As so often happens, the 1976 was a star among the older vintages, growing rather than fading as it sat in the glass, with earthy/chocolaty flavours not unlike an old Hunter shiraz.

Thereafter, the 1985, '91, '97 and 2000 were my top wines, the 1988 and '94 next in line. 1997 was Iain Riggs' first vintage, helping guide Seville Estate's long-term manager/winemaker, and the low yields and warm vintage produced an outstanding wine, seemingly significantly riper, richer and with more tannins than any preceding vintage.

Back at Coldstream Hills, the total crush has crept up to 686 tonnes, with 343 tonnes of pinot, 190 tonnes of chardonnay, 83 tonnes of sauvignon blanc and 70 tonnes of pinot gris, plus a few tonnes of semillon and pinot meunier. The next serious rain is not forecast to arrive until Sunday (April 14), six days away, and by that time all the pinot noir and chardonnay from the upper Yarra should be picked. The bureau can't quite make up its mind about another front coming through earlier, on Tuesday or Wednesday (April 9 or 10); one moment it says the change will be weak, the next moment it puts it back twenty-four hours and says it could be accompanied by storms. Nail-biting stuff, of course, but nothing new, and the quality of the wine so far made is truly exciting. We know the colour will be intense, and the flavours intense, but it is still impossible to tell how much mid-palate vinosity there will be. Just because the berries are small does not mean the flavour profile will be as we wish it to be.

APRIL 11   McWilliam's 125th Anniversary

Anniversaries? They are coming from all quarters, but the 125th of McWilliam's Wines (1877 to 2002) is an important one. Against the odds, it continues to be a family company, and it has survived various income tax assaults by the federal government, and a critical period in the first half of the 1980s when it was left floundering in the wake of changes then sweeping through the industry.

As Max McWilliam commented at one of the impressive anniversary lunches held around Australia in April, 'a consultant retained by us in 1987 said "the patient is very sick"'. The crux of the problem was its Riverina-anchored base, with only Mount Pleasant in the Hunter Valley providing any quality contrast. Even knowledge of Mount Pleasant was limited to the Sydney market, and there was no understanding of its core brand — Elizabeth — elsewhere in Australia or overseas.

Since then McWilliam's has moved far and fast. In 1989 it acquired Barwang in the NSW Hilltops region, increasing the plantings from 10 to 100 hectares. In 1990 it purchased a half share in Brands of Coonawarra, moving to full ownership in 1996, and dramatically increasing its Coonawarra plantings to 280 hectares.

Then in 1994 it acquired Lillydale Vineyards in the Yarra Valley, which, under the quiet control of Max McWilliam, has steadily increased production by supplementing the estate plantings with a network of contract growers spread throughout the valley.

It's not many companies which could present wines from seven decades during a structured tasting followed by lunch, mixing up rare classics from the past with wines of the present and future. Although suffering badly from the flu, I was determined not to miss it, and filled in the missing bits of smell and flavour from earlier tastings.

One of the classics was the 1963 Riverina Cabernet Sauvignon; when I tasted that wine in 1983 I wrote that it was 'absolutely magnificent, still retaining exceptional colour, body and richness'. Another twenty years on, it is still a freak wine, the colour developed but still strong, the secondary flavours (I think) a mix of chocolate, earth and savoury berry. It has to be said that subsequent vintages have been far less exciting.

The promise of the pale green straw colour of the 1979 Lovedale Semillon was fulfilled by the daisy fresh palate, even fresher than its 1986 counterpart. (At the other lunches the 1979 Lovedale was less exciting.) The 1958 Pedro Sauterne, the first commercially released botrytised wine made in Australia, cut through my flu with its rich perfume and blend of caramel and toffee apple flavours.

The pièce de resistance was the 1947 O'Shea Hermitage, provided by BRL Hardy from its famous 'black hole' museum, coming from a single barrel purchased from Mount Pleasant in 1948. A great bottle of a great wine, and a testimony to the strength the Australian industry gains from such open-hearted cooperation.

Back here at Coldstream Hills we are at the end of a week of wonderful weather, but with a significant change forecast for Friday and Saturday (April 12 and 13). Hurried arrangements are made to pick the cabernet from G Block, which, to everyone's vast surprise, has ripened before the Amphitheatre merlot or cabernet franc. Our suspicion that the early ripening is due to a low yield is confirmed when the block yields 6 tonnes, compared with an average of 12–13 tonnes and a horrendous 1999 total of over 20 tonnes (when rain pumped up the berries and bunches). This takes us through the 700-tonne mark, with a total of 206 tonnes of chardonnay, 384 tonnes of pinot noir, 87 tonnes of sauvignon blanc and 6 tonnes of cabernet sauvignon, the remainder with pinot gris, semillon, etc. We are also able to get all but a hatful of Deer Farm pinot noir picked; the remainder will have to take its chances over the weekend.

APRIL 14   Vintage: Starting to Count the Chickens

After two days of significant rain, mist and cloud, another sunny day, and the rest of the week, through to Friday (April 18), should remain the same. We're not there yet, but we are awfully close to finishing what should turn out to be an outstanding vintage. The paradox of a very cool summer and an early conclusion to vintage is entirely due to the tiny crops. Had the yield been normal, the grapes might never have ripened.

APRIL 16   Geoff Merrill, Melbourne

> It's always a big call to assemble a group of journalists to blind taste an elite group of wines which includes yours. As Geoff Merrill discovered, every now and then it doesn't work quite as well as anticipated.
>
> The occasion was the official Australian release of his ultra-premium 1996 Henley Shiraz at the snappy price of $150 per bottle. Not that the price is of great practical importance, for only 150 cases of the wine were made. But nonetheless it is intended as his ultimate achievement, and there are vintages (notably the 1998) to come.
>
> Merrill pulled no punches in the line-up, all eight of which were wines from 1996: Penfolds Grange, BRL Hardy Eileen Hardy Henschke Hill of Grace, Rosemount Balmoral Syrah, Tahbilk 1860 Vines, Merrill Henley and then the two top names from the Rhône Valley, Guigal Côte-Rotie La Landonne and Jaboulet Hermitage La Chapelle.
>
> This was the fourth time the wines had been pitted against each other; Henley had come second to Grange when judged by a group of 37 South Australian winemakers in January 2000, and more recently had come second to Balmoral Syrah in New York, and first in San Francisco, on each US occasion by a mixed group of writers and sommeliers.

Suffice it to say that on this occasion it did not fare so well, although there were split opinions on all the wines. In a sign of the times, my fellow journalists were more interested to hear the alcohol levels (once the wines were unmasked) than the prices. Paradoxically, though, most seemed happy with the apparent alcohol; only the Eileen Hardy admitted to more than 14°, weighing in at 14.5°, a long way short of the 16° monsters so fashionable in some quarters these days.

My tasting notes on the Henley included these words: 'Rich, round, harmonious; sweet berry/dark cherry; no hint of jamminess/over-ripeness. Great texture and length. Not overblown.' How did I rate such a wine sixth? Well, I did toss up between it and the Tahbilk for fifth, but on my third or fourth visit to the glass, the oak on the bouquet started to become a tad obvious.

They are cruel things, these comparative tastings, and seldom tell the whole truth, however interesting they may be.

APRIL 18   WINE AUSTRALIA, SYDNEY

Today I am off to Sydney to discuss the future of Wine Australia's location with the NSW government. Almost from the outset I have had reservations about the practicality of rotating the event between Melbourne and Sydney: in this day and age, four years between events of this kind is a generation. The Olympics and the soccer World Cup are in a different category, although the added value which Sydney has retained from the 2000 Olympics is certainly a factor in my view that Wine Australia should be held there every two years. Holding it in the same city at much the same time biennially makes far more sense, particularly when that city is by far the largest market in Australia.

More or less in tandem with these discussions have been negotiations and discussions with Event Management Pty Ltd and its chief executive/owner, John Kelly. Rightly or wrongly, probably rightly, the industry has taken the view that it should no longer underwrite the financial risk of the Wine Australia events, and it is highly probable that Event Management will be retained to run the events in 2004, 2006 and 2008. The financial upside for the

Winemakers' Federation of Australia is clear enough; only time will tell whether the standards can be maintained in the process.

APRIL 20   Vintage: Wines in the Barrel

It's been a very cool and overcast week, but without significant rain, and the grapes continue to come in. Indeed, so much so that we have crept — perhaps I should say dashed — over the 900-tonne mark.

Andrew Fleming and I take a walk around the pinot noir barrels today, and my enthusiasm about the quality of the vintage grows every time I taste the wines. Coldstream Hills A Block, Coldstream Hills G Block and parts of Denton Vineyard are outstanding, heading to Reserve quality, with Killara only an eyelash back. Down the other end of the spectrum, there isn't a single batch which would be ruled out of the picture for Coldstream Hills varietal at this stage. What is more, all are undergoing malolactic fermentation, and they never look at their best at this awkward adolescent stage. I have to stop myself throwing superlatives around the place until the wines have finished their malolactic fermentation, had a period of lees contact, and are racked.

BELOW

Coldstream Hills: blocks below the house.

The freak wine of the vintage to date, G Block cabernet sauvignon, looks as good in the barrel as it did on the vine. Part of the crush is still sitting on skins; the barrel-ferment component has now been in the barrel for some days, and is as good as its track record suggests it should be. I doubt that we will ever see a year again in which G cabernet is picked two weeks before Amphitheatre merlot and cabernet franc; more typically it is two to three weeks later. Amphitheatre merlot and cabernet franc, together with Deer Farm merlot, will all be picked Monday and Tuesday (April 22 and 23), as there is a threat of another front arriving on Wednesday.

APRIL 24   MELBOURNE

I am off to California for a few days, primarily to receive the Literary Award for 2002 from the Wine Appreciation Guild, but also to discuss the possibility of a long overdue second edition of my *Wine Atlas of California*.

APRIL 24   CALIFORNIA: LODI

My watch is suffering more jetlag than I am: it says it's April 25. No wonder I got an odd look when I signed a book today. It's all due to that weird experience of arriving in California before you leave Melbourne.

Even more unusual is the feeding routine. I had breakfast yesterday at 6 a.m., five hours before I had taken off from Melbourne an eternity before, and then didn't feel the least bit hungry until late afternoon, when my eyes were starting to close of their own volition. So I staggered across the street to a sandwich bar which offers every beer in the world, likewise cocktails, but also claims to be the greatest sandwich bar in the world. Amazingly, the latter could well be true: offered bread or roll, I opt for roll, which turns out to be a cross between a large French baguette and a sourdough loaf. In it is piled layer upon layer of warm, rare roast beef, with a little jug of red blood from the meat served alongside. Two large draught Heinekens prove the perfect company, falling not far short of the Krug I consumed in copious quantities on the flight.

Today, after a very interesting drive around Lodi — successfully establishing its own identity on wine labels, and for long a secret source of high-quality zinfandel for many of the best-known wineries in California — I am deposited at a Holiday Inn hotel for the evening, with Bruce Cass picking me up tomorrow morning. From the gastronomic high of yesterday's sandwich bar, I plummet to the absolute depths this evening. The problem is, the Holiday Inn is near to a freeway, has a closed amusement park opposite, and no other habitation, let alone restaurant, visible in any direction. So it's the Vallejo Café, the premier eating venue in the Holiday Inn, or nothing. Reluctantly I contemplate the entrée choices: Cheesy Movie Fries, Soprano Sticks, Some Like It Hot, Close Encounter, A Mexican, The Jigs Tumbleweed, Couch Potatoes, One Flew Over The Cuckoo's Nest or Sea Hunt, the last with the explanation that Lloyd Bridges swam with these tasty morsels on his popular TV show (twenty-plus years ago) — 'now you too can enjoy the bounty of the sea. Our calamari are deep-fried and served with our marinara sauce.' Calamari it is, I decide. Prime-time rib of beef is available only on Fridays and Saturdays (today is, I think, Wednesday), so I am left with the choice of Ponderosa Platter, The Godfather or Pretty Woman for the main course. 'Ponderosa Platter comes straight from the ranch made famous on the small screen but made for a hearty appetite. This ten-ounce steak is juicy and cooked to order, served with a baked potato and seasonal vegetables. Add mushrooms or grilled onions for $1 or more.' I take the Ponderosa Platter.

At this point I order my food and a bottle of Geyser Peak Cabernet Sauvignon, the wines by the glass being of exceptionally doubtful origin. Not long later the waitress triumphantly returns with a bottle of Geyser Peak Chardonnay which has thoughtfully been opened in the bar. Regretfully I tell her that what I want is red, not white; Cabernet Sauvignon, not Chardonnay. She returns to tell me that they don't have it, and intimates that perhaps the Chardonnay will be acceptable after all. When I say, 'No, I will choose another red', a bottle of Geyser Peak Cabernet Sauvignon suddenly appears from the wings. Gentle persuasion indeed.

A further, very long, wait ensues before my food is brought to the table: deep-fried calamari, piping hot and surprisingly tender on one plate, and on the other my steak, which I had ordered medium-rare (if you order rare in the United States you are as like as not to get it uncooked). Quite obviously, it had been cooked well before the calamari. Perhaps there was some miscommunication in the kitchen.

APRIL 25   A Day to Remember, Napa Valley

From one extreme to the other, to a degree only ever encountered in the United States. I am picked up in the morning by Bruce Cass and Elliott Mackey and we head out for a day in the Napa Valley, going from humble wineries in rented space in old warehouses through a succession of appointments culminating in the surreal mountain-top development of restaurateur extraordinaire Pat Kuleto.

The day starts with Donald Patz of Patz & Hall, on site at one of their principal contract vineyards, the Hyde Vineyard in Carneros. Larry Hyde, with a degree of disability not far short of paraplegic Patrick Campbell's, gets around his vineyard with a walking stick which he hitches in the back pocket of his jeans when he is not moving. Lean and wiry, Hyde's attention to detail in the vineyard

RIGHT
The Lodi Wine and Visitors Centre endeavours to lift the profile of the region.

APRIL

ABOVE
Lodi vines in spring curl like the crest of a wave.

has to be seen to be believed. It is, however, believed when I learn that Patz & Hall pay Hyde on a per acre basis, and that the payment is US$14,000 per acre. Double that and you get A$28,000 per acre, and with yields typically under 3 tonnes that equates to A$9–10,000 per tonne. Small wonder, then, that the Patz & Hall chardonnays sell for US$48, the pinots for US$50 a bottle. It doesn't really matter how you cut the numbers: the grape cost is a much higher percentage of the sale price than is the case in Australia, although I suppose you have to factor back out the huge difference in the tax on wine: 46 per cent in Australia and negligible in the United States.

From Patz & Hall we go to Turley Vineyard, owned by famous Napa Valley Helen Turley's brother Bill Turley, an emergency room physician who was one of the founding partners in Frog Rock. The winemaker here is Ehren Jordan, who came into wine with a degree in archaeology and, through a series of strokes of good fortune, learnt his winemaking on the winery floor in some particularly distinguished French and Californian wineries. He makes three labels at Turley: Nyers, Turley

ABOVE
Ehren Jordan, the creative and talented winemaker for Turley Vineyards (and others).

and his own label, Failla Jordan. He is one of those all-too-rare winemakers who seems equally at home with chardonnay, viognier, pinot noir and syrah grown in cool climates, and massive zinfandels grown in warm climates, which are the Turley trademark. His touch is exceptional; the trademark of all of his wines is the textural balance on the mid to back palate and finish.

From here to the Grace Family Vineyard for lunch, and the all-encompassing evangelism (and ego) of Dick Grace, which has grown in dimension since 1992. The price per bottle has risen to US$175, and the production is back over 400 cases, after hovering between 2 and 3 barrels (22 dozen bottles) in the latter part of the 1990s, following the removal of the main vineyard in 1994 because of oak root fungus. There is only one price for Grace Family wine, and it is all sold on allocation, with a hundred people on the mailing list and a thousand waiting to get on.

Now a disciple of the Dalai Lama, with whom he spends a week every year, Grace remains the same enigma as ever, raising much money for his charities, yet happy to retain all the trappings of wealth and literally basking in the glow of the good works he does. Very difficult for Australians to come to terms with.

Next we go up the mountainside to the top of Howell Mountain, where Robyn Lail has established Lail Vineyards; with the Inglenook family history behind her, and a joint venture with the famous French winemaker Christian Moueix at Dominus (also in the Napa Valley) ended, she and her husband have acquired a house and spectacular mountainside vineyard planted to cabernet sauvignon, and another block — opposite Dominus, on the valley floor — planted to merlot.

Back down the mountain to Napa City and a quick walk through the US$20 million Copia facility, the Napa Valley's answer to the National Wine Centre in Adelaide. This huge building sits on land donated by the Robert Mondavi family; a large part of the capital was also donated by Robert Mondavi. Like the National Wine Centre, no one seems quite sure exactly how it should be run and, like the National Wine Centre, it needs attendance levels far higher than it is getting. However, unlike the National Wine Centre, there is a largely bottomless pit of donated capital to support it. The name, incidentally, is a shortening of Cornucopia.

Then back into the mountains towards Lake Berryassa, veering off the highway and ascending more than 300 metres up through a private road to the fantasy land created by Pat Kuleto.

The 188-cm, 116-kg, generously bearded Pat Kuleto immediately fills every space he is in — even a 450-metre ridgetop of the 350-hectare Kuleto Estate, plus the Napa Valley floor and Lake Hennessey far below. At fifty-six, he has already lived a number of lives: he lost the tips of two fingers in a radial saw, emerged from bankruptcy in 1980, and in 1992 from a raging forest fire which destroyed his large ranch house in Calaveros County and all his and his wife Shannon's possessions.

Totally undeterred, he is nearing the end of his most ambitious project: the house, winery and 40-hectare vineyard project which are the 'conventional' pieces of Kuleto Estate. Less conventional are a 12-metre French riverboat sitting at the bottom of a series of fully functional locks running up a near-vertical mountainside gully, built (in part) because his six-year-old son had been entranced by a canal trip through France.

Nor do you often find a site which has consumed 3000 tonnes of rocks brought down from Lake County before being taken 450 m up to the winery and building site, or which is home to a grove of ninety-year-old olive trees saved when Stags Leap Winery wished to expand its vineyards.

Earlier this year, *Forbes Magazine* put the project cost at $40 million, and it is hardly surprising that Kuleto doesn't even pretend that it will ever provide a return of any kind. Indeed, he says offhandedly that the winery has a 35,000-case permit, but he doubts whether he will take production past 10,000 cases; he will probably sell the excess grapes from the plantings — currently 40 hectares, but still expanding.

This self-taught former carpenter and building contractor more or less stumbled into restaurant design and building in the 1970s, having had a brief stint as a waiter, completing more than 20 Refectory Steakhouses. In 1984 he created San Francisco's Fog City Diner; his 110th restaurant, it was a breakthrough in design and established his reputation nationwide. He has now designed over 150

ABOVE
Robin Lail's house high on the eastern mountains of the Napa Valley.

restaurants across the United States, and ventured as far afield as Indonesia and Japan.

Heading the list are three of San Francisco's most famous restaurants, and Kuleto is a partner in these: Jardiniere, Farallon and Boulevard. More recently, he opened Martini House at St Helena in the Napa Valley, where he is in partnership with Todd Humphries. A superb wine list with over 600 wines and equally wonderful food (I chose crispy sweetbreads, followed by lobster on roasted asparagus, then squab with wild mushrooms) makes it a powerful challenger to Napa icon restaurants such as Tra Vigne.

The winery won't be open to the public in the normal sense (the planning permit won't allow it, for one thing), but visitors will — by arrangement — be able to spend a whole day at the Estate, which is inevitably being described as a vini-viticultural Disneyland.

Finally, consider this in the land of the free: until recent changes in the law, Kuleto couldn't sell his wine to or through any of the restaurants in which he had a proprietary interest. Now he can sell to two — but only two — of them. Alice in Wonderland could not have provided a better storyline.

APRIL 26 THE WINE APPRECIATION GUILD'S WINE LITERARY AWARD

The Wine Appreciation Guild's Wine Literary Award for exceptional contribution to the literature of wine is an annual award, and has previously been won by writers such as Hugh Johnson and Jancis Robinson, among other very well-known names.

Over 1000 wines are presented for tasting throughout the day for journalists (and only journalists, interestingly — not the wine trade, and certainly not the public), and I assiduously work my way through as many as possible, chirping into my dictating machine, blissfully unaware at one time that it is not turned on. Very frustrating. A black-tie dinner follows; mercifully, it ends reasonably early, presentation and speeches all done.

APRIL 27 SAN FRANCISCO RHÔNE RANGERS

My plane to Los Angeles is not scheduled to leave San Francisco until 5.30 p.m., so I have several hours in which to attend the annual Rhône Rangers tasting, where virtually every producer in California with a Rhône-style wine in its armoury is represented. There must be

LEFT
The downstairs back door of Pat Kuleto's mountain-top house.

well over 500 wineries present. It's a massive affair, and I talk into the dictating machine against a veritable roar of background noise.

All this activity has been prompted by the possibility of a second edition of the *Wine Atlas of California*, but I'm not chicken-counting just yet; quite frankly, I think I'm mad to even consider it. (Postscript: I am still waiting to receive a proposition.)

APRIL 30   THE LAST SUPPER AT COLDSTREAM HILLS

A Wine Australia board meeting (by phone), then I fulfil my foolhardy promise to cook dinner for the 27-strong Coldstream Hills vintage crew, and to produce the wines for everyone's birth year. Not a lot of catching up on sleep here.

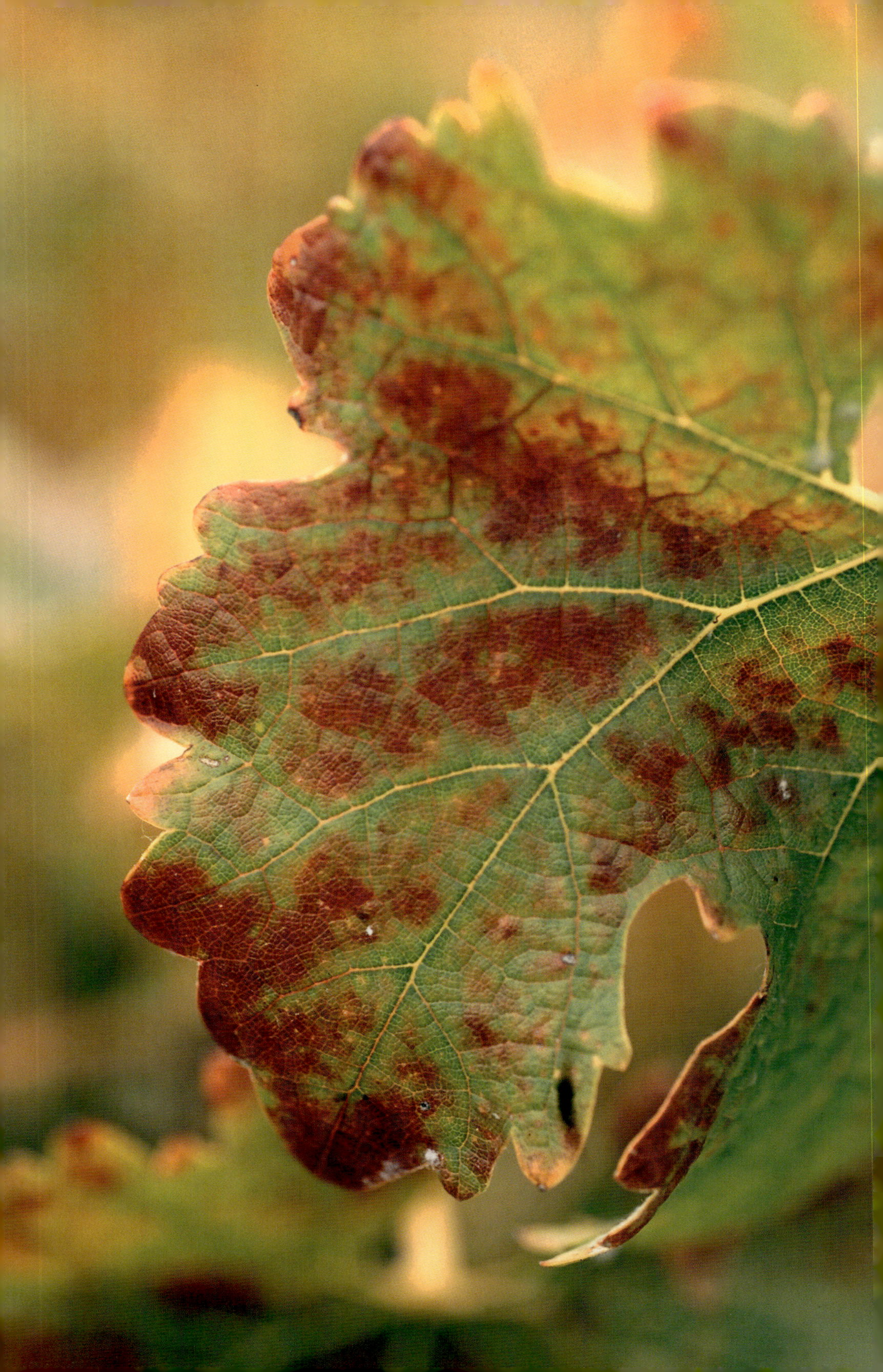

May

To France

Arrival in Monthelie

Market Day in Beaune

Simon Bize and La Bouzerotte

Hôtel Dieu, Beaune

Domaine Parent and La Ciboulette

Meursault and Hautes-Côtes de Beaune

Domaine Parent, Domaine Dujac and Domaine de la Vougeraie

The Vineyards of Burgundy

Domaine de la Romanée-Conti

Domaine Armand Rousseau

Maison Champy

Bouchard Père et Fils

Heading South

Avignon, Southern Rhône Valley

Relais Saint Victoire, Aix-en-Provence

Nice to Corsica

Calvi to Porto Vecchio, Corsica

MAY 1   To France

Off to France until June 7.

MAY 2   Arrival in Monthelie

Calendars are funny things. I left the 'last supper' before the vintage ports were served, but still in the early hours of May 1. And now here I am in Monthelie on May 2, having flown to Paris and caught the TGV to Dijon, changing there for the train to Beaune. It is a grey overcast day as Suzanne greets me at the station, having arrived earlier to spend time (and money) in Paris, her favourite city. As we drive to Monthelie and our house, the growth on the vines is remarkable, significantly more advanced than the same time last year. What is going on here, I wonder.

Going out for dinner this evening does not seem logical, so we buy two splendid duck breasts at the butcher in Meursault, then go to the supermarket in Beaune for the usual house requisites. French supermarkets are very different from those in Australia, with endless selections of cheeses, both pre-packaged and (better still) from a huge counter stretching half the length of the supermarket, matched only by the extraordinary range of Belgian, Czech, French and Dutch beers. From the vegetable section we choose minuscule French haricots vertes (green beans), smaller even than the smallest beans grown by the Vietnamese in Australia, and small white potatoes.

Suzanne has brought two small containers of caviar from Paris, one (like a miniature boot polish tin) called Caviar Pressé, the other Royal Oscietra. Radically different in texture and flavour, of course, but they both go well with the Billecart Salmon Champagne from our cellar underneath the house, as does the duck with a 1993 Vosne Romanée Les Suchots of J Confuron-Cotetidot, likewise from the cellar.

MAY 3   Ma Cuisine: My Favourite Beaune Restaurant

Another rainy day; in the course of arranging visits to our various friends in Burgundy, Jacques Seysses of Domaine Dujac comments that had the rain and cold change not arrived, they might well have been looking at an August harvest, an uncommonly early vintage. A figure of speech, perhaps, but it certainly underlines the unusually rapid early growth.

Tonight we are going to our favourite Beaune restaurant, Ma Cuisine, a tiny place with classically simple and inexpensive food, and a wonderful wine list put together by the chef/owner Pierre Escoffier and his wife, who is the daughter of Andre Parra, a Melbourne restaurateur who has now returned to Burgundy.

It turns out we have been very lucky to get a table at such short notice; the Escoffiers are going on two weeks' holiday, starting tomorrow. Suzanne has snails then quail; I start with homemade foie gras (sensational) followed by a tiny fillet of veal, cooked to perfection with mushrooms, marron (chestnut) and garlic together with fresh pasta, then a sinful slice of almond cake. The food (for the two of us) is 60 Euros, the wine 355 Euros, because after a half bottle of 1999 Monthelie Blanc (Louis Max) I cannot resist a bottle of 1993 Domaine de la Romanée-Conti Romanée St Vivant at 336 Euros (a little over A$500, but less than the wholesale price of the 1999 Romanée St Vivant when it comes onto the market later this year). Well, we had to celebrate our arrival here in some fashion, and it seemed a good idea at the time: fly now, pay later stuff.

The address for Ma Cuisine is Passage Ste Helénè; phone 03 80 22 3022. Closed Wednesday lunch, Saturday and Sunday.

MAY 4   MARKET DAY IN BEAUNE

It's market day in Beaune and, grey skies or not, there is never the least doubt that we are going. Across France there are many such markets, but Beaune is home base, and the largest gathering of people selling everything under the sun in our region.

The major part of the market, and that of most interest to us, is the food section. Stall after stall after stall rings the square outside the Hôtel Dieu; one has fresh morilles and slightly tired shitake mushrooms, and these go into the shopping bag first, the morilles

ABOVE LEFT
Market days at Beaune are a magnet for tourists and locals alike.

ABOVE RIGHT
Homemade saucisson of all manner of meats at the Beaune market.

making a noticeable dent in my cache of Euros. Then it's tiny, rosy-hued globe artichokes, more haricots vertes, fresh garlic (and I mean fresh, something almost impossible to find in Australia), onions, rosy-red tomatoes (not hydroponic, but with green stems still attached), spinach and strawberries.

Then to the even more serious business of cheese and meat. As ever, there are two giant mobile rotisseries filling the square with glorious aromas; a large rotisserie-roasted duck is added to the shopping. We move inside the market hall to consider endless possibilities for cheese and fresh meat. I have already bought a country terrine and homemade salamis outside. A huge rib of charolais beef is irresistible, as it was last year.

We have learnt that the best Epoisses cheese is made by Bertheaut, and that we should never buy the small round carton but should always insist on the large one. This advice came from Pierre Escoffier, when Suzanne enquired about the provenance of the Epoisses they serve at Ma Cuisine. When fully ripe, this gloriously smelly soft-rind cheese oozes onto your plate, like a super-charged camembert or brie, but with infinitely more flavour.

The final purchase is a large artisnal loaf, like a distended baguette. There is apparently a tradition that the bakers of France make artisnal (old recipe) bread at least once a week, not every day. Whether this is myth or fact, I am not sure.

While at the market, Suzanne learns about a wine bar-cum-bistro which has live jazz each Saturday night. The name is banal — Bistro Bourguignon — but we go there to book for dinner, and see for ourselves that the wine list is as good as we have been told. There are fifteen or so wines by the glass, all good, and a much larger list by the half-bottle and bottle.

We return that night, to cool jazz (piano and xylophone) played in an adjoining room which is set up for those who simply want to listen to the music, and have a couple of glasses of 2000 Chassagne Montrachet (good), followed by a bottle of 1999 JJ Confuron Nuits St Georges Premier Cru, which is as luscious a pinot as you could ever hope for, and very much typical of the best of 1999. It bears a striking similarity in terms of flavour and weight to the best Central Otago pinot noirs from 1999 and 2000.

MAY 5   SIMON BIZE AND LA BOUZEROTTE

More grey skies and another pattering of intermittent showers. We have made an appointment to see Patrick Bize of Simon Bize at Savigny-les-Beaune; Patrick did part of the 1981 vintage at Brokenwood, and was my assistant winemaker at Coldstream Hills in 1986 (back then my winemaking equipment was all at Yarra Ridge, which at that stage had not started to make wine).

We visited Patrick briefly last year and learnt that, just as he was about to be cast as the perpetual bachelor, he had met and married Tissa, a beautiful Japanese girl, and is now the father of two small children. He has also embarked on a major renovation and restoration of the cellars, which twelve months ago looked like a bombsite. Now, as in so many parts of Burgundy, brand-new stonework, new buildings and gravelled courtyards with flowers

ABOVE
The new winery building and courtyard at Domain Simon Bize.

everywhere are a symbol of hard-won prosperity — hard-won, that is, compared with the overflowing coffers of Bordeaux.

We taste all the 2001s from barrel; the wines have the finesse which has always been part of the Simon Bize style, but also have wonderfully sweet fruit. They are not as luscious as the 1999s, but have more mid-palate and structure than the 2000s.

Towards the end of the tasting I ask Patrick about a restaurant he recommended on our last visit, but which was closed when we finally found it. He says it is as good as ever and promptly makes a reservation for Suzanne and I for lunch. It is La Bouzerotte, situated on the D970 at Bouze-les-Beaune (03 80 21 30 26), and we must have tried to eat there last year on Monday evening or Tuesday, for this is when it is closed each week.

We have the 35-Euro menu, Suzanne commencing with pâté de maison and a white sweet pâté shaped like a tiny oval football, while I have gros ravioli (large ravioli) of snails and langoustine (lobster) with crème de l'ail (garlic sauce). The pâté is good, the white football altogether strange and too sweet, the ravioli ravishing. Served in a soup bowl, the flavour and texture are out of this world. Then follow veal fillet and mashed potatoes (Suzanne) and, for me, rabbit stuffed with kidneys, liver and mushrooms. The presentation of Suzanne's plate is simplicity itself; mine is baroque in the extreme, featuring the kind of three-deck structure found more often in the United States. On the top are two deep-fried, pressed-flat leaves of cabbage; then tiny string potatoes; then the meat. It simply gets better and better.

The cheese tray is excellent, with a festering Chambourcin (with its soft, orange rind and high butter fat content of 50 per cent) and a decadent Epoisses, and the usual gamut of other cheeses all the way from Brillat-Savarin (the ultimate in richness, made in Normandy, a triple cream cheese with 75 per cent butter fat content) to Chèvre (white goat's milk cheese which comes in all shapes, sizes and textures, from soft to hard, with a salty bitterness). The desserts which follow are, it must be said, not up to the standard of the rest of the meal, but we eat them anyway. It may have been better not to; it is not until 9.30 tonight that we can face anything more than a bowl of homemade French onion soup. I feel like an anaconda after a particularly large kill.

MAY 6   PHOTOGRAPHY IN BURGUNDY

The sun is out and so are my cameras, as I try to capture the vivid colours of spring, my only concern being a cloud which seems to have been personally assigned to me as I prowl around Pernand Vergelesses, St Aubin, St Romain and the southern outskirts of Beaune.

MAY 7   HÔTEL DIEU, BEAUNE

It doesn't matter how many times you visit the Hôtel Dieu in Beaune, its majesty is still overwhelming, its history mesmeric.

It was built in the middle of the fifteenth century, not long after the finish of the Hundred Years' War (in 1435) which so devastated France as the country sought to shake itself free of the Dark Ages. While peace had officially been declared, bands of mercenary soldiers still roamed the countryside, raping and pillaging. If this were not enough, a three-year famine began in Burgundy in 1436, and more than two thousand of Beaune's inhabitants were deemed to be destitute.

It was against this background that the Duke of Burgundy's Chancellor, Nicolas Rolin, decided to build a hospital for the sick or needy. Being a prudent (and extremely wealthy) man, he first asked the Pope for permission to proceed (it was to be run by nuns). Said permission was duly forthcoming, on 8 September 1441.

Preparation of the site began in August 1443. Rolin calculated the building would take five years to complete. In fact it took eight years; the chapel and cemetery were consecrated on New Year's Eve 1451, and the first patient was admitted the following day.

Rolin died in 1461, but his wife, Guigone de Salins, and his son, Cardinal Tehan Rolin (who had consecrated the buildings), took over the hospital's management and built on its fame. Over the generations, succeeding kings confirmed its privileges, and the Sun

RIGHT
The steeply pitched, tiled roofs of the Hôtel Dieu in Beaune.

King stayed in a large room on the first floor in 1658, which has ever since been known as the King's Chamber.

It was in this chamber that the gala dinner of the 2001 Academie Internationale du Vin excursion to Burgundy was held, with glorious wines such as 1990 Domaine de la Romanée-Conti Grands Echézeaux and superb food by Lucien Crotet of Hostellerie de Levernois, a nearby Michelin-starred restaurant (for a while disappointing, but now on the ascendant and well worth a visit).

Both Nicolas Rolin and Guigone de Salins gave specific vineyards to the Hôtel Dieu; over the centuries many others have followed suit, with the result that the Hospices de Beaune (as the larger institution has become known) is today the second-largest vineyard holder in Burgundy (Bouchard Père et Fils is first).

Each vineyard continues to bear the name of its donor (Cuvée Nicolas Rolin, etc) as well as its appellation contrôlée. (Appellation d'origine contrôlée, to give it its full name, is the French legislated system of designating and controlling all geographically based names of wine regions.) The wines are vinified at the Hospices, and are sold by the barrel at what has been described as the world's largest charity auction, on the third Sunday in the November following vintage (when they are little more than one month old). The purchaser is required to take delivery of the wine by no later than the following January, and is thereafter responsible for its maturation (élevage) and bottling.

Little or nothing of the viticultural and winemaking side of the business is apparent to the average tourist visiting the Hôtel Dieu. But it is also almost impossible to believe that the Great Hall, with its lines of scarlet-blanketed alcove beds running down the length of each side, remained in use for the sick until 1971.

MAY 8   Jardin des Remparts

Today (Wednesday) and tomorrow are holidays; today celebrating French victory day at the end of World War II, tomorrow Ascension Day. Half of France, it seems, is 'taking the bridge' by having Friday off, something the French are prone to do with even less excuse than on this occasion.

More than ever, the days revolve around food. After our monster lunch yesterday, we revert to our usual pattern of a fresh baguette and an array of terrines, pâtés, prosciutto, summer vegetables and cheeses. The butcher shop in Meursault is tiny, but all the terrines and pâtés are made on the premises and are mouthwateringly good.

Tonight we are going to one of the few one-star restaurants in Beaune, the elegant and spacious Jardin des Remparts, situated on the Peripherique (ring road) which circles Beaune. The evening starts promisingly enough, but soon descends into an abyss, the major problem being the far too few waiters. After much humming and hahing, we decide to have a full bottle of Aubert de Villaine's Aligote de Bouzeron to start with, followed by a full bottle of the 1998 Chambolle Musigny of Georges Roumier. Two glasses of the Aligote are poured, the bottle vanishes, and we then have a fifteen-minute sit-down strike until someone reappears to refill our glasses to accompany the course which has been sitting on the table for over

ABOVE
The apothecary at the Hotel Dieu; a lot less intimidating than the surgical instruments also on display.

ten minutes. We solve the problem by insisting that the bottle be left on the table so we can help ourselves. Much the same rigmarole occurs with the red wine.

The food itself is elaborate, some dishes very good, but others trying too hard and simply not working: for instance, the langoustines which Suzanne has, incorporating fresh ginger and lavender. The ginger and lavender flavours build up with each mouthful, finally completely obscuring the flavour of the langoustine. It was hard to suggest that at 219 Euros (A$350) we got our money's worth. However, it is highly regarded by some of the local vignerons. (10 rue Hôtel-Dieu, 03 80 24 79 41, closed Sunday and Monday.)

MAY 9   Domaine Parent and La Ciboulette

On my way to Meursault to buy a baguette for lunch, I bump into Milton Wordley (Australia's foremost wine photographer) once again — we had met in the street on market day. He's on my favourite corner taking pictures of the valley sweeping down to Auxey-Duresses, and says that in ten minutes he is going to a tasting at Domaine Parent in Monthelie with Paul de Burgh Day and his wife Geraldine plus Becky Wasserman's husband, Russell. I get the baguette and invite myself to the tasting, finding that Bill and Sandra Pannell (ex-Moss Wood and now Picardy) are also there. A gathering of friends, indeed.

Since 1997 the Domaine has been run by daughter Annick Parent on a full-time basis. Prior to that time she worked part-time as a psychologist in Paris and part-time at the winery with her father, Jean. Each has a number of vineyards in Monthelie, Volnay and Pommard, all small holdings, and with all the wines produced in tiny quantities. She has no permanent, full-time assistance in the winery and does much of the vineyard work herself — 'so I can get close to my vines,' she says.

All the wines are from the relatively lowly rated 2000 vintage — more successful in the Côte de Beaune than in the Côte de Nuits — but all have a stamp of elegance, length and balance. By far the most enjoyable at this stage is the Volnay Premier Cru l'Ormeaux, which is exceptionally supple and with lovely mid-palate fruit sweetness.

Tonight we go to La Ciboulette, given a red Bib Gourmand by Michelin: in Michelin's words, these are for restaurants which have 'moderately priced menus that offer good value for money and serve carefully prepared meals'. And indeed the food is far more convincing that that of the previous night; between us we have salad maquereaux (mackerel) — good; velouté aux asperges (asparagus in white sauce) — excellent; émince de pieds de veau tiède (finely sliced calves' feet) — brilliant, at once sophisticated yet provincial; cassoulette d'escargots (braised snails) — very good indeed; suprême de poulet fermier (free-range chicken in a rich cream sauce) — very good; estouffade de boeuf (beef cooked very slowly with a highly reduced sticky sauce) with fresh tagliatelle —outstanding; cheese and soupe de fraises (marinated strawberries) — both good. The food is accompanied by a half-bottle of 1998 Pouilly Fumé de Ladoucette and a 1999 Gevrey Chambertin Vielles Vignes of Goillot-Bernollin (a producer I have never heard of and who favours black and gold labels in the manner of some of Brian McGuigan's more gaudy efforts). Notwithstanding its unprepossessing appearance, the wine has all the plump, rich generosity of the 1999 vintage.

The cost? Only slightly more than half the previous night, at 140 Euros. Equally remarkable was the efficiency and speed of the two people working the front of house, the wife of the chef (Martine Demougeot) and a waiter, who literally flew, providing immaculate service to a restaurant packed to the gills with almost entirely French customers. We shall return.

The address is 69 rue Lorraine, telephone and fax 03 80 24 70 72, closed Monday and Tuesday.

MAY 11   Meursault

Meursault is the largest town on the 'golden slope' south of the city of Beaune. Pommard, Volnay, Monthelie, Auxey-Duresses, Puligny Montrachet and Chassagne Montrachet are all much smaller, but

ABOVE
The Monthelie vineyard of Domaine Parent in spring.

(like most of the famous villages of the Côte de Nuits) they share one thing in common: they all lie to the west of the N74, which might loosely be called the umbilical cord connecting all the communes of the Côte d'Or. Only a kilometre further east the traffic roars along the Autoroute du Soleil, the A6, which takes you from Paris to Lyon, and continues as the A7 until it meets the Mediterranean at Marseille.

So to visit any of these villages you have to make a deliberate turn off the N74 (assuming you have already exited the A6). Meursault, however, reserves some special tricks for first or second-time visitors. If you follow the signs suggesting you may be on the way to the town centre — a square ringed with the Gothic church, the splendid town hall (mairie), restaurants, small hotels, two boulangeries (bakeries), a butcher/charcuterie, micro supermarket and two paper shops — you will rapidly find yourself headed away from where you wish to be.

This is true whether you are approaching it from the N74 (to the southeast of Meursault) or (especially) the D973, which splits from the N74 just south of Beaune and takes you past Pommard, Volnay, Monthelie and Auxey-Duresses. You first pass a sign saying Autres Directions (other directions) and Centre Ville (town centre —

promising), but then must ignore a sign which comes one minor intersection thereafter and proclaims Toutes Directions (all directions) but is silent on the question of Centre Ville. If you then (for no apparent reason) go straight ahead and follow ever-narrowing unmarked roads until you enter a one-way road which twists past a blind corner, taking you literally underneath the square, you finally come across a small blue and white sign pointing to Centre Ville, a mere 50 metres up this tiny street.

In the centre of the square is a fountain ringed by a circle of (inevitably pollarded) plane trees. There is enough room for the square to fill with the mobile vans which travel from town to town for a market day, finishing around 12.30 p.m. In Meursault market days are Wednesday and Friday, offering all foods and — in spring — flowering potted plants in a blaze of colour.

The butcher has a large commercial kitchen at the back of his shop, where he makes an extensive range of sausages, salamis, pâtés, terrines (finely ground or chopped meat mixed with spices or herbs and compressed into an earthenware bowl, served sliced and always cold), rillettes (usually shredded pork cooked in its own fat, served cold, but spooned, not sliced) and so forth, all of which are seductively good. He is also a dab hand with choux-type pastry, making irresistible feuilleté de jambon (fine layers of pastry

LEFT
The butcher's display in Meursault: the ducks are to die for.

interleaved with ham) and feuilleté de saumon (salmon) which can either be eaten cold (good) or warmed up (dangerous, because if you warm up too much as an entrée there is every likelihood the main course will be largely uneaten).

If you purchase his duck breasts, as I have done on several occasions, the dilemma becomes acute. Each weighs around half a kilo or more; one divided into two is not enough, but one each becomes a duckathon. They come from ducks the size of turkeys, which I suspect have been force-fed for their foies, but it may be that they are just plain greedy. The poulet de Bresse I purchased the other day was also XXL size; it is sold complete with unplucked head, feet and innards. I gratefully accepted the offer of dressing (or removal) of these accessories — I imagine part, at least, was put to good use in that kitchen. Recycling is evident everywhere, from bottles to newspapers to tins (via receptacles identical in size to portaloos) and it doesn't worry me that I may have paid for the duck's innards twice.

But it is for its voluptuous white burgundy that Meursault is famous. All but 18 hectares of the total 370 hectares in production are Premier Cru. (The wines of Burgundy are classified both geographically by appellation contrôlée and by quality. The top quality is Grand Cru, a mere 1 per cent of the total area; then Premier Cru, accounting for 11 per cent; the remaining 82 per cent is commune or village. Strangely, the Premier Crus fall into two separate groups, one at the northern extremity of the commune, the other (larger and better known) at the southern extremity.)

Given time in bottle, Meursault develops a honeyed, nutty opulence and richness second only to the Grand Crus, with Geneverières and Perrières leading the way. Given a good vintage and producer, these wines can hold their own for forty years or more; they typically cast off awkward adolescence with five years of bottle age.

MAY 13 Hautes-Côtes de Beaune

I am sitting in the twilight in the back courtyard with an Epoisses which is trying desperately to escape by running away from the parchment sheet which once held it in slightly more solid form, and having dispatched a duck pilaf made with rice from Surinam and the remains of some of the very large and very local duck breasts which we had eaten half of the night before.

My only companions are the birds and the church bells now pealing in the background to mark the passing of nine o'clock. Steve and Sam Duquemin (friends who came to stay for a couple of days) left this morning to return to Jersey, and Suzanne took off to the Périgord (via forty-eight hours in Paris) at much the same time. So if last week was lazy, this one will be lazier still.

I have just returned from a forty-five-minute trip through the Hautes-Côtes de Beaune which took me from Monthelie to the little village of Nantoux and then (via the D23b) to the even smaller town of Mandelot. Both the Hautes-Côtes de Beaune and the Hautes-Côtes de Nuits lie above and behind the main slope of the Côte d'Or, with no villages of any renown, and any that are there usually awkwardly out of the way. The whole atmosphere here is very different, with a much lusher and greener landscape, only partly given over to vineyards; the rest is verdant pasture and crops. Oak forests, too, abound, and indolent white Charolais cows seem as happy lying sprawled on the grass chewing their cud as they do standing up for some serious grass mowing.

Late this afternoon, high cloud washed out the sun and I abandoned thoughts of a photographic trip. Then, almost without warning, the sun broke free of the high cloud, and I threw myself plus cameras into the car and headed off. The road is extremely narrow in parts, making photographic stops theoretically dangerous — the danger is alleviated only by the virtual absence of traffic.

All this seems entirely appropriate for a landscape which has changed little in hundreds of years. Gainsborough would have revelled in it, as would painters a hundred years before him. The poetic licence those painters would undoubtedly have given themselves to incorporate people, horses and so forth is matched by the 80–400 mm drop high capacity zoom lens of my Nikon, which can include or exclude particularly desirable or undesirable parts of the landscape. Ironically, it's also true that a feature which either

ABOVE
Hautes-Côtes de Beaune — narrow roads, tiny towns.

ABOVE RIGHT
Hautes-Côtes de Beaune vineyards above Mandelot.

particularly pleases or displeases the eye can appear quite insignificant when the picture is finally printed.

I have overcome the last signs of resistance from the Epoisses, now reduced to skeletal proportions, and my bottle of 1997 Hubert de Montille Volnay is fast disappearing — the light likewise. The birds have fallen silent, and now two officious town dogs are engaging in a brief verbal war presumably designed to impress their owners who — as ever — let the warfare continue without reprimand. When actually confronted, most of the dogs transform from snarling beast to simpering, fawning, tail-wagging friend, but it's always salutary to remember the smile on the face of the crocodile.

MAY 15   DOMAINE PARENT, DOMAINE DUJAC AND DOMAINE DE LA VOUGERAIE

Another glorious sunny day, with a windless but crisp start. While taking photographs yesterday afternoon (I am using film at an alarming rate) I happened to be standing beneath Annick Parent's office window, an enormous sheet of plate glass one storey up from the street. The office has a view out over the Auxey-Duresses valley similar to that of Coldstream. She saw me, and discussion led to an appointment for me to come by (with my camera, which I did not have last time) at nine o'clock this morning and buy some wine for my bin in the stone cellar under our house. The Parents' Clos Gauthey Vineyard and Winery were established in 1774, and now have various add-ons, including a most unusual pigeon house which looks like a mini chapel (around 1900) and, very recently, a refurbished office fronting onto the street (with the plate glass).

Murphy's Law being what it is, the 2000 Volnay L'Ormeaux is already sold out, but Annick takes pity and lets me have three bottles, and also three bottles of the long-since sold out 1996 Monthelie Clos Gauthey (out of twenty bottles remaining in the cellar). I buy another two dozen bottles of various 1998 and 1999 vintages from the tiny production, which seldom amounts to more than 1000 cases a year. The absence of 46 per cent tax makes the prices seem exceptionally low, the Monthelies selling for 13.5 Euros a bottle, the others ranging between 22 and 28 Euros per bottle.

From Domaine Parent it's on to Domaine Dujac at 11 a.m. My visit is timed to coincide with that of Dujac's largest US importer, Chambers and Chambers. It is owned by Jack Chambers and daughter Suzanne, and once again the wine world shows how small it can be. Jack Chambers was one of the founding directors of Chalone,

BELOW LEFT
At Domaine Parent: tools, not pigeons, in the pigeon house alcove.

BELOW RIGHT
The courtyard at Domaine Parent, the pigeon house on the right-hand side.

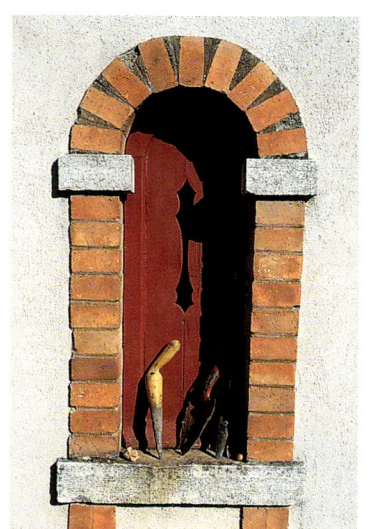

and for a number of years I received the Chalone shareholders group on tours to Australia at Coldstream Hills. And three weeks ago I was at Turley Vineyard, briefly saying hello to Larry Turley, Suzanne Chambers-Turley's husband.

Jeremy Seysses conducts the tasting, with occasional darts from behind barrels by father Jacques to briefly smell the wine we are tasting. The generational handover has commenced, but I don't doubt it will be many years yet before it is complete. The Domaine Dujac wines are much darker than usual (they are famed for being light-coloured, a lightness which entirely belies their intensity, finesse and length), and Jacques ironically observes that 'yes, they are dark; the problem is, so are all the pinots from the 2001 vintage'.

Lunch follows at the house; the Seysses' regular cook has recently had a baby, so the services of a former two-star Michelin chef are engaged. This chef gave up his thriving restaurant to teach cuisine at the university, but also to take on in-house lunches and dinners such as today's. After a lobster salad, crispy skin turbot is served with a red wine reduction sauce of quite extraordinary richness, texture and flavour. I cannot imagine what the initial volume must have been, for the sauce is every bit as thick as a concentrated demi-glaze, and ties in the fish to perfection with the magnum of 1969 Echézeaux (the first vintage of Domaine Dujac) casually produced from the cellar. I think (with encouragement from Jacques) I make up for the fact that others at the table seem preoccupied with eating, talking and drinking water.

The Echézeaux is an eerie experience. Nineteen years ago, when I worked at Domaine Dujac during the 1983 vintage, I was amazed at the freshness and condition of the wines (especially in large-format bottles) which Jacques produced from the cellar — they were from 1969, 1970 and 1971. Yet this bottle is precisely as I remember the same and similar wines nineteen years ago: fresh as a daisy, elegant, and showing no compost, game or other ancient smells. 'It is a testament to the benefits of non-intervention,' muses Jacques, pointing out that there was almost no equipment in the winery, and that the wine had spent only nine days in the vat before being pressed and taken to barrel.

From Domaine Dujac to Domaine de la Vougeraie, where next-door neighbour and part house owner (of our house, that is) Pascal Marchand is the general manager/winemaker.

Vougeraie (for short) only came into being in 1999, when the Burgundy magnate Jean-Claude Boisset put together all the estate vineyards which had come as parts of the string of negociant houses he had purchased over the previous ten years or so. The negociant houses — or companies — of Burgundy were all powerful until the advent of Domaine bottling (i.e. the bottling of their own wine by small producers) in the late 1920s/early 1930s. The negociant typically made some of its own wine, but most was purchased in bulk shortly after fermentation had finished. The erosion of negociant power was gradual; until the late 1970s only the best-known domaines bottled and sold their own wine direct to the consumer. Now it is the rule rather than the exception for those with precious Grand or Premier Cru holdings. Boisset's meteoric rise, and the size of the empire he has assembled, is still a cause célèbre. So is Vougeraie itself, for its vineyard holdings extend from near the bottom of the Côte de Beaune to the top of the Côte de Nuits, ranging from commune to Grand Cru holdings, and including the monopole (or exclusive ownership) of Le Clos Blanc de Vougeot, immediately adjacent to Clos de Vougeot and planted solely to chardonnay.

The spread of holdings gives Pascal Marchand a unique insight not only into the well-accepted notions of terroir (a French word which has no counterpart in English, and encompasses all of the physical attributes of a vineyard site, including soil, subsoil, aspect, degree of slope, sunlight interception, rainfall, humidity and so forth), but also into the way the particular climatic circumstances of each year impact on various parts of the Côte d'Or. He is the first to point to the dangers of generalisations (localised hail, small infestations of vine moths, or rather their caterpillars, mildew, botrytis, etc), but agrees with the view that in 2000 the Côte de Nuits fared much better than the Côte de Beaune (for the red wines), while in 2001 there is little relative difference between the Côte de Beaune and the Côte de Nuits. Just to complicate the issue, the Côte de Beaune produced consistently great white burgundies in 2000.

Pascal Marchand made a considerable name for himself during his fifteen-plus years in charge of the Comte Armand's Domaine du Clos des Epeneaux. He was installed there in 1985 with virtually no experience, but quickly justified the faith Comte Armand had put in this newly arrived French Canadian. Marchand was also lucky that, at the time, he only had one vineyard to work with: a 5-hectare holding of Pommard Clos des Epeneaux. It was not until later years that a few additional bits and pieces were added to the holdings in Volnay, Meursault and Auxey respectively. Even then, however, the total of a little over 9 hectares pales into insignificance compared to the aggregate 35 hectares of Vougeraie.

In the three vintages he has now spent at Vougeraie, Pascal's instinctive feeling for the differing cuvées he works with have come into full flower, and he has not been afraid to experiment. Thus in 2001, the 2.5–3 tonnes of Musigny pinot was de-stalked by hand, berry by berry, and then gently foot-stamped. The resulting wine is a far cry from the blockbuster wines he made at Comte Armand in the first seven or eight years, before he lightened off the style somewhat in the mid-1990s.

All being well, I am convinced that Domaine de la Vougeraie and Pascal Marchand are headed towards great things in the future.

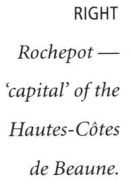

RIGHT
Rochepot — 'capital' of the Hautes-Côtes de Beaune.

MAY 16   HOUSEKEEPING AND MORE PHOTOGRAPHY

Despite the promise of another brilliant day (and a not-so-brilliant day tomorrow), I decide that I'm going to have to spend some time running an errand or two and dealing with some things which have just cropped up — some wine writing and a handful of postcards. So in the brilliant clarity of the morning I drive up to Vosne Romanée to collect a few precious bottles from the Domaine de la Romanée-Conti which I ordered last year (from the 1999 vintage) and bring them back to the cool of the cellar before the day warms up.

I then spend some time planning the finer details of what will be a one and a half day visit to Washington DC next month to attend a round-table conference, largely sponsored by the Comité Interprofessionnel du Vin de Champagne concerning both indications of origin issues (read Appellation Contrôlée for France, Geographic Indications for Australia and American Viticultural Areas for the United States) and trade agreements with the European Community. It's all a bit tricky, as I will have to fly directly to New Zealand on the way back, hopping from Auckland to Blenheim and arriving at Blenheim an hour and a half before the start of Cloudy Bay's long-planned Pinot Noir Weekend, to which I committed myself some time ago. (Postscript: the meeting ended up being postponed until later in the year, and fixed for a date which clashed with prior commitments.)

Apart from a quick dash to Meursault to pick up stamps for postcards and a baguette for lunch, I spend most of an increasingly warm — indeed hot — day indoors until 6 p.m., when I load my cameras into the car and head off to Rochepot and Baubigny on tiny back roads in the late afternoon light.

I think I have taken some beautiful photographs, but return home with a headache and a degree of ill-humour. Happily, I have a bottle of 1999 Chassagne-Montrachet Morgeot Premier Cru of Blain-Gagnard in the refrigerator to accompany the pork cutlets, morilles (small dark-coloured mushrooms), green beans and (more) rice which I have organised for the evening meal. As I literally wolf down the Chassagne-Montrachet, I once again marvel at the way wines tasted in their place of origin are invariably better than when tasted elsewhere. This is absolutely delicious, the pleasure as great with the second and third glass as with the first, and I wonder why we so seldom turn to chardonnay of any description — let alone white burgundy — at home, preferring riesling from Australia, Germany or Alsace, and semillon from the Hunter Valley. I resolve to buy some white burgundies from 2000 the moment I get home; if, that is, there are any left.

MAY 17   MONTHELIE

My 'home' town of Monthelie is one part of what I think of as my golden triangle in Burgundy, the other two points being Meursault and Beaune. You find it by travelling south-west from Beaune, briefly on the N74 and then — at a grand new roundabout — veering to the right (or west) and joining the D973, first passing Pommard, then Volnay, before reaching Meursault (off to the left) and on the opposite (right) side, Monthelie, half a kilometre down the C1.

Not many people are tempted to make the turn; it is a town without a single shop, and while it is home to over twenty wine

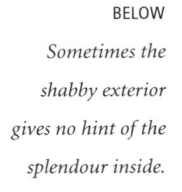

BELOW
Sometimes the shabby exterior gives no hint of the splendour inside.

The back garden of our house at Monthelie.

producers, Monthelie itself is a far less well-known appellation than its neighbours.

It is a hillside town, its name derived from mons or mont (hill), and more specifically, from Mont Olie. In 1078 Hugues I, Duke of Burgundy, gave Monthelie to the Abbey of Cluny, and it remained the property of the Abbey until the sixteenth century. Its status as a fiefdom is apparent from the fact that the oldest and dominant buildings are situated halfway up the hill, rather than on the top, which has sweeping vistas across the intervening valley towards Auxey-Duresses. If the town had a military history, one would expect a fortress (or the ruins of one) to be perched on the brow of Mont Olie.

The most significant building is the church, built at the end of the twelfth century under the direction of the Abbey of Cluny. Clustered around the church, and fronting narrow streets which run haphazardly across and up and down the hill, are vignerons' houses built in the sixteenth, seventeenth and eighteenth centuries. With one exception — the splendid early eighteenth-century Château de Monthelie — none of these was built with wineries or even significant cellars. Until the last thirty or so years of the twentieth century, almost all the grapes were sold to negociants, or sold as newly fermented wine.

It was not until the surge in prices in the second half of the 1970s (after the crash in 1973–75) that the less well-known growers were lured into producing and bottling their own wine, and into putting up roadside signs advertising tasting and sales in a manner familiar to Australian wine lovers. Then and now, the average Burgundian is far happier at work in his or her vineyard than in the winery, but cannot bear to see the negociants raking in the profits from their (the vignerons') year-round labours.

So it is that today I mentally divide Monthelie into three parts. On the brow of the hill is what I call Haut Monthelie, running along the rue de Beaune, with modern houses increasing in number as you near the D973, and wineries underneath or adjacent. The feeling here is amorphous: it could be anywhere were it not for the glimpses of views out to Auxey-Duresses and the occasional patch (or clos) of vines surrounded on all sides by houses.

The middle of the town closes in dramatically. The roads were never intended for cars — many are far too narrow to permit passing — but no one has had the gall to suggest that any should be made one-way. A number of corners are completely blind, and mirrors designed to tell you what lies around the corner are conspicuous by their absence. Despite this, most of the locals travel at frightening speed, with maximum reliance on divine providence (or intervention).

There are relatively few new buildings at the bottom of the town, where our house is situated, in the short rue de Dessous. According to the French dictionary, 'dessous' means underneath, beneath or underside, all of which are appropriate, because the houses on the opposite side of the rue have vineyards reaching up to their back walls. The street is so short that house numbers have never been assigned, and my suggestion that we should simply make up a number did not impress the locals. All of which makes giving directions to fellow Australians, or even to local tradesmen, somewhat hazardous. But given that the major source of noise in our back courtyard is the chatter of all manner of birds, Monthelie comes as close to perfection as an imperfect world will permit.

MAY 19 Le Charlemagne

May is one of the great holiday months for the French, and as today (Sunday) is Pentecost, the holiday is taken tomorrow. So yet another long weekend, with cars (and people) everywhere. Suzanne has returned and we go to Le Charlemagne for lunch, deliberately (and successfully) planning this so that it takes up most of the day. The food is as inspired as it was on our last visit, and we stagger out after 4 p.m. in a haze of gastronomic happiness.

An amuse-gueule (the food equivalent of an aperitif) arrives, a fine sliver of pâté-coated duck breast draped down the side of a small bowl in the bottom of which is a super-concentrated creamy bisque. Then comes the dégustation menu, starting with a feuilleté (layers of fine pastry) tart of snails with a tapenade (olive paste) and tomato base, surrounded by swirls of beurre blanc (a classic French sauce made of wine, butter, vinegar and shallots). Next is a stack of lotte (monkfish) interleaved with bay leaves, accompanied by tempura onion rings and a concasse (a coarsely chopped mixture) of aubergine (eggplant) and sweet potato. A rather less complicated dish follows: langoustine (lobster) and sweet tuille wafers with a fennel and dried olive sauce. The last dish challenges the 2000 Pernand Vergelesses Clos Berthet, a monopole of Dubrueil Fontaine, perhaps because of the power of the oil-based sauce.

A 1999 Bize Savigny Aux Vergelesses, however, is perfection with the next two dishes, the wine rich and with strong colour, yet full of finesse and length. The highly spiced pigeon is stacked with flavour, the puréed celeriac and string potatoes balancing the spicy meat; the caneton de Chalon (duckling) comes with the breast cooked rare and sliced, the confit of the leg shredded and layered in a potato stack.

After the obligatory cheese, we move to pommes sabayon (apple zabaglione), with tiny cubes of apple and nuts sitting on top of a crisp galette (pastry tartlet), a dried wafer of apple perched at right angles on top. The dishes seem complicated, yet the flavours and textures are in fact harmonious, the visual appeal and presentation certain to attract the attention of the Michelin inspectors.

Le Charlemagne's address is route des Vergelesses 21420 Pernand-Vergelesses. Telephone 03 80 21 51 45, fax 03 80 21 58 52.

RIGHT

*Lunch at
Le Charlemagne,
the fastest rising star
in the region.*

MAY 20 THE VINEYARDS OF BURGUNDY

Burgundy is an enchanted place, and never more so than in the full flower of spring through the month of May. All the pent-up energy trapped in trees, shrubs, plants and vines throughout the cold winter months — and by the uncertainty of March and April — is released in joyous abandon.

The growth of the vines' shoots, turning incandescent lime green in the late-afternoon light, is measured in hours rather than days or weeks. Tiny bunches of grapes appear overnight, and nature's sense of urgency is mirrored by that of the vineyard workers.

From early in the morning to late afternoon — more than twelve hours, for the days are very long — they are in the vineyards. The slowest task is the back-breaking removal of the unwanted shoots which festoon even the best-pruned vines. As those who visit Burgundy know, the vines' trunks are little more than 15 cm high, hugging the ground to capture the maximum warmth radiating from the red-brown soil and the prolific numbers of fractured limestone pieces dotting the surface.

Traditionally, and still most commonly, this removal of shoots is done by stooping, as if one were picking strawberries. Relishing any excuse to stand up and stretch backwards with hands on hips, every passing car or truck, old or new, French or foreign-registered, is carefully scrutinised.

However, some workers around the gentle slopes of the beautiful valley lying between Monthelie and Auxey-Duresses have come up with clever solutions. One group uses padded chair seats and backs mounted on a single set of rear wheels. They pull forward by stretching their legs out, digging in their heels and moving their chair to the next pair of vines. Since the typical planting density is no more than a metre between vines and a metre between rows, there is no problem reaching out for the vines. Another vigneron has adapted what looks like a ride-on lawnmower (again with a set of rear wheels), which reduces the energy requirement even more — but in neither instance is the need to observe passers-by perceptibly reduced.

Then there are the spindly, spider-like tractors, improbably high off the ground, which straddle the vine rows. At this time of year they may be ploughing the soil either side of the straddled row, or — more frequently — spraying copper and lime–sulphur mixtures. This is achieved by using lightweight booms which fold out and cover three rows either side of the tractor and are retracted at the end of the row for turning — the contraption is suggestive more of a praying mantis than a spider.

BELOW LEFT
Disbudding, or removing unwanted shoots, is back-breaking work if done the hard way …

BELOW
… or easy if some improvisation is used.

Activity has been especially frenetic this year because there was an unusually dry and (relatively) warm April, which warmed the soil and led to bud-break ten days earlier than normal. Curiously, while window boxes, scooped-out barrels and pot plants everywhere are ablaze with flowers, the roadside red poppies and row-end roses seem later than usual.

Nature has a way of balancing things, and the possibility of a late-August start to vintage (too early and too hot for comfort) has already receded, thanks to some cold and damp days and nights in May; it still looks as if it will be an early vintage, though, which normally bodes well for quality.

It hardly needs to be said that any number of misfortunes can occur between May and September, but 2002 has started with far greater promise than 2001, a vintage which kept vignerons struggling from start to finish. (Postscript: the 2002 vintage has in fact turned out to be superb, rivalling or exceeding 1999, ranking with vintages such as 1945.)

MAY 21   Domaine de la Romanée-Conti

Today we have one of the high points of our annual visit to Burgundy, a tasting at the Domaine de la Romanée-Conti. The pressure for visits to the Domaine must be bordering on the intolerable; quite how they manage it I do not know. The difficulty is exacerbated by the incredibly thin management structure: there are only Aubert de Villaine, his personal assistant, Jean-Charles Cuvillier, a receptionist/secretary, and Bernard Noblet, the winemaker. Obviously, there are cellarhands and vineyard workers, but none of these is involved in organising or being part of tastings; these are invariably run by Aubert and the ever-silent Bernard, who (however) misses nothing.

For the past decade, the wines of the Domaine (in barrel) have been stored in two separate cellars. Each vintage remains in the originally allotted cellar until bottling; the wines from the odd years (1993, 1995, 1997, 1999, 2001 and so forth) are stored in the oldest cellar, dating back to the twelfth and thirteenth century, when

Romanée-Conti itself was made by the monks at the Cluny Monastery, which was, until the early nineteenth century when it was largely destroyed, the most magnificent monastery in France.

The wines from the even years are stored in another cellar, also of great antiquity, the yet 'newer' cellars not being used for barrel storage. Says Aubert de Villaine, 'they obviously once knew far more about building cellars than we do today. And we have observed that the wine kept in the Cluny cellar always evolves better than the same wine stored in either of our other cellars.' It's the luck of the draw that determines which vintage gets which cellar, of course.

We are tasting the 2001 vintage, and it was no more easy for the Domaine than anyone else. The burst of extremely hot weather in the second half of August made the skins fragile, rather than toughening or thickening them, and when the weather turned cool and wet again in the first half of September, some degree of rot was almost inevitable. Aubert says, 'Our pickers have been working with us for so many years now that we were able to say to them, "Only pick the best bunches on the first pass through the vineyard", and then we sorted even these bunches in the winery. It is a practice we have had for some years now, and in 1999 the grapes from the second passage were so good they were mostly included in the final wine selection.'

It was a very different picture in 2001: between 35 per cent and 50 per cent of the potential wine was either discarded in the vineyard, discarded on the sorting table in the winery or declassified as wine after fermentation and a period of maturation.

As we taste through the six Grand Crus, Aubert de Villaine says, 'I cannot yet make up my mind whether the wines will be charming or austere.' They certainly have the refined purity and restraint which is the mark of the vintage, but for me the only two wines to slightly disappoint are the Echézeaux and the Grands Echézeaux. True, in the stratospheric hierarchy of the Domaine, these are the most minor two wines (reflected in their price), but they are often precociously appealing in their youth, and can develop just as magnificently with age as their more illustrious brothers and sisters.

The Romanée St Vivant is rich to the point of being almost burly, while the La Tâche, Richebourg and Romanée-Conti itself perform

ABOVE LEFT
The vines of Romanée Conti are the most valuable in the world.

ABOVE RIGHT
The humble entrance to a vinous Aladdin's Cave: one of the Domaine de la Romanée-Conti's barrel cellars.

exactly as one would expect, the silky finish of the Romanée-Conti putting it at another level, but all three with tremendous length and persistence of flavour. 'They also have that touch of green on the finish,' says Aubert, 'which I look for, as it gives the wines both character and authority.' It is indeed this exact character which I have always associated with the wines of the Domaine, and which has always made them (relatively) easy to pick in blind tastings, no matter how young or old they may be.

MAY 22   DOMAINE ARMAND ROUSSEAU

Today we are visiting the Domaine Armand Rousseau, first meeting with eighty-year-old Charles Rousseau, who is as sharp as a tack, discussing all sorts of things, and thereafter tasting with daughter Corinne, who these days effectively manages the sales and marketing of the estate's wines.

As is always the practice at Rousseau at this time of year, they choose not to show us the 2001 wines, which are still completing their malolactic fermentation and are full of gas. Instead, the focus is on the 2000 vintage wines, which are still in cask. We methodically work our way up from the Gevrey Chambertin (commune) wine at the bottom of the tree to Chambertin Clos de Beze and Chambertin itself at the very top. Corinne Rousseau says, '1999 gave us wines which spoke first and foremost of the vintage; 2000 has given us wines which speak first and foremost of the terroir they come from. All the differences between each vineyard and cru are very clearly defined, thanks to very pure fruit expression.'

And so it proves: the wines are very easy to understand, thanks to their openness and finesse. You progressively move up the scale from the fragrance of the Charmes Chambertin to another dimension of sweetness and flavour in the Clos de la Roche; then on to the spicy, aromatic plum and cherry of the Ruchottes; thereafter to the ripe, black fruits of Le Clos St Jacques; then the perfumed aromatics of the Clos de Beze, with its extra intensity and length, and having entirely consumed the 100 per cent new oak in which has been matured; and finally to the imperious power, strength and length of the Chambertin, which Corinne says is still opening up.

MAY 23   MAISON CHAMPY

Maison Champy, the oldest negociant house in Burgundy, was founded in 1720. It was acquired by Henri and Pierre Meurgey and partner Pierre Beuchet in 1990. My relationship with the Meurgey family goes back to the period between 1982 and 1985, when I was purchasing burgundies for David Jones. It was further cemented in

BELOW
The église at Gevrey Chambertin stands sentinel over the wines.

1994 when younger son Frederic Meurgey and (now) wife Anne-Sophie came to Coldstream Hills to work through the vintage. Frederic and Anne-Sophie now live in the Loire Valley, where Anne-Sophie's parents own Domaine de la Presle — and when we had dinner with Henri and Marie-Thérèse Meurgey on Tuesday night, we drank a number of wines made at Domaine de la Presle, including a fine, barrel-fermented chardonnay, unusual in the Loire Valley.

Maison Champy had been bought by Louis Jadot from the descendants of the founding family shortly before it was resold to the Meurgey/Beuchet interests; Jadot wanted the vineyards and some of the old, priceless stock, but neither the premises nor the brand. Notwithstanding its 270-year history, and its once-dominant position in Burgundy, Champy needed a great deal of care, attention and further expenditure, all of which have been lavished upon it since 1990, and all the knowledgeable writers about Burgundy recognise the continuing improvement in the quality and style of the wines since 1990.

After another splendid dinner at Ma Cuisine last night (including a bottle of 1996 Domaine de l'Arlot Clos de l'Arlot for the bargain basement price of 44 Euros), tonight we eat at Auberge du Vieux Pressoir in Evelle, in a typically indescribably beautiful part of the Hautes-Côtes de Beaune, the booking having been made on the recommendation and introduction of two friends Suzanne has made — they run a tiny shop offering just salads and tarts.

To say the Vieux Pressoir is off the beaten track is a masterly understatement, although it is only a relatively short distance from Monthelie. Not much larger (if at all) than Ma Cuisine, it offers an even briefer menu, with a choice of four entrées and three main courses. So far as we are concerned, we make the right choice: foie gras prepared in three different ways (natural, marinated in pinot noir, and infused with ginger) followed by côte de boeuf de Charolais, cooked to perfection and spectacularly infused with smoke from an open fire.

The wine list is a strange assemblage of labels and photographs, but features some serious wines, and I am delighted to find a 1993 Domaine de Monthelie-Douhairet Clos de Meaix Garnier to follow a half bottle of Saint Romain White Burgundy. The Domaine is owned by the ninety-three-year-old Madame Armande Douhairet, revered throughout the region for both her age and her sense of humour; the wines have been made since 1990 by the famous André Porcheret. Still immensely strong in colour, and admittedly still a little tough, the wine is a fine match for the côte de boeuf. The total cost is a mere 110 Euros. The Vieux Pressoir telephone and fax number is 03 80 21 82 16.

MAY 24   BOUCHARD PÈRE ET FILS

Somehow or other it seems appropriate that our final tasting should be at Bouchard Père et Fils, which, while not quite as old as Champy (established in 1731), is today by far the most important estate producer in the whole of Burgundy, with vineyard holdings of 130 hectares, of which 12 hectares are Grand Crus and 75 hectares Premier Crus. Just for good measure, Bouchard Père has exclusive rights to the production of another Grand Cru, La Romanée, which adjoins Romanée-Conti.

It was acquired by former Champagne supremo Joseph Henriot and his family in the spring of 1995, after nine generations of ownership by the Bouchard family. The expenditure by Henriot dwarfs that which has taken place at Champy: 94 hectares of vineyards came with the Bouchard purchase, and another 36 hectares have been added since, chiefly through the acquisition of Ropiteau in 1996, but with other acquisitions as well. Six years of continuous restoration of the magnificent cellars in the rue de Château in Beaune have been matched by similar expenditure in the vineyards, all with the single-minded intention of maximising the quality of the vineyards: a reasonably obvious strategy when you consider the capital value of those vineyards. At 130 hectares, it has twice as many vineyards as the next largest owner in Burgundy (the Hospice de Beaune), with the other large houses, such as Faiveley, Louis Latour and Jadot, further back.

In the Burgundian vintage, we start the tasting with eleven 2001 reds, finishing with Chambertin Clos de Bèze and La Romanée, then eight 2001 whites, finishing with Chevalier Montrachet and Montrachet. Joseph Henriot, who joins Bruno Pepin and ourselves at the end of the tasting, says that while he is more than satisfied with the 2001 reds, he is still unsure how the 2001 whites will turn out. From my point of view, I would have no fears for either.

MAY 25   HEADING SOUTH

We set out in mid-afternoon on a leisurely four-day drive down through Provence and across to Nice, where we will catch the plane to Corsica on the afternoon of May 29. The 2002 excursion of the Academie Internationale des Vins begins on May 30 and runs through to June 2. The principal stops we are intending to make are at La Pyramide in Vienne tomorrow evening, and the next night at Avignon.

MAY 26   LA PYRAMIDE, VIENNE

Our first visit (in 1982) to La Pyramide, then a three-star restaurant under the direction of the widow of its famed founder, Fernand Point, was in every sense a memorable one.

It was the centrepoint of a stretch of thirteen three-star restaurants in twelve days — in those magical times when the Australian dollar bought seven French francs, and prices were ridiculously low. Using our strategy of staying in the chambres (or rooms) of these restaurants, dinner, bed and breakfast cost between $150 and $300 for the two of us, the variable being the cost of the wine. So the seeming extravagance was not as great as it might appear at first sight.

The trifecta came with Auberge du Père Bise at Talloires (now only a one-star, but then three) on Saturday night, lunch at La Pyramide on Sunday, and dinner at Troisgros at Roanne on Sunday night. All might have passed without incident had it not been for a misunderstanding at Auberge du Père Bise when we arrived in our Renault A5, a decidedly down-market conveyance compared with the other cars parked nearby, and which impeded their progress while the misunderstanding was sorted out.

Our bookings had been made by the Comité Interprofessionel du Vin de Champagne (but at our cost, of course). Normally, we were greeted with much bowing and scraping, but here at Talloires there was no reservation. After written confirmation of our booking was provided, it turned out that yes, we had a table, but our room was reserved at a huge old hotel on the lake's edge half a kilometre away. Ruffled feathers smoothed, we returned to the car, ending the traffic snarl, and proceeded to the hotel.

The room was vast, the bathroom the size one might expect in a suite at the Ritz. We returned for dinner, and had half a bottle of champagne while we sat in the garden considering the menu. Then I was called to the telephone to speak to Kit Stevens MW, who was my courtier/broker for the French wines I was purchasing for my Australian clients.

When I returned, Madame (who was now more impressed with her guests) had produced another half bottle of champagne, on the house. We then proceeded to dinner, where we had a bottle of white burgundy, followed by a bottle of red burgundy, then half a bottle of sauterne which, because it was so good, was followed by another half. Bad idea actually, but it galvanised Madame into more largesse in the form of two giant glasses of Armagnac from 1938, which she had learnt was my birth year.

I manfully disposed of most of my glass, and tottered off to the men's, leaving Suzanne with her untouched glass. When I returned I found she had switched glasses and was in earnest conversation with Madame, who demanded to know why I had not drunk my Armagnac. Faced with an impossible situation, I did my duty, thereby adding half a bottle of Armagnac to the two and a half bottles of wine I had already consumed.

When, shortly thereafter, I endeavoured to lie down in bed, the whole world started to revolve in a fashion I had not experienced since my university days more than twenty years earlier. From those prior experiences I knew I should immediately sit upright, preferably within reach of the toilet. So I perched on the edge of the bath, waiting for the inevitable. At 6 a.m. I awoke lying on the marble floor of the bathroom, the early morning sun boring a laser hole in my left eye. I had not been sick — I had simply fallen onto the floor.

Two hours in bed did little or nothing for my state of health, and after a breakfast of black coffee and baguette, we set off for our lunch rendezvous at La Pyramide. I drove; to do otherwise would have been suicidal. All I could say again and again was, 'What a disaster. La Pyramide has a fantastic wine list, and I won't be able to face up to it or the food.'

We arrived, passed Madame, who sat silently in a small alcove near the door, and walked to our table. The menu and wine list were produced, and when I looked at the list, mind prevailed over matter. For among a treasure trove of magnificent old wines, at prices often less than those for current vintages, were a 1938 Louis Latour Corton Charlemagne and a 1938 Romanée-Conti (plus 1938 La Tâche and 1938 Richebourg), 1938 being my birth year — an abysmal vintage in Bordeaux, but good in Burgundy, with a reputation for late development. Due to the war, and the succession of great vintages from 1945 to 1949, it was seldom seen.

Indeed, I had never seen it at Christie's auctions, from which the Bulletin Place Front Row (Len Evans, Tony Albert, John Beeston and myself) had purchased many vintages of the Domaine de la Romanée-Conti, including 1948 La Tâche — but that is another story.

We had in fact come across a 1938 La Tâche on the list at the late Bernard Loiseau's Côte d'Or at Saulieu, then a one-star (now three). It was priced at 2300 FF, or a little under $400. We were at the start of our trip, and having commented to Suzanne that I had never seen the '38s come up for auction at Christie's, I said we simply couldn't buy it because we would never finish the trip.

We ordered a white burgundy, followed by a red, but before the latter arrived, Suzanne had insisted that we have the La Tâche: she would pay, and it would be my birthday present (then ten months away). When the bottle arrived in a wicker decanter, it became apparent it was quite heavily ullaged, and I wasn't prepared to take the risk. 'We have others in the cellar, please come and look.' I did, but there were no more '38s, so we passed.

It was just as well, for at La Pyramide we proceeded to have the large Menu Gastronomique, the Corton and the Romanée-Conti, all for 2100 FF, 200 FF less than the bottle of La Tâche alone at the Côte d'Or. I still have the empty bottles as reminders: the Corton with precisely the same label as today, its richly nutty, honeyed taste no less unmistakable, the Romanée-Conti from another planet.

As Louis, the venerable sommelier, teased the cork out of the bottle with his splayed fingers, a sixth sense warned me that something extraordinary was about to happen. As I smelt the wine he poured for my approval, Suzanne said, 'Why are you crying?' My first reaction was to indignantly deny that I was doing any such thing, but I then realised that tears were indeed trickling down my cheeks. It was an entirely involuntary reaction to the sheer perfection of the wine.

Over the next two years, we made repeated visits to La Pyramide, methodically drinking our way (with help from others) through the 1938 Domaine de la Romanée-Conti wines. There are only two tasting notes of 1938 burgundies in Michael Broadbent's *Great Vintage Wine Book II*, the first being for 1938 La Tâche. It reads: 'Clearly picked late. A warm, expansive autumnal maturity; and extraordinary chocolaty nose; distinctly sweet on the palate, exquisite, incandescent, lingering flavour. At La Pyramide, Vienne, thanks to James Halliday at a neighbouring table [five stars].'

We drank many other extraordinary bottles, and once again the admirable Michael Broadbent bolsters my memory with his indefatigable note-taking. '1947 Macon Vire, Clos de Chapitre, Moelleux, Jacques Depagneux. Interesting to note that this was a marvellous vintage in Beaujolais and Maconnais. This wine will have been made from extremely ripe grapes, possibly slightly botrytised. Pure golden colour; soft waxy nose; medium-sweet, very pleasant flavour, showing bottle age but held together with very good acidity. With James Halliday at La Pyramide, Vienne, Sept 1984 [three stars].' I would only add undoubtedly botrytised rather than slightly botrytised.

Needless to say, we drank all of La Pyramide's Romanée-Conti, much of the La Tâche and had made a determined start on the Richebourg before the Australian dollar started its fall from grace.

Other wines of note included a lusciously sweet 1945 Coulée de Serrant and 1937 Château Gilette Creme de Tête which, to my amazement, I learnt had not so many years previously been bottled and released. It sent me off to visit the Château, and to bring into Australia vintages starting with the 1953; again, a story for another day.

I visited La Pyramide's cellar on several occasions, and spied over a dozen bottles of 1806 Château Lafite which were then still on the wine list but were no longer for sale. A bottle had been sold in New York for a hundred times the price shown on La Pyramide's list, and the restaurant had hurriedly withdrawn theirs from sale.

Why were such great old wines sold so cheaply, and at prices less than current vintages? It had to do with the French taxation law, which meant that if the value of stock in trade increased by more than inflation, tax had to be paid on the increase even if the stock had not been sold. Thus prices were pegged to the initial acquisition cost plus (if the restaurateurs could be bothered to track and record it) a small inflationary increase.

And so at last I come to our sentimental return to La Pyramide twenty years after the first visit. When Madame Point died, the restaurant was closed down and sold, along with most of the old wine stock. Extra accommodation was added, but the floor plan and space of the restaurant were not changed. The chef is now Patrick Henriroux, and the restaurant has two very well-deserved stars.

We have the Menu de la Fête des Mères (Mother's Day menu), half a bottle of champagne, a bottle of 2000 Sancerre and a 1990 Guigal Châteauneuf du Pape. The service is impeccable, but far from tear-jerking. The closest I come to crying is when I turn to the library at the back of the wine list, which enumerates many of the great wines the restaurant once offered to mere mortals such as myself. The cost of the meal? About five times as much as we paid for that never-to-be-forgotten lunch.

MAY 27   AVIGNON, SOUTHERN RHÔNE VALLEY

As we head south on the A7 past Montelimar the scenery changes dramatically, as does the atmosphere. The air is filled with the scent of the scrubby bushes, the herbs and the flowers, all combining to give a distinctive spiciness. How appropriate that Montelimar should be the nougat capital of the world.

We have timed the journey to allow ourselves maximum time for exploring the wonderful medieval city of Avignon, which oozes history from every pore. We are staying at the Hotel d'Europe. Despite its Novotel-type name, it is in fact situated in a series of very old buildings located just within the ramparts which surround Avignon (12 place Crillon–8400 Avignon, telephone 04 90 14 76 76, fax 04 90 14 76 71).

We have lunch on the pavement outside a brasserie as part of an extended walk around the town. That evening, somewhat unadventurously, but having been thoroughly tempted by the menu, we eat at the restaurant (La Vieille Fontaine) in the hotel and have a truly excellent meal.

MAY 28   Relais Saint Victoire, Aix-en-Provence

After a few hours in the morning in Avignon, we are on the road for the relatively short trip to Aix-en-Provence.

We are now in the heart of Provence, and are staying this evening at the Relais Saint Victoire, which is 10 kilometres from Aix-en-Provence at a virtually nonexistent town called Beaurecueil. Michelin gives it the red bird symbol, promising absolute peace at night, and worth its weight in gold; the restaurant (and accommodation complex) has a Michelin star. Once again, we spend considerable time exploring Aix-en-Provence, in particular the narrow streets of the old part of town.

Returning to Relais Saint Victoire, the accommodation is modern, but without any character whatsoever and seems to have been built on the cheap. Nor are our spirits soothed as we enter the restaurant this evening, for it is jam-packed, largely by the occupants of a tourist coach. But when a dish of combined summer truffles and foie gras is placed before us we become a great deal happier, and the meal in fact goes from strength to strength (telephone 04 42 66 94 98, fax 04 42 66 85 96).

MAY 29   Nice to Corsica

We are headed to Corsica because of my membership of the Academie Internationale du Vin. One does not apply to join the Academie; one is nominated and seconded, and then entry is still discretionary. Its members include leading winemakers (the Chancellor is Jean-Pierre Perrin of Château Beaucastel, and its many European winemakers include Angelo Gaja of Piedmont and Jean Meyer of Alsace); chefs including Alain Senderens, owner of the three-star Lucas Carton of Paris (a particularly enthusiastic member); academics; and wine writers. Membership is predominantly European, of course, with members from all the major wine-producing countries, and all the proceedings are in French.

Each year the Academie undertakes a tour at the end of May or early June; last year it was Burgundy, this year it is Corsica, and next year it will be Piedmont. It also has a symposium in Geneva in December each year, at which lengthy papers are produced and delivered, once again in French. Unless and until I deliver such a paper I am a probationary or honorary member, although I pay the same annual fee (in Swiss francs).

MAY 30   Occupational Health and Safety, Corsica

The first official day of the tour of Corsica by the Academie starts at Bastia airport, where in fact we have arrived the day before. As much by luck as good management, we end up at the Hotel L'Alivi, which — inconveniently — turns out to be on the other side of the town of Bastia from the airport, but — conveniently — has an absolute waterfront position.

So it is that the early morning finds us having breakfast on our own terrace looking down into the crystal clear and utterly unpolluted waters of the Mediterranean. The water has similar clarity around the shores of southern Turkey and parts of Greece, but is very different from that of Australia. Small wonder that yachting is such a favoured pastime in these waters. By 8.30 a.m. it is already so hot that we retreat into the room, the continental breakfast only half consumed.

It is our taxi driver on our trip back to the airport who explains why Corsica is such a safe place to live, and why there is no crime. 'If we have a problem we sort it out ourselves. There is no need to involve the police.' End of bad guys, so it seems, and Omerta (the Mafia-like code of silence) flourishing in Corsica as it does in Sicily.

Just who the bad guys are depends on where you were born. The most visible sign of the deep resentment that Corsicans feel for the French (despite the fact that Corsica is part of France) is that all the major road signs, originally written in both French and Corse, have been defaced so that the French names are obliterated. Thus it was that many of the French Algerians, the so-called 'pieds noirs', who were settled in Corsica by the French government after Algeria became independent, were 'bombed' (suffered physical injuries, destruction of property, etc) and, sooner or later, forced to return to the French mainland.

Our chief Corsican host, Christian Imbert of Domaine de Torraccia, turns out to be one of the few exceptions. With a craggy, leonine head, and of well above average build, he was a big-game hunter in Africa during his time in Algeria. When he came to Corsica in 1964 and realised the problem, he opened up his extensive armory of high-powered hunting weapons and taught all his farm workers how to shoot with deadly accuracy. This solved the problem of both persistent (protection) tax collectors and locals who might otherwise have sent him back to the mainland. Thirty-eight years later, he is universally accepted and liked.

The next thing that becomes immediately apparent is that the program for today, while listing a seemingly unreasonable number of places to visit, is conspicuously silent when it comes to time. Thus it is impossible for us to run late, even though we find the main course at dinner this evening being served shortly prior to midnight. Somehow or other, our two very large buses, apparently designed to completely occupy the narrow, twisting roads on which we travel with no possibility of any oncoming vehicle getting past, find their way up and down incredible mountainsides without any major

RIGHT
Bastia harbour: the old and the new, the small and the big.

FAR RIGHT
The leonine, silver-haired Christian Imbert, owner of Domaine de Torraccia.

incident. The closest is at a local graveyard, where one of the locals watering the flowers on a relative's tomb has to scurry back to her car and remove it from the road so that the bus can proceed.

With a clear blue sky throughout the day, the scenery is invariably majestic yet incredibly varied, with a wild beauty similar to that of parts of the Douro Valley in Portugal. What seems to be a wild goat, with massive curved antlers, standing on the point of a rock high above the road, is a partial symbol of the day.

As well as the expected winery visits, the program takes in a fourteenth-century and a fifteenth-century église (church) at Mirato and at San Martinu, although we somehow or other missed a planned stop at the Cathedral du Nebbio. At the second of the two églises, we are entertained by five men singing unaccompanied music termed 'polyphonique'; they are the Confraternitia San Martinu Ti Patrimoniu, and when they briefly continue their singing outside the church, we realise that the incredible sounds they are able to make are not entirely due to the church acoustics, good though they are.

Most of the white wines offered during the day have come either from muscat or (predominantly) vermentino, the latter also known as malvoisie de Corse. Vermentino is considered the one truly noble white grape variety of Corsica, and one maker in particular — Clos Colombu, whom we visit late in the day — shows just what a good wine can be made from it. However, the very large bunches and high juice ratio do not encourage any tricks in the making of the wine. One that we tasted had been given skin contact, which simply made it bitter, and it is perfectly obvious that any attempt to introduce oak would be a disaster.

All the wineries we have visited are relatively small, and have been family-owned for generations. However, we learn that the younger generation has typically had formal training in oenology, and that there are discussion groups and workshops held across Corsica which are designed to share knowledge of new technology and techniques. For all that, the wines we see today would have great difficulty in competing in international markets without even greater subsidies than they already enjoy. One of the particular problems for Corsica is the cost of freight from the island to the mainland, but this is not the root cause of the problem. Rather it is that these are country wines made by country people in a very warm climate, even though it is clear that there are significant site climate differences, due in particular to rain shadow patterns in the lee of high mountains.

LEFT

Snaking wine hoses on the floor of Corsica's largest cooperative winery.

We are getting to bed at 1 a.m. with a 7 a.m. start tomorrow, and the promise of an even longer day as we make the lengthy journey from Calvi to Porto Vecchio. If the weather and the scenery are in any way as good as they were today, I for one won't be complaining.

MAY 31   Calvi to Porto Vecchio, Corsica

Somehow or other we struggle onto the buses after the 7 a.m. wake-up call and head off back across the middle of Corsica towards Aleria, which is on the east coast. We are meant to stop at a winery called Clos Mandry but, for reasons unexplained, we do not. I spend the next two hours fast asleep; during the few moments that I am awake, the scenery is no less spectacular than yesterday, but no amount of willpower is going to keep my eyes open.

After three hours we arrive at the Cooperative d'Aleria. Here we endure an excruciating tour of a 1950s era cooperative, including the obligatory bottling line, and lengthy inspections (and explanations) of various pieces of winemaking equipment. The fact that the explanation is in French is, so far as I am concerned, quite immaterial. The one salient fact that emerges is that this is the largest of three sites that have been combined to make a single cooperative, which produces 60 per cent of the total production of the island, or 2.7 million hectolitres out of a total of around 4.5 million hectolitres. Much of it is aimed at the bottom end of the French market, with chardonnay, merlot and cabernet now coming alongside the indigenous varieties, and actually having some recognisable, albeit light, varietal character.

I am stopped in my tracks by Christian Imbert saying to me, 'You see, there are two types of wineries in Corsica: the modern facility such as this, and the rustic little places run by families in the hills and the valleys.' I'll certainly buy the rustic little places, but the idea that d'Aleria is a modern winery takes my breath away. The good news, as it were, is that while Aleria is situated on the coast, you look back towards the mountains, the peaks of which still have appreciable snow.

Thereafter we visit the site of a Roman village which has been excavated (after a fashion). All I can say is that Turkey has no cause to fear the threat of archaeological tourism posed by Corsica, although an adjoining museum does have a marvellous display of bronze and pottery objects excavated both here and elsewhere in Corsica.

The reason we spent three hours at the Cooperative (which included an al fresco lunch) was the fact that the museum was closed from 12 until 2 p.m., and the whole day proceeds in similar slow motion. Tonight we are eating at the splendidly named Moby Dick, and everyone is putting on their best clothes, which in the case of several noble Spanish and German couples who are part of the Academie, seems highly superfluous, as they have been flaunting different ensembles taken from vast suitcases at every opportunity. At least the dinner is starting at eight o'clock, and while I doubt that it is to be an early night, it can't be worse than last night. The weather, incidentally, continues to be spectacular: not a cloud in the sky and the sunshine brilliant from early morning until late at night. Once you get into the shade it doesn't seem so hot, but the sun has a scorching clarity and I have entered the fashion stakes with a hat fashioned out of a knotted handkerchief, having cleverly left the sun block in my large suitcase in the bowels of Nice airport.

On the way to Porto Vecchio our bus happens to pass a policeman standing at the side of the road. A hurried stop, and then a lengthy discussion involving the bus driver, Christian Imbert and the policeman ensues. It turns out we are obtaining special permission to take the two buses into the old part of the town, which has narrow cobbled streets. It helps that everyone knows everyone else, and that the policeman's sister happened to be Christian Imbert's secretary for a period of time. The old city does not disappoint, although in this country of startling beauty, it is easy to run short on superlatives.

We go back to the vast Moby Dick restaurant for the gala dinner of the trip, the main course being a splendid bouillabaisse, accompanied by endless variations of Vermentino, and it's well after midnight before we start to head towards our respective hotels, faced with yet another early morning start.

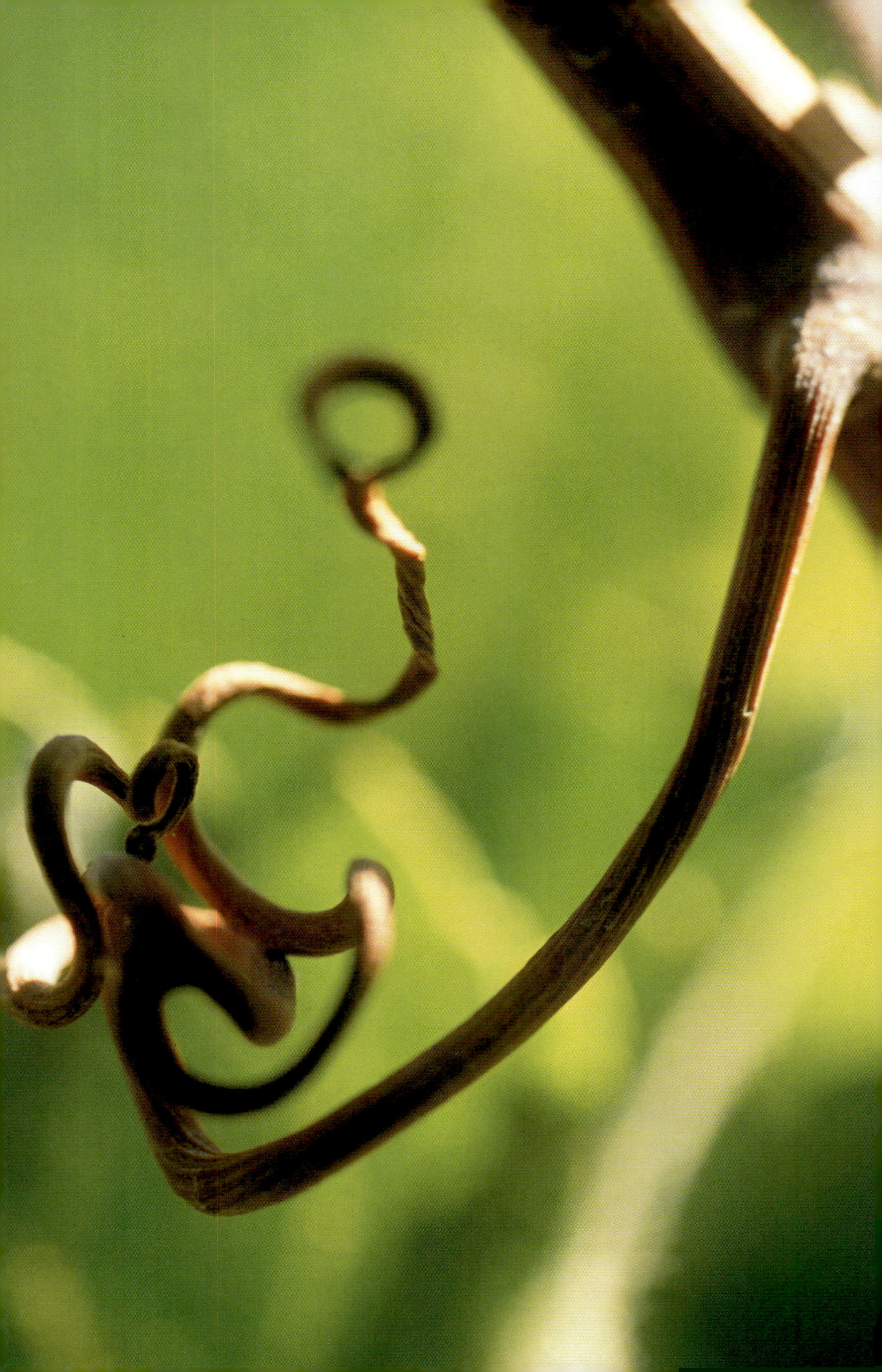

June

Domaine de Torraccia

Au Trou Gascon, Paris

Home Again, Yarra Valley

Yarra Valley: Wildlife

Tyrrell's Vat 47 Vertical, Sydney

Coldstream Hills Classification: The Crunch

Cloudy Bay, New Zealand

Marlborough Sound

Pruning, Coldstream Hills

More Pruning, Yarra Valley

JUNE 1   Domaine de Torraccia

Part of the proceedings of the Academie is a symposium which, so far as I can understand it, discusses the region we have been visiting and its wine. Fortunately it is held adjacent to the open deck of the Moby Dick, where breakfast is being served, so my failure to participate in the formal part of the proceedings does not cause undue notice.

We now head to the spectacular little town of Bonifacio, perched on a rocky promontory, but with deep green–blue inlets providing natural safe havens and marinas for the innumerable boats.

From here we head to Christian Imbert's Domaine de Torraccia, which is 10 kilometres north of Porto Vecchio. Slowly we learn more of this quite remarkable man, who utterly belies his seventy-three years of age and has a personal history full of romance and intrigue. His father was a tobacco grower in Africa, and presumably left a substantial inheritance; Christian himself may or may not have been a member of the French equivalent to the CIA; may or may not have served in the French Foreign Legion; but was married to a well-known American actress who had starred on Broadway, but whose precise identity remains unknown; and who began the development of Domaine de Torraccia in 1964.

In some ways de Torraccia is similar to Pat Kuleto's amazing development in the hills above the Napa Valley. Certainly the backdrop is every bit as grand — indeed, more so — while taming the rocky mountains and planting 43 hectares of vineyard, 25 hectares of olives and 2.5 hectares of apricots was every bit as daunting. Christian originally tackled the task by hand, quite literally, but moved to progressively larger pieces of machinery — which, their job done, remain in evidence in various spots around the winery.

From the high point of the vineyard the sea is disarmingly close by on one side, and mighty granite mountains rear on the other side. The day is calm, the sunlight fiercely brilliant, and it is not until we are treated to a bottle of 1995 Oriu Reserve that we learn that the genesis of this wine was winds of 130 kilometres an hour which swept across the vineyard in May 1995, removing all signs of growth, and giving birth to a much reduced second crop.

In total, the property covers 125 hectares and has, if Christian Imbert is to be believed, five-thousand-year-old archaeological foundations and — somewhat less believably — two-thousand-year-old olive trees next to the house which, along with various huge umbrellas and converted yacht sails, provide shade for the ninety or so people gathered for lunch.

It is difficult to convey the sense of history and untamed nature which the property oozes from every pore. Parts of it are strongly reminiscent of the Douro in Portugal, although the profusion of wildflowers and the innumerable scents are to all intents and purposes identical to those of Provence.

The meal which follows the hour-long amble around the vineyard ridgetops must have taken (without any exaggeration) days to prepare. It starts with thick black sausages made predominantly from pigs' kidneys, called figatelli, cooked on an open pit similar to a South African brai, filled with the glowing embers of gnarled vines and olive wood. These are sliced into 3 cm long pieces and placed in crusty pieces of baguette of similar length; it seems that the balance between bread and sausage is an essential part of the dish, for any attempt to take only a piece of sausage is firmly rebuffed.

At much the same time, massive platters of two different types of prosciutto/jambon and equally large platters of very obviously handmade salamis circle ceaselessly. For many of us, this would have constituted the meal, but these are just appetisers. Tables laden with various seafood salads and carpaccio of swordfish come next, again constituting a substantial meal.

Then the barbecue pit is called into action to cook cutlets of free-range pork accompanied by a Corsican version of polenta (dark brown, heavily spiced and with a chocolate-like taste) and ratatouille. Another meal. Then comes brocciu, a fresh local cheese, in various forms: as a scoop in the centre of a plate, topped with eau de vie (brandy, or 'water of life') and sugar, and also hidden within two types of beignets (small bread rolls).

The saving grace, or so it seemed at the time, was that the lunch, along with countless bottles of wine, was served over a four-hour period. By the time a winery tour had taken place, and the two buses

RIGHT

Lunch at Domaine de Torraccia.

were filled, it was half past five, and we had a three and a half hour drive to Ajaccio over some of the most spectacular scenery encountered in the entire trip, the net result being arrival at our hotel, the Dolce Vita, around 9 p.m. In theory we were then to deposit our luggage and turn back for another fifty minutes' drive to a winery we had passed on the way, which was providing dinner. Discretion proved the better part of valour for at least some of us; Suzanne and I were retracing our steps by train the following morning to return to Bastia and had a 6.30 a.m. start awaiting us. So we ate a simple but delicious meal on the terrace of the hotel.

JUNE 3 AU TROU GASCON, PARIS

Au Trou Gascon has been a Paris landmark restaurant for more than twenty years. How much more I don't know, but I can vouch for the twenty years, for it was in 1982 that Suzanne and I first attempted to eat there. 'Attempted' because we were stranded on the other side of Paris in stationary traffic, blocked by a US Presidential motorcade. When our taxi finally arrived, an hour late, our table reservation had been given away and, despite all our entreaties, that was that.

We were staying at the Hotel Ritz that night — a special treat paid for by Suzanne — and we returned there to seek help from the concierge, reckoning that he would have more pull than most. The upshot was a booking at the famous three-star Le Taillevent (with its massive wine list), which you might say was a fairly good outcome. The problem was that the booking was for 11 p.m., and we were ultimately shown to our table after midnight.

After twenty years I am prepared to let bygones be bygones, especially given Stephanie Alexander's view that the food at Au Trou Gascon was (or is) still some of the best in Paris, so we make a booking, and this time arrive ten minutes early so that there can be no misunderstanding.

Both then and now the wine list figures prominently in my mind. It has always had a great reputation for its diversity, and in particular for its wines from Gascony and the south of France. Twenty years ago, too, it was one of the pioneers of wine by the glass, although time (in Australia, at least) has caught up with it.

As the moment comes, my courage fails me as I wade through page after page of southern France wines (as far south as Corsica and Domaine de Torraccia) from vintages up to fifteen years old. So I opt for sentimental choices, which do, however, partially reflect the diversity of the list: a glass of Manzanilla to start, then a 1979 Bonnezeaux (half to accompany the hors d'oeuvre of rillettes d'oie

LEFT

On the train from Ajaccio back to Bastia; a proud stationmaster's flower boxes.

(goose) and my foie gras entrée, a 2000 St Aubin Pucelles of Domaine Roux (which twenty years ago I had brought into Australia for David Jones' Connoisseurs Club) to accompany Suzanne's asparagus, poached egg and sea urchin roe (this bald description giving no hint of the brilliance of the presentation), then a 1997 Cornas of Jean Luc Colombo to accompany our main courses.

Suzanne's choice turns out to be a hundred-octane confit of duck à la maison; against all the odds, she devours every bit of it. I have veal kidneys presented in a towering stack with crunchy potato galettes and wild mushrooms — the kidneys cooked exactly as I have ordered them, rosy pink.

We still have half the Cornas to drink, so we have the two cheeses on offer. Two? Yes, no trolley of well-trodden clichés here: one is goat, the other a twelve-month aged sheep cheese which has the crunchy, sweet-and-salt flavour and texture of good parmigiano. Quite wonderful.

Our paths meet with the dessert — feuilleté of wild strawberries, a classic dish when the fraises du bois are in season — matched with the other half of our Bonnezeaux. I have to admit that all this chopping and changing really tests our sommeliers. If there was only one it would be no problem, but there are more than one, all with a messianic zeal to empty the bottle into the nearest convenient wine glass. You get used to it in France, but it is a trifle disappointing when it occurs at a restaurant such as Au Trou Gascon.

Will I go back in the future? Yes, armed with more research on the megastar makers of the south of France. Au Trou Gascon is in the twelfth arrondissement, 40 rue Taine, telephone 01 43 44 34 26.

JUNE 6   HOME AGAIN, YARRA VALLEY

Our flight from Paris arrives half an hour early, at 4.20 a.m. In the manner of hospitals, we have been awoken two hours earlier for breakfast, so it will be a long day. Suzanne stays at the terminal with our luggage, while I go off to the long-term car park to retrieve my Subaru B4, praying that the newly installed fourth replacement battery in the car (which I have only owned for five months and which has been perpetually plagued with battery problems) will have lasted the five weeks. When I use the open button on the remote as I approach and there is no response, I fear the worst, and, indeed, the worst happens. One and half hours later the RACV arrives, but on connecting the battery via jumper leads, the anti-theft devices all spring into action. Try as we might, using all the codes and every trick in the book, the car continues to howl and we finally give up the fight.

Suzanne catches a taxi to town, and I one to Coldstream Hills ($90 taxi trips are always well received by taxi drivers), and once again the Subaru goes off to Eastdale Subaru for in-patient care. (Postscript: a redesigned immobiliser ex the Subaru factory finally resolved the problem.) The day dawns cold but clear, and as I arrive back home and look out over the valley, there are still patches of vivid yellow and gold here and there, although most of the vines are now bare. As ever at this time of year, the grass gleams emerald, the remaining golden vineyards a vivid contrast.

All I can do today is arrange the piles of correspondence, magazines and so forth into some form of battle order so that I can deal with them over the next couple of days. I'm never quite sure whether it should be depressing or reassuring that my absence has barely caused a ripple; most surprising of all is that world affairs are more or less precisely where they were when I left (one of the glories of staying in Burgundy is that one might as well be on a desert island when it comes to news of the world), the terrible tit-for-tat suicide bombings and reprisals in Israel and Palestine continue in the same fashion.

JUNE 11   Yarra Valley: Wildlife

As I write these words, seven or eight of our resident flock of vivid red and blue crimson rosellas are energetically chasing each other around the ground immediately outside my office, squabbling over birdseed which is in fact primarily intended for an even larger population of tiny red-browed finches, little olive green birds with vivid red beaks and a slash of scarlet at the base of their tails. The

RIGHT
Amorous echidnas — love is a many-prickled thing.

birdseed is also much appreciated by Australian bronzewings, who grow fatter each day (if they knew my thoughts they would feed elsewhere), and ring-necked doves. The primary food source is a suspended bird feeder, but there are always seeds spilt or distributed on the ground as well as in the feeder.

The finches flutter down from the trees above like leaves falling in autumn; then an unseen puff of wind scatters the leaves upwards back into the branches. The false alarm over, the process repeats itself. Photographing this avian ballet is impossible, partly because of the green-tinted glass of the office and partly because the feeder (and additional water bowls and seed bowls) are in shade throughout the day.

At the bottom of the hill, and directly in line of sight with the rosellas, a family of nine kangaroos is moving around the wall of the Turkey Nest dam. Today is the Queen's Birthday holiday, so there has been no agricultural equipment in use, and the kangaroos will eventually come up to the house, where every now and then they provide photographic opportunities, one giving rise to the 2001 Coldstream Hills label. (Each year a different photograph is used on the Coldstream Hills wines; all but a couple of the early vintages have been taken by me.)

JUNE

As well as wedge-tailed eagles in the hill behind, and several resident wombats (alas, many with a form of mange which can strike even young wombats, making them a pitiful sight), we have become home to a number of echidnas. The other day I was able to photograph one standing on its hind legs drinking out of a dish intended for the birds in the fernery on the upper side of the house, and yesterday (for the first time ever) three echidnas suddenly appeared immediately outside a back window near the kitchen. It transpired that two of them were males seeking the affection of a female which, I can only assume, was on heat. One suitor was preferred, but in the tangle of spines it was unclear to me whether we should expect an immediate increase in the echidna population. I am sure that Ogden Nash has something to say on the subject.

ABOVE

Crimson rosellas come to feed at the house every morning and afternoon.

LEFT

Winter, looking across the Amphitheatre.

131

JUNE 13   TYRRELL'S VAT 47 VERTICAL, SYDNEY

Today I fly to Sydney for a vertical tasting to commemorate the thirtieth vintage of Tyrrell's Vat 47 Chardonnay. The tasting begins with the 1971 and ends with the 2000 vintage, so the mathematics are correct.

Tyrrell's Vat 47 Chardonnay was the wine which provided the fuel to launch a thousand containers. Much of Australia's early success in the export market can be directly attributed to this wine, but for decades it also set the standard for the super-premium category of the variety.

Chardonnay had been brought to Australia in the early 1830s by James Busby, who catalogued it as white pineau or chaudenay, and was successfully grown by Col Laraghy at Smithfield on the western outskirts of Sydney, at Mudgee and at Penfolds HVD (Hunter Valley Distillery) Vineyard.

As its name suggests, HVD was established (in 1908) by a consortium of local growers for the production of spirit. It went into receivership in the early 1930s and was managed by Penfolds until that company purchased the vineyard in 1949.

For no obvious reason, chardonnay was planted on the HVD vineyard in 1923, and the table wine made by Penfolds from the planting was labelled White Pineau. In 1944 Frank Penfold Hyland decided to blend it with semillon and changed the name to Pinot Riesling. (Semillon was called Hunter Valley Riesling at that time.)

In the mid-1960s Murray Tyrrell was introduced to (French) white burgundy by the noted art dealer, bon vivant and wine judge Rudy Komon. With much relish, Murray Tyrrell used to tell how he jumped the fence at night and stole cuttings of the HVD chardonnay in July 1967. It seems this may have been an embellishment of the real story; namely, that Penfolds refused to sell cuttings to him, but that the vineyard manager 'facilitated' the supply and was protected by the theft story.

Whatever be the truth, a little under a hectare of chardonnay was planted on the Apple Tree Block of the Short Flat Vineyard in 1968 (the cuttings having taken root in a nursery in the intervening year) followed by a little over a hectare in 1970.

The first Vat 63 Pinot Riesling (adopting the Penfolds name) was made in 1970, the first Vat 47 in the deplorable, rain-sodden vintage of 1971. It and the 1972 were made in exactly the same way as Vat 1 Semillon: fermented in stainless steel and early bottled.

In 1973 Murray Tyrrell purchased his first (Nevers) oak barrels from Demptos, in which components of the 1973 were matured. The 1972 had won a gold medal at the Royal Brisbane Wine Show in the year of its vintage; the 1973 received precisely the same treatment as the early vintages of Grange: utter rejection, and 6 points out of 20. The senior judge said, 'It is either badly oxidised or the best white wine I have ever seen.'

The 1973 went on to win a Championship trophy and ten gold medals, setting the path for the prolific show successes of the following vintages. By 1978 Tyrrell's had moved on to barrel fermentation, but it was another ten years before this became standard practice, especially among the large wine producers — it is costly, space inefficient and requires constant, barrel-by-barrel monitoring. Lees stirring came later still, but once again Tyrrell's was at the forefront.

The tasting of the three decades demonstrated that five to ten years is the likely outer limit for safe cellaring, but with the wines ready to roll right from the word go. Moreover, there is no closed or dumb period as there tends to be for semillon or riesling.

But just to prove the rule, the exceptions were the 1984 (still rich, complex and succulent), the '79 (fresh, long and fine, a great Hunter vintage), the '73 (powerful, multi-flavoured, excellent texture and length) and the '71 (a freakishly good bottle, still crisp and lingering).

A final word of warning. Two bottles of each wine were used, and with several of the wines (most notably the 1984) there was considerable variation. In other instances the cork had failed, and the wines showed extreme oxidation/madeirisation. So remember the time-worn adage: there are no great old wines, only great old bottles.

JUNE 17   COLDSTREAM HILLS CLASSIFICATION: THE CRUNCH

Today I was meant to be in Langhorne Creek tasting five decades of Stoneyfell Metala, but the formal classification day for the majority of the Coldstream Hills wines from 2002 takes precedence. The

RIGHT
House block chardonnay in winter; above the fog line.

Coldstream Hills team of Andrew Fleming, Greg Jarrett and myself is joined by Philip Shaw and Peter Taylor as we work our way through innumerable samples.

The background of tiny yields is ever present, and some tough decisions will have to be taken on the sauvignon blanc components available which are not of Yarra Valley origin, even though in most instances they have been made at Coldstream Hills. There are eleven samples in all, and unfortunately two of the larger batches from the Yarra Valley, from the Yarrawalla Vineyard, simply do not stack up. In one sense this comes as no great surprise, for this is a problematic vineyard at the best of times. On the plus side, the components that are included are excellent, and the view is that this is the best sauvignon blanc of all the Southcorp group brands.

The tempo increases with seven batches of chardonnay which have tentatively been identified as the basis for about 1000 cases of Reserve Chardonnay. The lots have all the hallmarks of top-flight Yarra chardonnay, intense and long on the palate; the one problem is that three of the batches are still slowly fermenting, and are carrying residual sugar. If (as hoped) they can be fermented dry, they will be included, but as we move into thirty-nine different batches identified for the standard Coldstream Hills Chardonnay, it is obvious that there are several components here which could go into Reserve if the slow ferments do not run through to dryness.

Of the thirty-nine samples, ten are either rejected outright or rejected for the time being — some of these, too, are still to finish their fermentation. The likelihood is that there will be 10,000-plus cases of excellent wine, fulfilling the promise of the vintage.

We then move to pinot noir, with sixty-two individual batches to be tasted. The six lots earmarked for Reserve Pinot Noir are exceptional: Coldstream Hills Amphitheatre A Block and two parcels from our upper Yarra vineyard Deer Farm are absolutely outstanding, and the other three are likely to contribute to the overall complexity of what should be a very high-quality reserve wine.

It is when we move into the forty-eight samples for the varietal pinot noir that the character of the vintage really comes rocketing through. It is true that eight lots (amounting to around 20,000 litres) have already been rejected, but under normal circumstances a number of the wines tentatively earmarked for varietal would either be rejected outright or left with a substantial query. After all, the

BELOW

Yarra Valley in winter: ever-changing light.

wines are barely through malolactic fermentation, many are full of gas, and this is close on the worst time of the year to taste the wines; it is for financial and accounting reasons that a preliminary decision on inclusion or exclusion has to be made now.

The utterly remarkable feature is the consistency of the quality. There is a total of 173,000 litres, and only a single barrique experiment of 220 litres is under serious question. This was an interesting trial of total barrel fermentation — the crushed grapes were placed in a barrel with the head (or end) knocked out; the result was an exaggerated carbonic maceration character with gamey/vegetal overtones. In the context of the overall blend, it could add a touch, but making an entire wine this way would be out of the question.

It is with these varieties (along with pinot gris) that the excitement of the vintage rests. Merlot was a failure, and while G Block cabernet sauvignon has once again come through with flying colours (amazingly, picked before the Amphitheatre merlot and most other merlots which normally ripen far earlier), the rest will have to transform themselves in barrel over the next twelve months if they are to make the grade.

All this is a reflection of an ultra-cool vintage, or, if you like, a reversion to what was once considered to be a normal pattern before the run of hot vintages since 1997 which have so favoured the later-ripening (Bordeaux) varieties.

JUNE 22   CLOUDY BAY, NEW ZEALAND

With its mountain backdrop, immortalised by the Cloudy Bay label, Marlborough is a beautiful place at any time of year. Most tourists prefer to come in spring, summer or autumn, knowing that the temperature rarely rises above 30°C even at the height of summer, and also aware that the winter days can be very cold and intermittently rainy. Though it's not always so, I must admit that it seems quite incredible that only yesterday, when transferring from the international to the domestic terminal in Auckland, I was being literally blown off my feet, my wheelie bag careering away on a mission of its own with me still attached to the end of it, the rain whistling horizontally over my head.

The sky is a pale but brilliant blue, with a few patches of cotton wool white clouds clinging to some of the mountain tops and high valleys, the air crystal clear, and the wind no more than a puff. The main activities of the day are taking place inside, starting with the international tasting of pinot noirs, due to last two and half hours, from 11 a.m. to 1.30 p.m., then a leisurely glass of Pelorus, and lunch from 2 p.m. till close to 4 p.m., featuring extra bottles of all of the pinots tasted earlier in the day. Lunch for the hundred-plus people who are attending the tasting is served in a marquee, with a caterer fighting the usual miniature kitchen (for this number of people) and doing a spectacular job.

I am the after-lunch speaker, and attempt to collect the strands of what are the signposts signifying a great pinot noir, and what are not (colour, tannins, extract and so forth). Some of it is nebulous stuff; more substantial are the planting statistics, which in New Zealand have trebled since 1996 to 1491 hectares, and in Australia have doubled to 4142 hectares. Making international comparisons, the United States has 4400 hectares and the Côte d'Or 6440 hectares, with surprising similar yields per hectare except in New Zealand, which is lower (at 5.3 tonnes per hectare) because of the high percentage of very young vines.

> The format of the tasting is precisely that of its parent's (Cape Mentelle) annual cabernet sauvignon tasting, which was first held in 1982. Imitation being the sincerest form of flattery, the annual Cullen chardonnay tasting and the nouveau-riche Xanadu merlot event (this will be its second year) carefully follow precisely the same pattern.
>
> Line up three flights of seven wines each in a partially evacuated barrel hall; pour one flight at a time at waist-high tasting tables with all present standing to taste; conduct the assessment of each flight in near-silence (the Kiwis are more prone to twitter during the tasting than Aussies); after twenty minutes move to an adjacent room so that the next flight of seven wines can be poured, and while this is happening, invite two serious tasters to comment on the previous bracket.
>
> This is repeated twice, with different speakers, so all twenty-one (or twenty) wines will have been dissected. Before you start the

tasting you know the identity of the wines, thanks to a carefully researched and written monograph, and you know the vintage (1999); what you don't know is the order in which the wines have been served.

There are then two ways in which the tasting can be approached: the young bucks not only write tasting notes but try to guess the identity of each wine. The old bulls (like myself) content themselves with analysing as precisely as possible how the wine looks, smells and tastes, and don't try to pin the tail on the donkey.

Indeed, with my wine show judging in the background, I actively try to exclude any guessing about the origin or maker of the wine. I barely glanced at the background notes to get a general feel about the field, and didn't refer to them again. All I retained was the knowledge that France, New Zealand, Australia, California, Oregon and South Africa were represented, the last with a single wine, the other countries with more. All of which goes to prove that even a little knowledge can be very misleading, for the only wine I instinctively 'recognised' was a coal black, extractive wine, which I took to be South African — it wasn't: it was Californian (Talley Vineyards).

BELOW
Cloudy Bay lunch on the Marlborough Sound.

The benchmarking is not done numerically. The two speakers on each flight typically give a general indication of the wines they liked most, and occasionally lash out at a wine they don't like at all. But this is in no sense a wine show or competition, and although many of those present did allot points (and hence rankings), there is no attempt to collate these.

For what it is worth, my three top wines in the first bracket were Mugnier Chambolle Musigny (tightly knit, complex, needing time); Seresin (fragrant, silky and stylish); and Saintsbury (broodingly powerful black plum, demanding time).

In a stylistically uneven and challenging second flight, d'Angerville was top (controversial, very powerful, some bottles — not mine — variously considered corked or aldehydic); Dry River (which I described as slightly ponderous or elephantine, but crammed with flavour) second; and Drouhin (fragrant forest floor aromas and textured with fine tannins) third.

The last bracket (of six wines) was superb: it was all but impossible to separate five of them, but By Farr (fragrant, slippery/sappy), Mongeard Mugneret (understated, but marvellous length and intensity), and Rousseau (beautifully balanced, pure fruit and great length) just edged out Rex Hill Reserve (spotlessly clean, fragrant sweet fruit) and Bindi (a beautifully proportioned mix of sweet and savoury fruit).

A blink of an eye and a few cleansing ales later, and we are assembling for dinner at the Hotel d'Urville, where I am staying. The d'Urville occupies one of the two significant buildings in Blenheim surviving from the nineteenth century, having withstood earthquakes and being now protected under National Trust legislation. In its prior life it was the Public Trust office, with massive steel-doored vaults on the first floor which have been converted into several of the eleven rooms. The mix-and-match blending of nineteenth-century and late twentieth-century décor has been done with great flair; this is a small hotel of genuine international class, the double-room rate of NZ$270 no doubt proving irresistible to those with US dollars or other such currencies. Despite being situated in the centre of Blenheim, noise is not a factor. It also has a comprehensive website at www.durville.com.

As the meal proceeds to demonstrate, the restaurant provides high-class, imaginative food, which is accompanied by Cloudy Bay Te Koko 1997, Cloudy Bay Chardonnay 1997, Cloudy Bay Pinot Noir 1997, Cape Mentelle Cabernet Sauvignon 1998 (which somehow or other doesn't make it to my end of the table) and Cloudy Bay Late Harvest Riesling 1996.

I dash upstairs to the television in my bedroom every now and then to check on the progress of the two rugby union test matches being played; all in all, it's a great night.

JUNE 23   MARLBOROUGH SOUND

By 9 a.m. we are on our minibus for a rapid tour around much of Marlborough, looking at the further outposts of the Cloudy Bay vineyard empire and somehow or other making our way up to the top of Joe's Knob (named in honour of Joseph Henriot, former chief executive of Veuve Clicquot, the owner of Cape Mentelle Cloudy Bay) with its panoramic views across the sides of the valley, both up on the hillside and on the typically (but not universally) flat vineyard land. I marvel at how beautiful the region is in winter. True, we are blessed with yet another glorious day, illuminating the now largely bare canes from last year's growth, which have a particular glowing russet orange–brown colour, contrasting with the emerald green grass and the deep blue of the mountains behind. Time and again I have to repress the desire to ask the driver to stop, as one picture postcard view follows another, and another, and another …

Two hours later we're at Cloudy Bay winery once again, here tasting components of the Sauvignon Blanc, Te Koko and Chardonnay from 2002, with a second look at the upcoming releases of 2000 Cloudy Bay Pinot and Chardonnay and 1999 Te Koko — wines which were served at the welcome dinner on the evening of Friday, June 21 when, like lemmings, we congregated on an outside balcony at Cloudy Bay and were frozen into statues before someone had the bright idea of moving inside.

From the tasting we drive to Picton to board a high-speed catamaran which takes us to Ivan Sutherland's boathouse in a secluded part of the Marlborough Sound. Here we're treated to a substantial array of older vintages. For me the standout wine (both in terms of quality and in terms of its being unexpected) is the 1992 Sauvignon Blanc — sheer perfection. We talk about the development curves of sauvignon blanc, agreeing that at three or four years of age it becomes decidedly difficult, with spikes of herb, grass, asparagus and green capsicum, then progressively changing from five years through to (in this instance) ten years, when it acquires a gently honeyed taste and feel, the greener aspects there only to keep the wine fresh on the tongue. And indeed it is the remarkable freshness and harmony of this wine which is so outstanding. It is an experience few people have, simply because conventional wisdom has it that sauvignon blanc is best when young, a view reinforced by the ugly patch it then goes through. Mind you, I doubt that every Cloudy Bay vintage is as brilliant as the 1992 is now.

JUNE 26   PRUNING, COLDSTREAM HILLS

Pruning has been underway now since the beginning of the month. I became an expert pruner at Brokenwood, but notwithstanding that I spent virtually every weekend in the period from June to September hard at work, it took me considerably longer to learn how to prune than it did to learn the art of winemaking.

Pruning in the winter in the Hunter Valley was intensely therapeutic. While the mornings are very cold, necessitating jumpers and mittens, by 10 a.m. the jumper is gone, and by midday the shirt is, too. I became absolutely engrossed in the job, with the concerns and worries of big-city law practice a million miles away. It is, in its purest sense, an art form, the satisfaction being magnified when you solve the problem of a particularly difficult vine, leaving a perfect shape as you move on to the next.

Yarra Valley winters are far less benign, and the first 5-hectare planting in the Amphitheatre under the winery was on slopes varying between 20 and 30 degrees gradient. Despite this, in the first three years Suzanne and I alone pruned the vineyard; we had to recognise, at the end of the third year, that the task was beyond us. In that year I finished the last block by getting up at first light each morning and pruning for an hour or more before rushing back to the house to get changed and catch the train from Lilydale to the city and my law practice, repeating the process (if light permitted, which it often didn't) when I returned in the afternoon.

These days at Coldstream Hills, hand pruning is an entirely different affair. First, a mechanical pre-pruner (like a mechanical hedger) rumbles up and down the vine rows, cutting off all the high growth that is surplus to the needs of the next growing season. Then, half the job already done, the pruners arrive with pneumatic secateurs powered by a compressor on a tractor sitting at the end of the vine row, with hundreds of metres of air hose rolled on neat spindles. The soft sounds of 'sssh-snick' fill the air as four to six pruners work their way down adjoining rows, the umbilical cords of

BELOW
Historic gulf station on the outskirts of Yarra Glen.

ABOVE

Pruning the cherished A Block pinot noir in the Amphitheatre.

the secateurs growing ever longer. The job is done not only far more quickly, but also without the bogey of RSI. (The danger of accidentally pruning a finger is in fact minimal, because only the cutting hand comes into play.)

JUNE 29   MORE PRUNING, YARRA VALLEY

Winter has well and truly arrived, with yesterday's gale force northerly winds making the 9°C midday temperature seem much colder still. Today the winds have gone, and in their place come alternating bursts of heavy rain and improbable sunny periods. Indeed, from our house high on the hillside you can see rain on the Healesville side of the valley and bright sunshine (and blue sky) over Yarra Glen.

I vividly recall coming out to the valley in July 1983 (shortly after moving to Melbourne from Sydney) to help Louis Bialkower plant some of the first vines at Yarra Ridge. The sky was a faithful reproduction of a Gainsborough painting, with towering cumulonimbus clouds in a pale blue sky on one side, and shafts of rain coming from dark clouds on the other. Today is a replay of that sky.

The grass is as vividly green as any English or Irish landscape, the bare vines' canes ranging from burnt sienna to russet orange. Up close, water droplets glitter like diamonds, and shimmering spiderwebs are similarly festooned with a silver tracery of droplets.

The pruning team (largely Cambodian) works methodically on, seemingly oblivious to the weather, so far removed from the humid heat of their homeland. They arrive at first workable light and continue until dusk. As long as they are working, they are making money, and they are happy. Their employment is not the result of positive discrimination: Australians are by and large simply not prepared to work when it's too cold and wet (or too hot).

In California, Mexicans fill the same role; in Germany, it's the Polish and eastern Europeans (German law futilely proclaiming that the majority of the workers must be German citizens); in France it used to be the Portuguese (France has recently passed legislation which makes it illegal for any person to work more than thirty-five hours a week, from chief executives down to messenger boys), but with Portugal now part of the EU, the wage disparity has lessened.

When Australia adopted equal pay for women, part-time vineyard work for mothers during school hours quickly disappeared, leading to machines doing much of the work — mechanical harvesters, mechanical pruning, and now leaf trimmers, wire lifters and so forth. We choose to hand-prune and hand-pick because there is still a viable labour force, but how long will it last? It is more expensive than doing it all mechanically, but it's not the cost that is the issue. It simply comes down to finding people who are prepared to learn the skills required, and to work in all weather conditions.

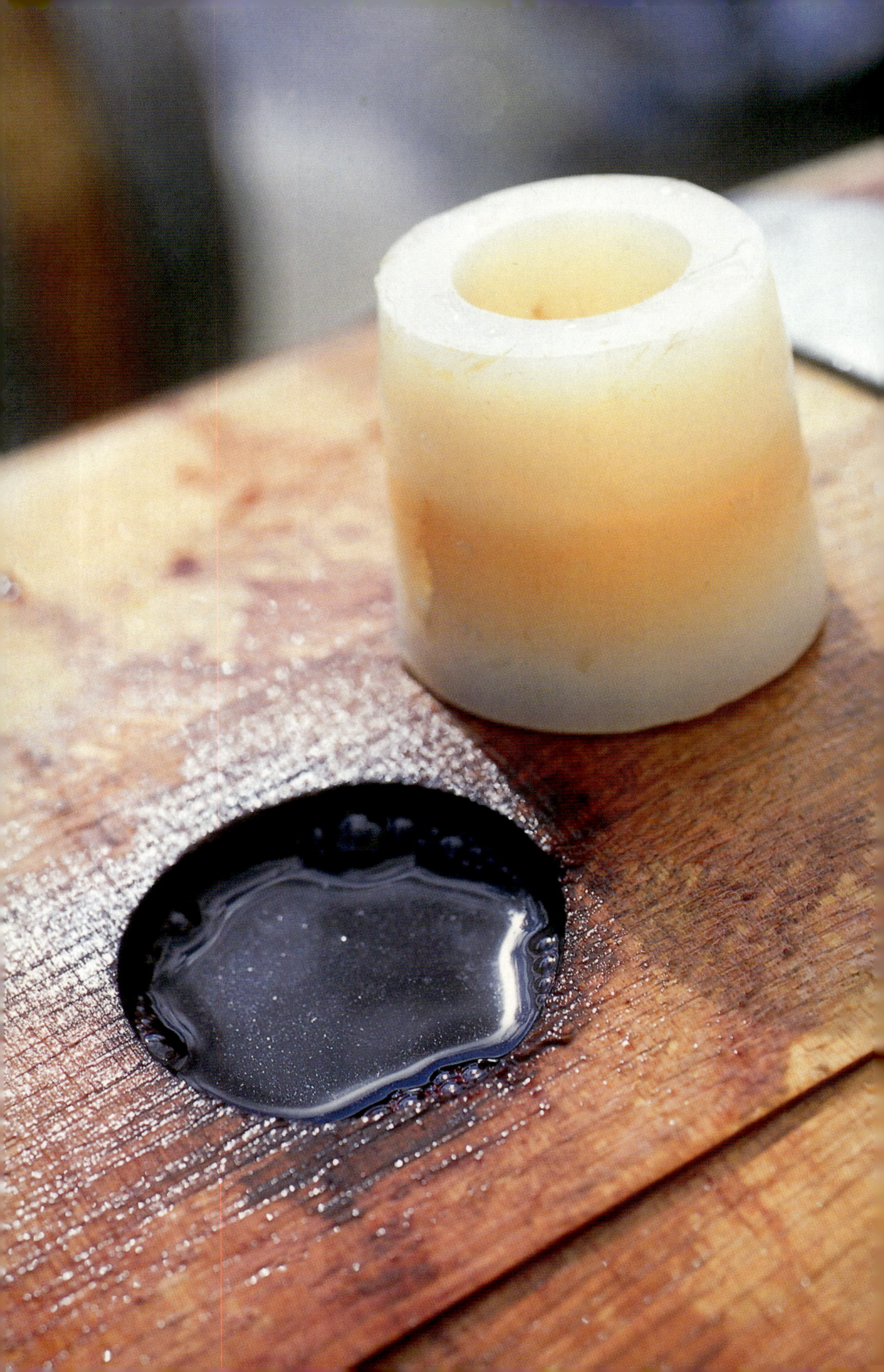

July

Brokenwood, Sydney

Sydney and the Hunter Valley

Howqua-Dale, Victoria

Brisbane Hilton Food and Wine Masterclasses

Chablis: Laroche

Riesling: Vickery and Grosset

Perfect Pinot: Oregon, New Zealand and Australia

Moss Wood: Blue-blood Cabernet

Oporto, Portugal

A Century of Vintage Ports: 1963 to 1863

A Fast-changing Cork Industry

Return to Australia

Scotchmans Hill by Helicopter

Tim Adams; Back to Melbourne

Shaw & Smith, Melbourne

Yarra Valley

Two Decades of Petaluma Coonawarra

Château Latour 1920 to 2000

JULY 1   Brokenwood, Sydney

It is ironic that I should be among those receiving an invitation to attend a spectacular function marking the launch of the 2000 Brokenwood Graveyard Shiraz, when the two Brokenwood partners who are also wine journalists and authors do not. One is the other surviving co-founder of Brokenwood, John Beeston (the other two were the late Tony Albert and myself); the other is Nick Bulleid MW, who supplied the background material for the stylish A4 booklet which was provided to those attending the launch dinner, and who has authored an excellent book on the Hunter Valley. The reason they are not invited is to avoid discrimination between the numerous Brokenwood partners, who would all give their eye-teeth to attend.

Lifestyle journalists — wine, food and/or travel — are often envied by their readers. But for most it is no more or less than a job, one which may be done professionally or not. Often I think it is the latter, simply because (as a group) we are variously jaded, satiated, cynical or just plain spoilt.

Those seeking our attention need to come up with an angle, a hook on which to hang a story. A new release of a wine at a restaurant with the winemaker in attendance may have been enough twenty-five years ago, when it was something of a novelty (especially if the restaurant was trendy), but no longer.

Unless, that is, it is organised with the exceptional flair of this release dinner. The invitation came in a black envelope, addressed using beautiful calligraphy. Inside was a vertically folded black and cream board in the shape of a cross, and at the bottom were the words '2000 Brokenwood Graveyard Vineyard Launch'. Closer inspection of the cross revealed the words 'horizontal' (across the board) and 'vertical' (down the board).

Inside was an invitation to a vertical tasting of five vintages ('00, '98, '94, '91 and '86) of Graveyard Shiraz, matched with a horizontal of ten of its peers. The venue? The Crypt, St James' Church, Sydney. Where else would you gather to consider the merits of the Graveyard?

The horizontal tasting matched the respective Brokenwoods, Seville Estate and Hanging Rock (2000); d'Arenberg Dead Arm and Jaboulet La

Chapelle Hermitage (1998); Wynns Michael and Guigal Rotie Brune et Blonde (1994); Wendouree and Eileen Hardy (1991); and Grange and Henschke Hill of Grace (1986).

The tasting concluded, but the wines retained (and the Graveyards topped up), we repaired for pre-dinner drinks (Champagne or Pike's Ale), then returned to the dinner. But this was no ordinary dinner: five of Sydney's leading chefs each prepared a course to match one of the five Graveyard vintages.

Sensibly, the tasting order was reversed, starting with the 1986 and finishing with the 2000. Older wines are typically more complex, aromatic and lighter in body; younger wines are more robust and powerful. When undertaking a vertical tasting in the absence of food, there is usually a case to be made for either order of progression, and experienced tasters may well take opposite starting points. But once food comes into play, it is self-evident that there needs to be a progression from more subtle to fuller-flavoured dishes, the challenge intensified in this instance by the need for all to match full-flavoured (to put it mildly) red wines.

Tim Pak Poy of Claude's matched the superb 1986 Graveyard (still well and truly in the prime of its life, combining complexity, generosity and elegance) with venison Martini, the most imaginative dish of the night. Presented in a martini-type glass, braised venison lay on top of morels and chestnuts, with a sliver of prosciutto on top. Then, after all the coupes were on the table, they were topped with an alcohol-infused venison consommé.

Neil Perry of Rockpool presented pan-roasted Illabo lamb saddle (in a ballottine-type roll) with rape and almond chilli and bread salsa with the 1991 Graveyard. The baby lamb was cooked to perfection, though there was a question about the level of spice given the lighter style of the wine (the product of a drought year) with only 12.8° alcohol, significantly lower than all the others.

The 1994 Graveyard is in transition from youth to maturity, neither one nor the other, but was beautifully supported by Peter Gilmore's (of The Quay) Persian spiced squab, white mulberries, chestnuts, chestnut mushrooms (the size of five cent pieces and culled from 5 kg of these rare mushrooms). The squab was at the cutting edge of rare, just as I most enjoy it, the dish very well balanced and lifting the profile of the wine.

It's a big leap from the 1994 to the 1998 Graveyard, the latter densely coloured and still bursting at the seams with luscious dark plum and cherry fruit cradled within a web of perfectly balanced tannins and oak. Serge Dansereau, of the Bathers' Pavilion, rose to the challenge (as he always does) with roast loin of hare, spiced confit of beetroot, homemade blood pudding and caramelised onion, the hare even rarer than the squab, but meltingly tender. A dish every bit as luscious as the wine.

The grand finale — and the reason for the culinary pyrotechnics — was the 2000 Graveyard served with Szechuan-cured duck breast, cauliflower, cumquat and what the menu described as coffee bean, but was in fact Valrhona chocolate. By sheer chance, several of us had been discussing the mistaken view that chocolate and red wine are well matched, the object of criticism being a chocolate soufflé so matched (elsewhere).

But as an ingredient in a sauce using blood and/or a rich reduction of vegetables and/or meat it does indeed work, even with a wine as stupendous as the 2000. The vintage is regarded in the Hunter Valley as the best for thirty-five years (perhaps rivalling the 1965) and it comes as no surprise to find the Brokenwood winemaking team of Iain Riggs and PJ (Peter James) Charteris tagging it as the best ever.

JULY 2   SYDNEY AND THE HUNTER VALLEY

Following a Wine Australia meeting and a sponsors' lunch at Fox Studios, I am headed to the Hunter Valley, where over the next two days I am to join Len Evans and a few others to taste just under five hundred budget and mid-priced Australian wines. Our task is to winnow out of these two separate offers of a dozen bottles each (six white, six red) at two price points. The wines will be primarily offered through *The Australian* newspaper, but also through Liquorland/Vintage Cellars' own direct mail offers. A tasting such as this falls unambiguously into the hard work category, with no romance of any kind attached to it. At least I am staying with Len and Trish Evans, and will have a chance this evening to catch up with a group of the best young Hunter Valley winemakers over dinner at Blaxlands Restaurant, run by Len and Trish's daughter Jodie Evans.

JULY 4   HUNTER VALLEY

As expected, the tasting is hard work. However, it seems to me that the twenty-four wines selected offer exceptional value for money, and that the lower-priced segment of the industry is in good health, whatever English journalists may suggest to the contrary. The one problem is a growing tendency to leave residual sugar sweetness in red wines, and a not-so-new habit of doing likewise with chardonnay. It's hard to know how much this is meeting the demand of the marketplace on the one hand, or simply covering up the lack of intrinsic flavour on the other. Len Evans and I take the view that it doesn't really matter: a dry table wine should be just that.

Before and after the day's tasting I am chauffeured around the valley by Len; against all the odds, so it seems, the rate of development shows no sign of slackening. A massive new golf course and housing estate, partly owned by course designer Greg Norman,

BELOW

The Pokolbin Village shopping centre; once there were vines here.

has been commenced at the north end of McDonalds Road. The first hundred home sites sold so quickly the developers have brought forward stage two of the residential development even though the golf course is not yet quite complete. The site chosen for the golf course is splendid, on gently rolling hills with an expansive view across the valley to the hills of the Barrington Tops, and Norman has moulded the course into the natural contours.

Developments of this kind to one side, the number of restaurants continues to proliferate, as does the choice of hotel accommodation. Land values have increased to $25,000–$35,000 per acre for bare land, which makes the $1000 per acre we paid for Brokenwood back in 1970 seem a great bargain. When I remember that the terms of the sale (a Crown Land sale) required 10 per cent of the purchase price to be paid each year over ten years with interest at 4 per cent, the gulf seems even greater. Yet when we made that purchase, it was regarded as a totally outrageous price, and we ourselves had declined to purchase a much larger block only 12 months previously (in 1969) at $96 an acre.

JULY 5–7   HOWQUA-DALE, VICTORIA

I am spending the weekend at Howqua-Dale Gourmet Retreat, founded by Sarah Stegley and Marieke Brugman twenty-five years ago. When Sarah and Marieke aren't leading gastronomic tours in places all over the world, they host twelve people at the retreat for the weekend.

On some weekends the accent is predominantly on food and cooking demonstrations given by a celebrity guest chef, with a lesser emphasis on wine. Taking part in the preparation of the food and working with the chef in the large open kitchen is the main activity — apart from, of course, devouring the dishes when cooked.

At other times there is roughly equal emphasis on the food and the wine, with a structured wine tasting taking the place of formal cooking lessons, and with the guest chef and guest wine expert (me, this time) cooperating in the planning of the weekend and, of course, in the presentation. The last weekend I participated in was with the great Sydney chef Tetsuya Wakuda, whose dishes and cooking style make the choice of wine very easy.

On this occasion my food partner is Sandor Palmai, who established the Landhaus in the Barossa Valley. Still relatively young, he is an imaginative and inspirational chef, and it was not simply a case of looking at the recipes and choosing the wine: his input in earlier discussions was vital. It was just as well we took the trouble, for it turns out that the members of the group are highly intelligent and all passionately interested in wine.

JULY 12 BRISBANE HILTON FOOD AND WINE MASTERCLASSES

This is the eighth Brisbane Hilton Food and Wine Masterclass weekend, and it seems I have participated (as a presenter) at all of them. The format is the same as for Melbourne (where it all began) and Perth, but this evening — Friday — breaks the pattern of previous years, which featured a very large black-tie dinner in the Hilton Ballroom with a major charity auction. I cannot say I am distressed that it is not happening, particularly given that on Sunday afternoon I am headed to Portugal via Singapore and Frankfurt, with absolutely no need for a dinner suit.

Instead I am having dinner with Gary Steel of Domaine Wine Shippers and Michel Laroche of Domaine Laroche, one of the most important chablis producers. The three of us are presenting a morning session (on Laroche, of course) and the idea is that we will plan the session.

In fact we don't quite get around to it; four others join us as we eat at Lat 27 Restaurant, and an entirely unexpected array of dazzling wines is brought along. We have 1990 Bollinger, a magnum of 1995 Laroche Grand Cru Chablis (Reserve l'Obedience ex Blanchots), 1985 Chambertin Clos de Beze of Armand Rousseau, 1983 Chambertin Clos de Beze of Faiveley, 1985 Romanée-Conti, 1983 Château Petrus and 1982 Château Mouton Rothschild, onto which are tacked bottles of Krug and Louis Roederer after the meal.

The menu includes a lemon risotto with prawns, which seems the obvious match for the chablis; warm quail salad for the burgundies;

and rump of lamb for the Bordeauxs. But do we really wish to have the wines in that order? The dilemma is neatly solved by the decision to stick with the risotto and chablis to start, then have the two Chambertins with the quail, the two Bordeauxs with the lamb, and then have the Romanée-Conti on its own at the end of the meal as the ultimate palate cleanser — no cheese, just the wine.

It turns out to be an inspired decision. The chablis is impeccable (I came to know it well over the ensuing two days) and easily accounts for the perfectly cooked risotto. The Chambertins perform precisely as one might expect: the Rousseau spicy, savoury and intense, yet light-bodied; the Faiveley bigger, stronger, but less elegant.

The 1982 Mouton is cassis-laden and succulent, the 1983 Petrus with a tapestry of flavours and awe-inspiring length; I much prefer it to the 1982 Petrus, however great the reputation of the 1982 may be.

But it is the 1985 Romanée-Conti which sets the evening on fire. 1985 was a vintage which caused great excitement at the time: a perfect growing season led to the healthiest crop seen for decades. I was in Burgundy during harvest, and there was no sign of botrytis or mildew anywhere. The longer perspective shows that the vintage was in fact too perfect, the yield too high, the wines lacking intensity and developing far more quickly than anyone imagined at the time.

However, Romanée-Conti will almost inevitably rise above the reputation of the vintage, especially when it is one such as 1985. The bouquet really defies description, it is so scented with such an amazing array of aromas: violets, truffles, wild strawberries, black cherries, plums, sandalwood, spice, cedar, vanilla — yet no one character dominating, the balance shifting each time I go back to the glass. It is so satisfying, so perfect, I toy with the absurd idea that I should not break the spell by tasting it: will it be an anticlimax? Sanity prevails; I do indeed slowly sip it, and it is no anticlimax.

I go to sleep on cloud nine, but am awoken at 4 a.m. by the pounding in my head, and resort to the Vitamin B and Disprin I should have taken before I went to sleep. It's an age-old trap: the better you feel before going to sleep, the greater the need for prophylaxis.

JULY 13 CHABLIS: LAROCHE

Most events which are held year after year have a natural life cycle, eventually running out of enthusiasm and becoming tired. Not so the International Pinot Noir Celebration of Oregon, nor — if this year is anything to go by — the Brisbane Hilton Food and Wine Masterclasses. All things considered, the Vintage (or Wine) Room has the strongest array of sessions for many years.

The five sessions each day commence with 'Champagne Ruinart', presented by Guy de Rivoire; then 'Chablis: The Real Thing', with Michel Laroche; 'Masters of Riesling', presented by John Vickery and Jeffrey Grosset; 'Perfect Pinot', with Steve Cary of Oregon, Clive Paton of Ata Rangi, New Zealand, and Phillip Jones of Bass Phillip; finishing with 'Marvellous Moss Wood', with owner/winemaker Keith Mugford receiving largely unnecessary support from myself.

The chablis session is simply great: Michel Laroche is a natural, speaking fluently and with perfect timing on his nine wines — but as the hackneyed cliché puts it, the wines really speak for themselves.

It is all too easy to forget that Chablis is part of Burgundy. Geographically, it is far closer to Champagne than to Beaune, the epicentre of the Côte d'Or. It is equally easy to roar past this northern outpost as you travel south on the A6 or the TGV. Small surprise, then, that it is often overlooked in Australia by Burgundy lovers, or by those searching for a white wine which is not fat, alcohol-sweet or overoaked.

There was a time, indeed, when chablis very nearly went out of existence — the once mighty plantings shrank to a mere 500 hectares in the 1950s. They have since grown to 4500 hectares — still well short of historical highs — causing near civil war between traditionalists who argued that plantings should be restricted to the classic marine-derived Kimmeridgian chalk soils and those who claimed that they should be permitted on the related but different Portlandian soils.

This focus on terroir is, of course, the modern mantra for French winemakers trying to establish the unique nature of their wines, and arguing that the place of origin is of far greater importance than the grape variety. The latter can be found anywhere, the former is by definition unique. But in the case of chablis, there is an immediate and profound character which can only be explained by its terroir, its place: the cleansing, lingering, minerally acidity which marks the finish of all chablis, young or old, humble or great.

There are several Grand Crus, totalling a mere 100 hectares in all. Les Blanchots represents 14 hectares of the total, and Laroche owns 4.6 hectares. Here subtlety is the key word when discussing the layers of flavour and texture, the finesse ensuring a ten- to twenty-year cellar life.

At the peak of the pyramid comes Laroche Les Clos, $150 a bottle compared with the $100 for Les Blanchots. Totally barrel fermented (one-third new oak), it is a wine of exceptional complexity (apple and citrus blossom aromas, mineral, citrus and apple flavours) which will live for ten to twenty years or more. Before you get too excited, only five hundred cases are made each year, and Australia's allocation is five cases.

JULY 13   RIESLING: VICKERY AND GROSSET

Amazingly, the 'Masters of Riesling' session brings John Vickery and Jeffrey Grosset onto the podium for the first time, and they obviously enjoy the experience. They have chosen their ten wines with great imagination and skill, tracking four different topics: the exceptional quality of the 2002 vintage in the Clare Valley (the Leo Buring Watervale DWF18, looking as good as it did earlier in the week); three 2001 wines (Grosset Polish Hill, Mount Horrocks Watervale and Orlando Steingarten Eden Valley), to show the style differences of these three regions; 1998 Richmond Grove Watervale under cork and Stelvin respectively (the great closure debate); then 1996 Orlando St Helga, 1994 Grosset Watervale, 1992 Mitchell Watervale and 1984 Seppelt Eden Valley, to show the development curve of riesling as it ages in bottle.

The best-laid plans of mice and men notwithstanding, I (and some others) prefer the Richmond Grove with the cork to that under Stelvin. The latter has a toasty character which was slightly intrusive, where the former has finer, purer fruit and more honey on the palate. Were it not for the distinct colour difference — the Stelvin wine with more green hues — I would have sworn the glasses had been poured the wrong way around. Behind the scenes, however, nine bottles of the 1996 St Helga (with corks) are opened to obtain four good, one acceptable and four spoilt bottles — this for a wine with a natural lifespan of around twenty years.

JULY 13 PERFECT PINOT: OREGON, NEW ZEALAND AND AUSTRALIA

'Perfect Pinot' features two outstanding vintages from three countries: 1999 Oregon and 2000 New Zealand and Australia. Stephen Cary speaks for Oregon and, for that matter, for the whole world of pinot noir. Well over twenty years ago, when he was a wine wholesaler, he founded the Steamboat winemaker conference, an integral part of the International Pinot Noir Celebration (IPNC), which brings together sixty or so pinot noir makers from around the world to discuss the myriad issues relating to every aspect of growing and making pinot noir. It takes place in a 'closed shop' environment on the beautiful Umqua River, famous for the steelhead fishing of Zane Grey and countless others who have followed in his footsteps. (Closed shop because journalists are barred: I attended many such meetings wearing my winemaker hat, but with a vow of journalistic silence.)

The other segment of the IPNC is held at McMinville, in the north of Oregon. This is a two and a half day public event, so popular that the tickets, costing US$1000 each, are sold by ballot, demand far exceeding supply.

Stephen Cary did the vintage at Coldstream Hills in 1991, and we also share a love of fly fishing — in his case it's an all-consuming passion. Very cleverly, he has built a three-pronged career: photographer, winemaker for Yamhill Valley Vineyards, and fly fisher for anything that moves in water, fresh or salt.

He chooses three top-end Reserve wines: Rex Hill, with a tight black cherry, herb and spice bouquet, then a totally unexpected silky/velvety mouthfeel showcasing pure fruit; Cristom, with spice, herb and ripe cherry aromas, both the bouquet and palate showing the synergies to be gained from the incorporation of 50 per cent whole bunches when the innate character of the fruit is concentrated enough to carry the stem tannins; and the complex and powerful Yamhill Valley, with savoury/gamey notes and the structure to sustain long ageing (I just wish he wouldn't use synthetic corks).

Clive Paton responds with three New Zealand classics: Felton Road from the Bannockburn sub-region of Central Otago (highly focused dark plum and cherry, silky tannins, great length); Neudorf Moutere Home Vineyard (fragrant, exotically spiced, long, lingering, savoury finish); and Ata Rangi (by far the richest and most powerful of the three, with all manner of aromas and flavours to emerge as the wine ages in bottle).

Finally it comes to the turn of a flu-stricken and nearly voiceless Phillip Jones (just returned from China with a particularly nasty strain of Asian flu, pre-SARS) to present three ex-barrel wines from 2001 — a so-called Pinot Rosé, Village Pinot and Belrose Pinot. The three wines come from three different blocks, but are made in precisely the same way. If anyone wishes to see terroir in action in Australia, here is their chance. While there is some similarity between the Rosé (which really isn't a rosé at all, having far more stuffing than a conventional rosé) and the Village, the Belrose is from another world, infinitely deeper and darker in colour, still with strong purple tints, the fruit sweet and lush, the tannins ripe.

The other Australian representative is the 2000 Yering Station Reserve, which earlier this week won the Pinot Trophy at the London International Wine and Spirit Competition for 'Best Pinot Noir in the World', which really means best pinot noir entered in that competition. Nonetheless, it is a neat coincidence, for Ata Rangi has won the Trophy an amazing three times, and Coldstream Hills has also won it (in 1998, with its 1996 Reserve). Yering Station winemaker Tom Carson's first exposure to the Yarra Valley was at Coldstream Hills, and the style of the Yering Station Reserve Pinot is very similar to that of Coldstream Hills, albeit with a touch more oak.

JULY 13   MOSS WOOD: BLUE-BLOOD CABERNET

My last formal vertical tasting of Moss Wood took place almost eight years ago, covering the 1992 to 1973 vintages. So the opportunity to taste the eleven vintages from 1991 to 2001 (plus the '83, included for good measure) is very welcome.

Moss Wood is one of the blue-blood classics of Australia. Its site is unambiguously distinguished, identified long ago by the foremost terroir (climate and soil) scientist Dr John Gladstones. The Margaret River climate has a general propensity to produce complex, structured, tannic cabernet sauvignon which nonetheless has a velvety richness — softness even — to its mid-palate. Nowhere, however, is that character more evident than at Moss Wood. Regardless of the vintage conditions, the wines have a generosity which makes them a pleasure to drink at almost any stage of their development.

There have been changes to the wine over the years: while the cabernet sauvignon component has never been less than 90 per cent, cabernet franc and a dash of merlot were introduced at the end of the 1980s, the merlot effectively replaced by petit verdot (since 1998). While the precise composition varies a little from vintage to vintage, it averages 92 per cent cabernet sauvignon, plus 4 per cent each of cabernet franc and petit verdot.

Mugford has also discontinued the intermittent Special Release versions (the last was 1994), which were kept in oak for an additional six months, now applying the 'Special Reserve' technique to all the cabernet sauvignon: it is kept in small oak for two years, and then given an additional year in bottle prior to its release.

I depart to Portugal via Cairns immediately after lunch the following day, so cannot (as usual) participate in the repeat Moss Wood session on the Sunday afternoon.

JULY 15   OPORTO, PORTUGAL

I am ensconced in a suite at the Porto Carlton Hotel, right on the waterfront, looking directly across the Douro to Vila Nova de Gaa, the home of all the port lodges. It is a perfect day, not a cloud in the sky, the temperature in the mid to high 20s, no hint of humidity and a brisk sea breeze blowing up the river.

Having (finally) arrived at the hotel just before noon, and had my first shower and change of clothes in a little under forty hours, I go on a combined photography and food mission. A spur of the moment decision takes me into one of the small, granite-walled restaurants which hug the quay not far from the hotel; I choose it simply because it is less obvious than many of the others. With memories of some great meals in Alentejo on my last trip, I order Pork Alentejana. An ice-cold beer in an all-too-small glass arrives along with a wicked plate of sliced blood sausage, small green and black olives, and a spiced bread/cake cross, the density of rye bread but cut in cubes and much sweeter. It is a specialty of northern Portugal, called brao.

Having consumed one piece of the spicy blood sausage, it seems to me there is little point in hanging back, and I place my faith in the will of Allah. The plate much diminished, and several beers later, the Pork Alentejana arrives, an oval ovenware dish piled high with tiny pippies, cubes of pork, and golden cubes of fried potato lurking underneath in the sublimely intense sauce. Truly, this is one of the great peasant dishes — if that is the right description — I have ever had, rivalling a blanquette de veau (rich, creamy veal stew) which Suzanne and I stumbled across on the French Swiss border at a tiny roadside café twenty years ago.

One part of the mission accomplished, I walk for the next few hours up and down either side of the river and ultimately decide that I will keep the climb to the top of the town for another day.

It's now four o'clock and I am wrestling with the choice of having a couple of hours' sleep or sticking to my usual battle plan of forcing myself to stay awake until the end of the evening. The problem with this is that we are not leaving the hotel until seven o'clock this evening to drive to the Vinho Verde region, with dinner starting around nine o'clock (if we are lucky) and a midnight return to the hotel (again, if we are lucky). Previous trips to Portugal and Spain mean I am forewarned, but I don't really think I can say I am forearmed. What can you do if you are part of a group in the hands of the Portuguese?

It's seven o'clock, and we are meant to be leaving for dinner at the Quinta de Asevedo around an hour to an hour and half distant by road. By some mystical process, we are also due to arrive for dinner

LEFT

Old houses cling to the steep Oporto hillside above the River Douro.

BELOW

One of the many restaurants and bars along the quayside of Oporto opposite the Port lodges.

at the Quinta by eight o'clock. With the South African members of the group leading the way, we manage to delay departure with several beers, and don't set out until 7.40 p.m., which also happens to be rush hour out of Oporto. If this were not enough, our guide — Raul d'Alva — is armed with a highly coloured and quite striking map produced by someone's computer, which turns out to bear no relationship at all to the way we are meant to go.

After inching our way out of town and onto less cluttered roads, our minibus makes a number of U-turns before we finally arrive at the Quinta shortly before 9 p.m. It turns out to be a magnificent and very large house which had remained in family possession for centuries until being sold and then quickly resold to the Guedes family, owners of SogrWe, who over the ensuing three years spent millions of dollars in its restoration, and who actually use it as a family house on weekends, plus guest room accommodation. The various ceilings, all wood-panelled with incredibly complicated but wonderful designs, are something to behold.

The dining room and the granite table, constructed from slabs taken from lagars (open fermenters), is massive, easily accommodating the twenty guests — there would be room for thirty without crowding. Apparently someone in the public relations department asked whether the table could be moved slightly to one side for a function; a medium-sized crane might have just been able to accomplish the task. While lunch today (and prior visits to Portugal) are proof you can eat wonderfully well, the food at formal dinners can fairly be described as idiosyncratic, the matching of food and wine likewise.

JULY 16   A Century of Vintage Ports: 1963 to 1863

This morning we are embarking on the tasting which has lured me to Portugal; true, it is in part a leap of faith, because all I know is that the tasting will be a mix of Vintage, Colheita and Garrafeira vintages, the youngest 1963 and the oldest from the nineteenth century. The trip itself has been sponsored by Apcor, the cork promotion arm of the cork industry and the Portuguese government (one is never sure precisely where the money comes from) but also, equally significantly, by the major Portuguese port firms: Ferreira, Niepoort and Burmester (which now also includes, by acquisition, Sandeman and Offley). It is these firms which provide what turns out to be a once-in-a-lifetime tasting. The vintages represented cover the very greatest classic years: 1963, '47, '37, '34, '27, '22, '12 and 1863.

Some of the greatest and oldest wines in the tasting are put into context by the events of the year in question.

In 1947 India and Pakistan proclaimed independence, with bloody religious battles breaking out in Kashmir and elsewhere. The Bell XI aeroplane broke the sound barrier for the first time, and the Cold War between Russia and the West began.

The '47 Ferreira Vintage Port (served from a magnum) is a wonderful wine. It has an exceptionally complex bouquet, with hints of spiced Christmas cake allied with clean spirit; while the flavours on the palate are well and truly into the secondary spectrum, the life, and above all else the length, of the palate is outstanding.

Two superb Colheitas (a vintage tawny port style) came from the year 1937, as Hitler was beginning his campaign of annexation across Europe.

Burmester Colheita (bottled 2001) is a glowing tawny; it proclaims its class from the very instant it is smelt, very complex and intense, with a wonderful array of aromas, yet spotlessly clean and pure. The palate lives up to the bouquet: fantastically intense, with long, lingering acidity. A great wine, unmarred by volatile acidity.

Niepoort Colheita (bottled in 1977) is also golden tawny, fractionally lighter than the 1934. The intensely fragrant bouquet has nuances of citrus and prune, a long, intense palate tracking the bouquet, particularly with hints of preserved citrus peel. Less showy than the 1934, but harmonious and elegant. Because of the difference in style/mouthfeel, it is difficult to rationalise any difference in quality rating.

1934 was the year in which Stalin's slaughter of millions of Russians began; in Germany, Hitler cemented his control by making trade unions illegal. Roosevelt's New Deal was launched in the United States, and Salazar strengthened his grip on Portugal.

Once again, two magnificent wines: first Niepoort Colheita (bottled 1981), which is golden tawny; it has a powerful and intense bouquet with some volatile acidity; contrary to expectations, that volatility is less evident on the mandarin/cumquat flavours of the palate. This manages to combine smoothness and intensity to a remarkable degree, sustained by welcome acidity.

Ferreira Vintage has exceptional colour, bright and clear, every bit as deep as the 1947. The bouquet is intense yet elegant, complex yet fine, very pure and lightly spiced. The palate has absolutely perfect texture and balance, with gentle spice and raisin flavours providing a lingering sweetness.

1912 is described by Michael Broadbent as 'the last great classic vintage of the period', although what period he is referring to I am not sure.

Niepoort Colheita (bottled 1977) is bright golden tawny; a complex multi-spice bouquet with a touch of earthy spirit; the palate super-intense and long, almost overwhelming in its attack, but with a cleansing aftertaste. What a wine. Incidentally, all the Niepoort wines use a full natural cork regardless of their style or vintage. This deserves more than five stars, but then so did one or two others in the tasting.

In 1863 President Abraham Lincoln issued a decree abolishing slavery, but the civil war between the northern unionist states and the southern confederate states was to continue for another two years.

Hot weather through the entire summer produced what was regarded by the long-deceased Ernest Coburn as one of the best vintages ever for the Douro. It was also the last vintage before phylloxera began to decimate the vineyards, which means that it was produced from old vines planted on their own roots on the old terraces.

Ferreira Vintage is distinctly olive, but still vibrant, lively and clear. The bouquet is very similar to a high-quality Madeira of similar age, free of even the slightest hint of decay; nuances of mandarin skin and spice. The palate has quite amazing mouthfeel and balance, and is like the bouquet, unbelievably fresh and zesty. It has developed to the stage where it is simply very great old wine, its vintage port ancestry now lost in the mists of time. To give it only five stars is a gross injustice.

JULY 17   A FAST-CHANGING CORK INDUSTRY

The two and a half hour drive down to Alentejo and the principal cork forest area, where Amorim and Subercor have set up their multi-million-dollar new factories, takes us from temperatures in the high 20s to 40°C.

The economics of the cork industry are far from clear. There has been a A$20 million investment by Subercor in a state-of-the-art factory with a high degree of automation, radically reducing the number of people employed in the latter stages of cork manufacture. On the other hand, stripping the trees (as ever, an amazing sight), getting the stripped bark to an intermediate holding point where it is briefly stockpiled, then taking it to the factory where it is unloaded off semitrailers by hand then restacked by hand (typically in very high temperatures), makes one wonder. It seems that there have been savings due to automation, but that these have been offset by rising cork prices. Here the expectation is that cork prices will fall over the next few years, said to be the law of supply and demand, but how this actually works in this case I am not sure.

The most impressive feature by far of the visit to Subercor is the establishment of an audit trail from the forest to the finished product. The piles of bark are identified before any treatment process has started, and electronic tagging takes over early in the piece — tagging not of individual corks, of course, but of batch numbers, which typically cover in the region of 30,000 corks.

The precise technical advances of each major producer are regarded as secret cork business, notwithstanding some cooperation on R&D. The new boiling tanks at Subercor exist alongside two of the old versions, and here too the technical advances are massive, with stainless steel water towers where the water is filtered through 25 micron filters, its chemical analysis continuously monitored via computers in use both here and in the treatment phase.

The forest we see being stripped is in fact owned by the local municipal council, as a result of a gift of the property by the family which previously owned it, and the stripped cork will be sold to the

ABOVE LEFT

Stripping the cork from trees is both very hard and highly skilled work; the axe must cut to precisely the right depth.

ABOVE RIGHT

The raw cork bark is piled high at the factories soon after it is removed from the forest.

highest bidder. As ever, I am amazed at the agility of the cork strippers as they climb up the trees, axe in hand, and their ability to continue working in relentless 40°C heat.

Lunch is wonderful: after an assortment of local cheeses, cured ham, sausage, chopped liver and marinated octopus, the main course is of wild black-footed pig (or boar). The meat is cut in thin strips in an identical fashion to wagu beef (which was served at the Brisbane Masterclass dinner for the presenters) and the end result is eerily similar. The pork has a similar degree of fat within the meat itself, which acts as a self-basting factor, giving the slices (grilled over charcoal) an inbuilt marinade.

It is virtually impossible to guess where the great closure debate will be in ten or twenty years' time, or whether, indeed, there will be any debate at all. Natural cork has remained supreme for three hundred years; it has only been in the last twenty years of the twentieth century that its role has been questioned, and even then only in limited sectors of the market. The fact that after four thousand years of wine production, a technological revolution led to the glass bottle and the cork does not give the cork eternal primacy.

I am not an apologist for cork; I have no shares or equity in cork companies, nor am I paid any money by those companies or their organisations. In 1995 I accepted an invitation to travel to Portugal with Peter Leske, then of the Australian Wine Research Institute, to look at the cork industry. Neither of us was keen to make the visit; we were well aware of the disinformation given to previous larger groups of journalists and wine trade members.

We came back to Australia even more disillusioned than when we left and both published scathing accounts of the trip, Peter in scientific journals and I in the press.

We saw outmoded factories, some like a scene out of a Charles Dickens novel, received no real information from the official research organisation, CTCOR, and were even told that part or all of the Quercus (the code-name for the research project) results might not be made public.

Seven years further on, there has been a total turnaround in attitude. Massive investments in entirely new factories have been made, and radically new processes have been introduced to create a multi-stage sequence from the tree in the forest to the cork in the bottle.

The change in attitude on the cork production side is more than matched on the winery customer side, both occurring at bewildering speed. Australian winemakers have started to talk of banning the use of 'bits of tree bark' in their wines, while the Portuguese suppliers sometimes talk of 'the campaign for survival'.

While it may seem that this has all happened overnight, and that the issue is simply one of TCA (trichloranisole) cork taint, the dynamics and time lines are far more complex.

For the time being, the real contest is between natural cork, technical corks and Stelvin screw-caps. I am confident that the stringent new procedures and processes, the tough certification scheme introduced in 2000 (upgraded in 2001, and further upgraded in 2002), the decreasing amounts of chlorine left in the environment of the cork forests from pesticide and other sprays, and the establishment of new cork tree plantations in controlled environments will lead to the elimination of TCA and the other two less frequently encountered taints, guaicol and geosmin.

But no matter how quickly (or slowly) that situation is reached, will it be too late? For certain wine styles — most notably riesling, but also semillon, sauvignon blanc and other aromatic white wines — I suspect the fight is all but over. All makers of top-class Australian riesling expect their wines to last for at least twenty years, and improve for at least half of that period. Unfortunately, experience shows that natural corks will have an unacceptably high incidence of faults — chiefly taints and oxidation — over this timeframe.

I have seen repeated evidence of these faults in major riesling and semillon vertical (or museum) tastings over recent years. The traces of sugar in riesling exacerbate the problem, but semillon also suffers. Conversely, corks in red wines (which have no sugar) are typically more robust, and can hold the wine in exemplary condition for incredibly long periods of time.

Last year I took the lead role in spending $78,000 on a single cork, or, if you prefer, a single bottle of wine: a double magnum of 1865

Château Lafite, which had never been recorked, although the top of the neck had been rewaxed in the 1930s. (The precise history of the bottle was known, and it had spent the first hundred years of its life in the cold English cellar of the Earl of Rosebery.) The obvious questions were: was the cork tainted, and had it kept its seal? The answer to both questions was favourable: the wine was utterly magnificent.

However, Australian cellaring conditions are a long way from those of English castles, and the active auction and secondary market in Australia means that storage conditions are often unknown — ignorance in this situation is likely to be bliss. So unreasonable demands are often made on the cork, demands which the Stelvin can better resist.

That said, Stelvins do not freeze the wine in time, making it a perpetual Peter Pan. The majority of the changes in wine which occur over time do not require oxygen to fuel them, and there is in any event a small amount of dissolved oxygen present in wine when it is bottled. So storing wine in hot conditions will destroy or prematurely age it even if it does have a Stelvin cap.

But does this really make Stelvin a better overall closure than taint-free one-piece corks or technical corks? I don't believe so, but then my lifetime experience with wine has been preconditioned by the use of cork. For me, a long cork (54 mm) coming out of a twenty- or thirty-year-old bottle of well-cellared red wine in prime condition (the cork, that is) is part and parcel of the experience of fine wine. Two generations on, the answer may well be very different.

JULY 17 · OPORTO

The nomination (some years earlier) of Portugal as European cultural city of the year for 2001 unleashed a frenzy of building activity and road repairs, which was in full swing when I visited last year and which shows no sign of abatement today. From dawn to dusk road workers labour away outside my hotel, directly under the three large windows of my room which look out over the River Douro. Aeroplane earplugs do a fine job of noise abatement, but I know the sound of each piece of equipment intimately.

Oporto's narrow cobbled streets, running every which way on the steep hillsides, are made even narrower by the omnipresent building and roadworks. A new code of conduct emerges as cars and trucks, denied the opportunity to park conventionally, simply stop in the middle of the road. As the traffic builds up behind, the first sign is a short beep on the horn, designed to lure the missing driver back to the parked vehicle. If within a minute or two there is no progress, a longer blast (deafening if a truck is blocked behind the parked vehicle) follows.

If this fails, all the blocked traffic starts horn-blowing, and out saunters the missing driver with a smile (not the least sheepish), and a casual wave of acknowledgment rather than apology.

Roadworks to one side, parking is forever at a premium, which has given rise to a swarm of volunteer parking attendants. Regardless of the time of day or night, their uniform is the same: a filthy and tattered pair of jeans, and what may or may not be the remnants of a shirt held in one hand but never worn. Without having the faintest idea whether the approaching car is wishing to find somewhere to park or simply to find a path around the would-be parking attendant, they leap out onto the road, gesticulating wildly with shirt

The Port Lodges of all the famous producers huddle together on the hillside of Oporto above the River Douro.

in one hand, and either pointing to imaginary parking places or energetically trotting off making 'follow me' signs.

When the restoration and building work will slow down I have no idea. Obviously, there is still a significant cash flow coming from Brussels and from the Portuguese government. Happily for the future of Oporto and its budding tourism industry, most of the money is being spent on the renovation of existing buildings, rather than on tearing down the old to make room for the new. Even now, and regardless of the building and traffic chaos, it is a great city to visit, not overly expensive (even with Australian dollars) and compact enough (population 600,000) to encourage exploration on foot.

The food, too, has much to commend it. It is all about flavour and richness, and robust dishes which appeal directly to the stomach. There are a no mind games or tricky presentation outside one or two French-accented restaurants. Most typical are the family seafood restaurants sprawling along the shoreline towards Matosinhos. As Raul d'Alva (our host) says, 'If the quality of the food is not up to the mark, the restaurant will soon close. Word of mouth is very powerful, and you won't find any restaurants like these in guidebooks.'

We are eating at an Oporto equivalent to the older-style but good Chinese restaurants in Australia. A huge tank of live crabs and lobsters sits near the door, while fresh fish and pre-cooked king prawns and crabs are reflected in mirrors above long trays in the front of the open kitchen.

We start with two dishes of king prawns, sweet yet salty, then a crab with claws big enough to do battle with a Queensland mud crab, then a large bream, cut across its body into steaks and chargrilled, accompanied by a giant pot of rice and beans in an intensely smoky tomato-based sauce (soup, really), the taste coming from smoke-cured ham.

The service — from two brothers who simply have to be the owners — proceeds at a frenetic pace, plates appearing and disappearing in a flash, glasses likewise, but it's still after midnight before we exit.

Vinho Verde, at its best penetrating, fresh, crisp and bone dry, with a limey acidity, is a very logical wine to have with cold, fresh seafood. It has to be said that there are also harsh, volatile, over-sulphured versions, and (given that there are hundreds of producers) little hope of choosing the best unless you are with a local.

But never, ever be tempted to choose a red Vinho Verde; the oxymoronic name only hints at what is to follow. So vivid is the purple colour that if you blend it with 50 per cent water, the colour is still deep. The alcohol is only 10°, the pH way under 3, and the acidity at some frightful level. The impact is like a mouthful of needle-sharp tacks in a bath of concentrated acid.

JULY 18   RETURN TO AUSTRALIA

The more I see of Portugal, the more I like it, but all good things must come to an end, so I begin the long trip home via Frankfurt and Singapore, in the thoroughly familiar interior of a Qantas 747.

JULY 22   SCOTCHMANS HILL BY HELICOPTER

As I drive into Melbourne from home, the Yarra Valley floor is white with frost, the temperature 0ºC as I pass Mount Mary. It's an ominously cold start, for I am soon headed to the Bellarine Peninsula, itself a cold place when the wind blows. Scotchmans Hill has laid on two helicopters, which depart from the helipad opposite the Crown Casino on the Yarra River. The purpose of the day is the launch of two single-vineyard wines at the top end of the Scotchmans Hill portfolio.

While I have heard much about the combined Scotchmans Hill and Spray Farm enterprises, I have never made the long trip to the tip of the Bellarine Peninsula, so the helicopter ride is irresistible.

From the air you realise just how dramatic the transition is from the flatlands to the rolling hills at the end of the Peninsula. But one glance at the tortured shapes of the few old trees, and the ocean that completely surrounds the Peninsula, tells you this is indeed a windy part of the world, buffeted alternately by northerlies and sou'westerlies.

Nonetheless, the climate is quite different from that of the Mornington Peninsula on the other side of Port Phillip Bay, chiefly because the rainfall is much lower here, at only 550 mm per year. In keeping with the powerful business acumen of David and Vivienne Browne, Scotchmans Hill entered into a long-term contract giving it access to unlimited water from the Geelong wastewater treatment plant. This so-called grey water is pumped along a 7-kilometre pipeline installed and paid for by Scotchmans Hill, and it guarantees the ability to irrigate in the increasingly common drought years.

Spray Farm is without doubt the jewel in the crown of the Scotchmans Hill group, and one of the best historic cellar doors in the state. Particularly striking is the contrast between the white-painted sandstone of the large house and the red convict-made sandstock bricks of the adjoining coach house and stables. The contrast is striking, but not discordant; it simply adds interest to the site.

The Brownes cautiously began the establishment of their vineyard in 1982, planting a little under 1 hectare each of riesling, cabernet franc, gewürztraminer and chardonnay, an eclectic choice based on now-outmoded advice. To be fair, though, there were no other vineyards on the Peninsula at that time.

As their experience grew, so did the plantings, eventually reaching today's 53 hectares. The first vintage was 1986, and in 1988 Robin Brockett, New Zealand-born but Charles Sturt-qualified, was appointed as full-time winemaker.

Three years later, when production was around 10,000 cases, David Browne gave his wife Vivienne the keys to a new four-wheel-drive vehicle as a birthday present. 'Did I ever mention Plan B?' he asked, and Vivienne duly started retail distribution in Melbourne, with 40 cases at a time loaded in the back of the car.

Local knowledge was, if anything, even more important when the nearby National Trust Spray Farm homestead (built in two stages, beginning in 1851) came onto the market in 1994. It was in a sad state of disrepair, having been abandoned for decades at various stages, and the restoration was both lengthy and expensive.

Spray Farm now houses the corporate offices of the group, a courtyard café and two large dining rooms. It hosts all manner of events, from small conferences to an annual series of outdoor concerts (since 1995) attracting 10,000 patrons each year, and (since 1999) the Spray Farm International Horse Trials, said to be the pre-eminent equestrian event of its kind in Australia. It is open every day for lunch (12.30 to 3 p.m.) and from 10.30 to 5.30 for light refreshments. Unusually, the excellent wine list has a wide choice of both local and imported wines.

Spray Farm has also given its name to Scotchmans Hill's second-tier wines, produced in part from estate-grown grapes in the Geelong region. The third tier is Swan Bay, which simply carries a Victorian appellation. All up, production has grown to 65,000 cases, and Scotchmans Hill believes it is the largest family-owned producer of pinot noir in Australia.

Clare Valley — a place of many quiet corners.

JULY 23   TIM ADAMS; BACK TO MELBOURNE

The morning starts with vertical tastings of Tim Adams' Clare Valley Semillon and Cabernet, each spanning the 1990–2000 vintages. It is a deliberately eclectic choice of varieties, for Tim Adams could equally well have chosen riesling and shiraz, for which the Clare Valley is better known. However, on the principle that old news is no news, and because he strongly holds to the view that the region is well suited to semillon and cabernet (the latter is in fact a blend of around 85 per cent cabernet sauvignon and 15 per cent cabernet franc), he chooses these two wines. Equally courageously, he includes all the vintages, resisting the temptation to omit the less successful years.

In each case the style has evolved over the decade, in no small measure reflecting the increasing use of better-quality oak. Thus between 1990 and 1992 the semillon was part fermented and matured in a mix of German and American oak; between 1993 and

1998 in American oak; and since 1999 in French oak. But in each case, around 60 per cent of the wine is stainless steel fermented, the balance oak fermented, and the two components blended shortly before bottling.

Clare Valley semillon bears little or no resemblance to Hunter Valley semillon, even though some of the major plantings of the variety used clonal material sourced from the Hunter Valley. In Clare, the finished alcohol is usually 13º or above, compared with the 10.5 to 11º in the Hunter Valley, the higher alcohol being balanced by significantly higher acidity. It is that acidity which complements the richness of the wine, and the powerful honey, toast and nut characters it soon develops.

The cabernet has graduated from a mix of shaved American and French hogsheads to 100 per cent French, 40 per cent of which are new. Here my best wines are the 1999, with fragrant blackberry earth and gentle oak spice, soft, chewy tannins and ripe fruit providing lots of texture and weight on the palate; the 1998, which is smooth and clean, with a mix of sweet cassis, berry and dark chocolate flowing through to a long, silky finish; the 1996, with excellent colour, a complex mix of powerful but balanced blackberry, cassis, chocolate and earth, rounded off with ripe, silky tannins; the 1994, with clean, clearly defined varietal fruit ranging from blackberry and blackcurrant to fine leather, the intensity boosted by relatively high acidity; and the 1990, which is fresh, elegant and harmonious, fruit-driven and still full of life.

JULY 23   SHAW & SMITH, MELBOURNE

From the Tim Adams tasting (which extended into lunch for most of those present) I dash to the annual Shaw & Smith yum cha lunch at Sharkfin House in Little Bourke Street. And a full house it is, brimful to overflowing with the trade and a smattering of journalists. It is time for the annual release of the Shaw & Smith Sauvignon Blanc, in this instance the 2002, paired with the release of the 2000 Merlot. It is in sharp contrast to the cerebral chardonnay exercises which go on with the release of the Shaw & Smith Chardonnay, but a little light relief can go a long way. The wines are, of course, exemplary; in a sign of the times, even though the 2000 Merlot is better than the 1999, the price has been reduced, not increased. The crisp, tangy 2002 Sauvignon Blanc will, once again, sell out before the next vintage becomes available. Says Michael Hill-Smith MW, the Smith of Shaw & Smith, 'Even before the wine has been officially launched, 65 pallets have gone whoosh out the winery door.'

JULY 24   YARRA VALLEY

It is one of those magical winter days. As first light dawns there is an unbroken sea of fog covering the valley floor below, with the mountains on the far side rising above it. During the morning the fog starts to thin out, lingering longest over the course of the Yarra River, and even at midday there is still a thin band (almost like a smoke haze) hugging the river and the base of the mountains. Here at Coldstream Hills there is brilliant sunshine, and although the thermometer has climbed to only 6ºC by 10 a.m., you do not notice the cold; rather it is the crisp clarity of the air that is the overriding impression. And within another hour, with the temperature not much above 10ºC, it actually feels quite warm in the sunshine.

JULY 25   TWO DECADES OF PETALUMA COONAWARRA

Once a teacher, always a teacher, and a good teacher will ensure that there is plenty of interaction and involvement in the classroom. So if you attend a tasting run by Brian Croser, be prepared to think and to express your opinions.

He recently ran tasting classes in Brisbane, Sydney and Melbourne with the title 'Defining Coonawarra since 1979', using eleven vintages of Petaluma Coonawarra (the cabernet-based red) to pose and answer three questions: What/where is Coonawarra? What is the definitive Coonawarra wine style? Are the wines better in cooler or warmer years?

The first question was pure Dorothy Dix, revolving around the $5 million legal battle to define the boundaries of Coonawarra, which is still under appeal. (Postscript: since finalised.) Petaluma no longer has

ABOVE
Fog shrouds the Yarra Valley most mornings in winter.

an axe to grind, for its two vineyards (including Sharefarmers, which was originally excluded) are within the new boundaries.

However, Croser suggests that a far, far wider boundary, taking in Mount Gambier to the south, St Marys to the west and Wrattonbully to the north, is logically sustainable, and could be equated to the Bordeaux region, which has even greater soil and climate variation than would be found in 'Greater Coonawarra'. He knows, however, that it's not going to happen, the appeal being raised on narrower issues, but he was able to aim a few verbal blows at the establishment, which had unsuccessfully sought to exclude the Sharefarmers vineyard.

Fraught with debate though the boundary issue is, the question of the definitive wine style is even more tendentious. Should it be elegant, medium-bodied, fruit-driven, with more length than volume, comparable (in style terms) to the wines of the commune of St Julien, in Bordeaux's Haut Médoc? Or should it be rich, full of dark fruit extract, oak and tannin, capable of living for many decades? Those who know the Petaluma wine style will have no difficulty in guessing that Brian Croser's fervently held views favour the former not the latter style. However, one of the remarkable features of the Petaluma Coonawarra is that it spends over eighteen months in 100 per cent new French oak, and that one vintage (the 1988) was double-oaked, i.e. transferred to a second set of new barrels when it was twelve months old. Despite this, the oak is so well integrated that it seldom comes through as a single, obvious facet of flavour.

The third question required the eleven wines to be grouped into three categories. The cool vintages were 1979, '87, '95 and '98; the warm were 1988, '91 and '92; the warmest were 1982, '90, '99 and 2000. The room (in Melbourne, with close to a hundred people present) was then asked to indicate (with a show of hands) which group they preferred as a whole.

Those supporting the warm group edged out the coolest, with the warmest a long distance back in third. The other cities came to different conclusions, the most curious being Sydney, which placed the warmest group in first place.

Perhaps 'curious' is the wrong word, for I am sure many had favourite wines coming from each group; for myself, 1979, '95 and '98 from the cool group, 1988 and '92 from the warm; and 2000 (potentially, at least) from the warmest.

JULY 26–28   Château Latour 1920 to 2000

The genesis of this upcoming weekend was the acquisition and — more importantly — consumption of a double magnum of 1865 Château Lafite on 24 November 2001. It was the greatest red wine I have ever tasted, and I cannot believe I shall ever see its like again. As a nostalgic look back over my shoulder, part of my article originally published for *Wine Magazine* follows.

There it was, on the cover of Christie's End of Season Fine Wine catalogue for Thursday, July 19, 2001: a double magnum of 1865 Château Lafite, the dumpy, slightly crooked hand-blown bottle with the slip label applied by Christie's when it was first offered for sale on May 31, 1967.

The wine had been purchased by the Earl of Rosebery and laid down in his Dalmeny House Cellar in 1868. It had lain there undisturbed for a hundred and one years, except for the application of a new wax seal by Berry Bros in 1932. It and twelve other double magnums had been regarded as undrinkable by the Earl when first tasted, and presumably it was for this reason that the bin had remained untouched.

ABOVE

Chateau Lafite 1865 and a few magnums to keep it company.

When sold by Christie's in 1967, the catalogue described the bottles as 'All with perfect appearance; no ullage'. One had been resold by Sotheby's on May 21, 1975, and had since been stored in the air-conditioned cellar of an Austrian collector. Coming back to Christie's for its last sale, the catalogue said, 'The double magnum remains today in wonderful condition … level base of neck.'

My extreme interest in the wine was prompted by the sharing of a 750 ml bottle of the same wine in 1977 at the first Single Bottle Club dinner, and by three bottles of 1865 Château Kirwan, the last at a much more recent Single Bottle Club dinner. Small wonder Michael Broadbent describes 1865 as 'more consistently reliable than any other pre-phylloxera vintage', for all the various bottles were superb.

But this double magnum was potentially another thing again, for it is well known that the larger the bottle, the better the wine will age over long periods of time. So I looked at the ultra-conservative estimate of £12,000 to £18,000, and my mind started working. If I was able to secure the bottle for £25,000 (the very least I could imagine the wine selling for into the US or Asian markets), the dollar cost — including Christie's buyer's commission — would be around $78,000. If twenty-six of us shared the cost that would be $3000 per head for a decent-sized glass (about six and a half persons per bottle, in other words).

A few faxes, emails and phone calls later I was able to establish that there was no shortage of people as crazy as myself, so I began the process of establishing exactly how I would bid for the double magnum. Should I get someone to be present to bid; should I be a phone bidder; or should I simply send a written bid with a maximum of £25,000?

Over the past thirty years I have made numerous purchases from Christie's, but not one of this magnitude. After some back and forth emails, it was agreed that since I had an absolute limit of £25,000 (and perhaps didn't trust myself not to get carried away) there was little point in phone bidding; I would simply leave Christie's to do the work.

I learnt subsequently that as the bidding increased, the floor bidders fell away, leaving two phone bidders against me. One dropped out, and the sequence of bidding steps meant that my bid (rather than that of my phone opposition) was £25,000, and at that precise point the last phone bidder dropped out. A single step higher and he/she/it would have been the purchaser, myself the underbidder — a position I have often occupied.

The next issue (other than the small matter of payment) was to form a view as to whether or not I should endeavour to have the bottle recorked before arranging for its transport to Australia. Christie's were horrified at the very thought, assuring me that the cork was fine, but I have had personal experience of corks falling in when old wine is moved. In the end, I decided prayer was the best solution, and the rest

LEFT

The first sniffs …

— as they say — is history. Not only did the cork stay in position, but it was very difficult to extract. The heavy wax seal had done a superb job, the cork remaining supple and relatively moist; only the irregularity and widening of the neck posed problems for its extraction.

Had I not opened the bottle on the sideboard at Tower Lodge in full view of all the other twenty-five attendees, I doubt whether they, or even I, would have believed the wine was more than fifty years old — like a wine from the three great Bordeaux vintages of the 1940s (1945, 1947 or 1949) which had been cellared in immaculate conditions.

Having extracted the cork, the wine was decanted using a syphoning technique I had seen employed by Jacques Seysses at Domaine Dujac many years before. A fine piece of syphon tubing was bound to a glass rod (in fact a 1-ml pipette) with the bottom of the tube 5 mm above the bottom of the rod.

The syphon was established, and it was immediately possible to tell whether the wine was clear or not. If it had been unclear, the tube would have been moved up on the rod, and the process restarted. In fact, it was clear and bright, and virtually all the wine was decanted at the first attempt. The tube was then lowered by 2 mm, and the rod moved off the slight punt in the bottom of the bottle towards the side. Still the wine was clear, initially suggesting that there was little or no sediment. Once the bottle was tipped to pour out the remnants, however, it became clear that there was in fact a lot of relatively coarse sediment; it was simply that the syphoning (which took ten minutes) had worked perfectly.

The aromas coming off during this process, and the astounding colour of the wine, made it obvious that something beyond all expectations was on its way. The colour of the wine in each glass confirmed that the sheer volume in the magnum decanters had not played optical tricks on us: it was deep red, with no sign of fading or browning on the rim.

Then the bouquet, unbelievably profound and complex, with blackberry, cassis, plum, spice, truffles (some said fresh mushroom) and violets. Everyone in the room had different descriptors, none of them failing to strike a chord.

Once tasted, the wine's marvellous texture and line became obvious, with fine-grained, lingering but soft tannins running through to the finish. At this point, the reputation of the vintage and the Earl's description coalesced. In Cyril Ray's book, *Lafite* (Christie's Wine Publications), the Château's own contemporaneous summary of the vintage described it as good and ripe (the September 6 starting date was the second earliest in the whole of the nineteenth century), but hard, and needing a long time to soften. At the time, the softer, more charming 1864 was regarded as the better vintage — but no more.

As the wine evolved in the glass over the next few hours, its sweetness and ripeness became progressively more evident, and the unanswerable question of varietal composition came up for discussion. There was much interplanting of varieties prior to phylloxera, and the proportion of each variety was not recorded. What is known is that malbec was far more widely planted than it is today, and while Cyril Ray (in 1968) quotes the then Chef de Culture (viticulturist) who started work at Lafite in 1908 as saying that the malbec had been removed because it was not suited to the gravels and sand of Lafite, its presence in the 1865 seemed obvious.

Those who kept the remnants in their specially engraved Riedel Bordeaux glasses (1865 Château Lafite Double Magnum) for several hours found that not only did the wine change and evolve, but it lost none of its richness and freshness. It was matched, incidentally, with a whole round of Parmigiano Reggiano, simply cut into quarters.

Was it worth the money? No one doubted that for a minute, but I did not tell them that another of the Earl of Rosebery's double magnums had been sold by Sotheby's in 1974 (the year prior to ours) for £500.

Will this weekend-long tasting of seventy-seven vintages of Château Latour come as an anticlimax? It shouldn't, if only because it is so different from the Lafite dinner, and it includes some of the greatest wines made in the twentieth century.

As the last flight of the last dinner is poured, and we settle down to the 1961, '59, '45, '29 and '28, every one of us knows we would have been prepared to pay the cost of the entire weekend for these sublime wines alone (plus the equally sublime 1949 from the previous flight).

Just as had been the case with the double magnum of 1865 Château Lafite, it was the cover of the Christie's auction catalogue for a Finest and Rarest Wine Sale on December 6 and 7, 2001 which lit the flame. It was a picture of all the greatest Château Latour vintages of the twentieth century: 1928, '29, '45, '47, '49, '55, '59, '61, '62, '66, '70, '72, '78, '82, '85 and '86.

In fact the photograph was part of a single offering of seventy vintages between 1920 and 1997, missing only the miserable vintages of 1927, '30, '31 and '32, plus the 1991, '92, '93 and '96. The estimate was £12,000 to £18,000, which seemed far too low. Armed with the knowledge that sixteen of those who participated in the 1865 Château Lafite dinner were prepared to pay $5200 each for the wines, a bid at the top end of the estimate was made.

Fortune smiled on us once again, for we purchased the lot for only £13,000, which, with the buyer's commission included, resulted in a cost per head of only $2750, or an average of $568 per bottle. If this seems a lot of money, yes it is, but in the same week a 46-vintage collection of Penfolds Grange was sold at auction in Australia at an average price of $5000 a bottle. Moreover, when the 2000 Château Latour arrives in Australia next year, the retail price will be over $1500 — if, that is, you can find a retailer with the wine available in the first place.

But it's one thing to have seventy vintages of Château Latour available, and another thing to do justice to them. Early on in the piece, Len Evans and I decided that the wines would be tasted over two lunches (Saturday and Sunday) and two dinners (on the same days), with around eighteen to twenty wines per sitting.

We assumed, incidentally, that we would be able to source the missing vintages from the 1990s, although we never dreamt we would be able to procure the 2000 vintage — proclaimed by Robert Parker as the greatest ever, and more believably by Château Latour as the best since 1945. (Our success in finding the missing vintages from the 1990s, plus the 2000, lifted the field to seventy-seven wines.)

ABOVE
The amazing colour of the 1865 Château Lafite.

Next came the issue of deciding the order in which wines would be served. It seemed fairly obvious that we should finish on the Sunday night with the greatest wines, but that was only the start of the chess game. The next step was to agree that the least highly regarded vintages would be served with the lunches; it was Len Evans who hit upon the idea of having the first day's lunch (the weakest group) at a side table, with the actual tasting prior to the lunch (with micro-pours), leaving the group to drink their preferred wines during lunch.

At the Sunday lunch and at the dinners, the wines were served in flights of four to six in chronological order, from younger to older. But because we had effectively divided the seventy-seven vintages into four quarters, it was unusual for sequential vintages to be placed next to each other.

How did the wines get grouped? The best vintages were easy; over the years Len and I had tasted all the older wines on various occasions, and there is no shortage of reference material for these. However, the lesser-known vintages were more problematical, particularly given the reputation Château Latour has for producing better than average wine in poor vintages. So in the end we relied heavily on Michael Broadbent's *Great Vintage Wine Book II*, both for comments on the vintage weather and overall rating, and for notes on each wine of the year in question.

I cannot pretend that the lunch wines on either day were particularly memorable. There is no doubt that the great advances made in Bordeaux over the past twenty years, and in particular over the past ten years, have lifted the quality of the wines of lesser vintages. Ever increasing prices and profits have led to better viticulture, more rigorous selection of grapes, better winery technology (temperature control being non-contentious, concentration machines more contentious), far more new oak, and better husbandry of previously used oak.

Thus it has been said by many observers that the poor vintages of the 1960s and '70s (1963, '65, '69, '72, '74 and '77) will never occur again. Moreover, further back in the past, there were equally poor vintages for which there was no adequate response.

If there was a general description of the poorest vintages in this tasting, it was the green fruit flavours and tannins, and particularly marked acidity not balanced by either fruit or (interestingly) alcohol. We could not be certain, but it did seem that many of the weaker, oldest vintages were deficient in alcohol.

The first lunch brought together 1993, '91, '84, '74, '72, '69, '68, '65, '63, '56 '54, '44, '42, '41, '40, '39, '38 and '35. It was hard work; of the younger wines, the 1993 and '91 stood out, earning 88 and 91 points respectively. Of the older wines, the 1956 was a surprise packet, still with unexpected weight and flavour (86 points), while the 1942 (87 points), '41 (85 points) and '40 (85 points) all attracted favourable remarks.

The lunch on Sunday was, if it were possible, even more disappointing. Flight 1 brought together the 1997, '94, '92 and '87; Flight 2 1980, '79, '77, '76 and '73; Flight 3 1958, '57, '51, '50 and '46; and Flight 4 1936, '33, '25 and '22.

Here the 1997 (88 points), already delicious and to be drunk sooner rather than later, and the '94 (88 points), the reverse of the '97, with powerful tannins which may or may not soften before the fruit disappears, were the best. The 1980 (85 points), showing obvious development in a vegetal, cedary/earthy spectrum, and the aromatic '76 (86 points), with its sweet flavours, were followed by a dismal run of wines until the rearguard of the '36 (86 points), '33 (85 points), '25 (84 points) and '22 (86 points). Here the elegance of aged cabernet sauvignon came through to a lesser or greater degree, and the wines were balanced, although precariously, all having passed their best-by date.

If lunches were the bad news, the dinners more than compensated with good news. At the very last moment we were able to obtain a couple of the recent missing vintages from Château Latour and — almost miraculously — a bottle of the 2000 vintage, which had been bottled only one week earlier. Thus we became the first people outside the Château management to taste what is an undeniably magnificent wine.

The first flight started with the 2000 (99 points), then the '99 (96 points), '98 (93 points), '96 (97 points), '95 (92 points) and '90 (97 points). Tasting a red wine only a week after it is bottled, and at the tail end of its around-the-world flight, should put the wine at a huge disadvantage. Latour Managing Director Frederic Engerer showed enormous faith in his newborn child, and the faith was rewarded: the wine is sheer perfection, with seamless flavours, perfect texture and structure, and great length. It had a new world look about it, but as the years go by, it will increasingly assert its unique place of origin.

The 1999 is another totally seductive and easily accessed wine, exuding dark cassis and violets, with ripe, sweet, cedary tannins. The 1996 is a classic statement of restraint, with great concentration and power, the perfect balance making it quite certain that the intense cassis flavours and silky tannins will flower with another six to ten years in bottle. That timeframe is certainly supported by the 1990, voluptuous, flowing and elegant, with a perfectly balanced, long, lingering finish proclaiming its sheer style. It will live for decades, but there is no crime in drinking it now.

Flight 2 grouped 1989 (94 points), '88 (95 points), '86 (91 points), '85 (90 points), '83 (93 points) and '82 (89 points). The hot vintage showed through in the rich, ripe cedary, spicy 1989, with its particularly sweet tannins and the suggestion of some extra alcohol. The 1988 was strongly supported by all present, the bouquet with pure, concentrated blackcurrant/cassis cabernet fruit, the palate following suit, surrounded and supported by powerful but not astringent tannins. If ever one of the younger Latours is destined for a long life, this is it. All in all, a totally impressive flight, only the 1982 showing some of the schizophrenia evident on earlier tastings, and the suggestion of possible bacterial action (brettanomyces).

The third flight of 1981 (90 points), '78 (87 points), '71 (88 points), '67 (88 points) and '60 (91 points) were good rather than great, the '71 showing some cork taint (as, incidentally, did the '79 and '92), but pointed as if the taint wasn't there. The surprise was undoubtedly the fragrant 1960, perfectly balanced and absolutely at its peak, with cedary aromas and a sweet palate.

The final flight brought together the 1937 (87 points), '34 (86 points), '24 (90 points) and '23 (93 points), the '37 exceeding expectations (not too tannic), the '34 under-delivering (thinning out slightly on the finish with piquant acidity), the '24 smooth, supple and quite Burgundian, the '23 prodigiously dark in colour and rich in spice plum pudding flavour.

ABOVE
The Lafite dinner;
Suzanne Halliday centre right.

The first flight on the Sunday night presented the 1975 (91 points), '70 (96 points), '66 (94 points), '64 (91 points) and '62 (93 points). Every time I taste the 1970 it gets better, on this occasion showing totally classic and intense blackcurrant and cassis fruit in highly aromatic bouquet which, quite literally, sings a chorus, the palate adding a dash of chocolate, silky smooth, yet with great structure and length. The 1966 is in full flower, with a fragrant spice and cassis bouquet, then a wonderful explosion of fruit on the mid-palate before a supple finish.

The pace lifted with the second flight of 1955 (97 points), '53 (89 points), '52 (92 points), '49 (99 points) and '48 (90 points). The 1955 has retained excellent colour and remarkably youthful berry and mint aromas, the palate crammed with luscious, fleshy fruit and soft, lingering tannins on the finish.

By common consensus, the 1949 was one of the greatest wines of the entire tasting. We must have been lucky and received a particularly good bottle, for this exquisitely proportioned and utterly seductive wine has almost unbelievable length and persistence of flavour, relying on the fruit core rather than tannins. I felt it was more akin to a great Lafite in style; some agreed and some disagreed with that proposition, but — as I say — no one faulted the quality.

We knew we were approaching the crescendo with the third flight, offering the 1947 (90 points), '43 (94 points), '26 (94 points), '21 (97 points) and '20 (unfortunately oxidised and vinegary, the cork having failed).

The performance of the 1943 justified its reputation as by far the best wartime vintage, the medium-bodied palate with unexpected finesse and harmony, prompting the comment 'a great drink'. The 1926 and '21 were in a different league, the '26 with amazingly deep colour, hugely powerful prune and dark plum aromas and a massively rich and ripe palate with similar prune and ripe plum flavours. Had it not been slightly affected by dank cork characters, it would have been given even higher points.

The 1921 opened with hyper-rich, hyper-sweet mint and berry aromas, the fragrance growing as the wine sat in the glass, the very complex palate with velvety sweet fruit, still with excellent length.

Like most people, I am given to moments of introspection, when I wonder how and why it is that wine can sustain lifelong fascination and job satisfaction. The fourth flight of the dinner provided a comprehensive answer to those questions, bringing together the 1961, '59, '54, '29 and '28. Every one of the five wines was magnificent, making the process of awarding points seem almost tawdry. However, have applied the discipline of coming up with points for the other wines, it had to be continued for these.

Over the years I have had a couple of bottles of very poor 1961 Latour. On this occasion the wine more than compensated for all the disappointments, showing just why 1961 and 1945 are often rated as the two greatest postwar vintages. Holding superb colour still, the exceptionally vibrant and aromatic bouquet offered dimensions beyond all the preceding wines, the palate with layer upon layer of almost juicy fruit held together by impeccable tannins. If recorked and well cellared, this wine will not have diminished by 2061, and will probably live late into the twenty-first century. I parsimoniously gave it 99+ points, only because it still hasn't peaked.

The 1959 (97 points) has always been regarded as one of the most classic Latours, causing Michael Broadbent to write that 'the wine is virtually indestructible'. A slight touch of wet cork character initially dulled the bouquet, but the wine shrugged off the problem, displaying cedar, briary, cigar box, sweet cassis and supple tannins coalescing on the perfectly structured palate.

1945 is rightly regarded by Broadbent as measuring up to the great 1865 pre-phylloxera vintage, and the 1945 Latour (98+ points) showed why. Once again, there was a faint sandshoe 'bottle stink' (as the English call it), which soon blew off. (All the wines in this bracket were decanted and poured immediately, working on the Len Evans principle that you can wait for the wine, but the wine will not wait for you if it has been decanted too early.) Having comprehensively thrown off that initial uncertainty, the superb colour, vibrant fruit aromas and an almost viscous, ultra-smooth entry into the mouth, then merging into perfectly weighted tannins, proclaimed a truly great wine.

In his *Great Vintage Wine Book II*, Michael Broadbent commented, in giving the 1929 the maximum five stars, that 'one is tempted to add a sixth star'. I can fully understand why, for this wine was the greatest of the greats, and I had no second thoughts about giving it 100 points. Intensely aromatic, with a mix of berry, leaf, spice, mint and coffee, it is sheer perfection in the mouth, with supple, silky texture and tannins providing perfect harmony and balance, the length and persistence of the finish and aftertaste quite awesome. Yet it is best described as medium-bodied, and has a lot in common with the 1949. It also demonstrated that no matter what Robert Parker and others may say to the contrary, modern technology and viticulture cannot provide wines of greater quality and character than this.

The 1928 (98 points) brought up the rear, exactly placed. The colour is much deeper than the 1929, the bouquet still youthful, with potent, classic cassis, cedar and cigar box aromas. It is on the palate that the legendary strength of the wine manifests itself; it is a monumental wine in every way, with immense power and huge tannins, the volume significantly bigger than the length (and in this respect the opposite of the 1929). Writing in 1990, Broadbent opined that the wine had 'another half century of life', and I wouldn't doubt that for one moment. The question is, will it ever come into the perfect balance of the 1929 and '45?

I fear that I shall not have the opportunity of answering that question, but at least I have been able to frame it, hoping that somewhere in the years ahead another group of besotted wine lovers will be able to do so.

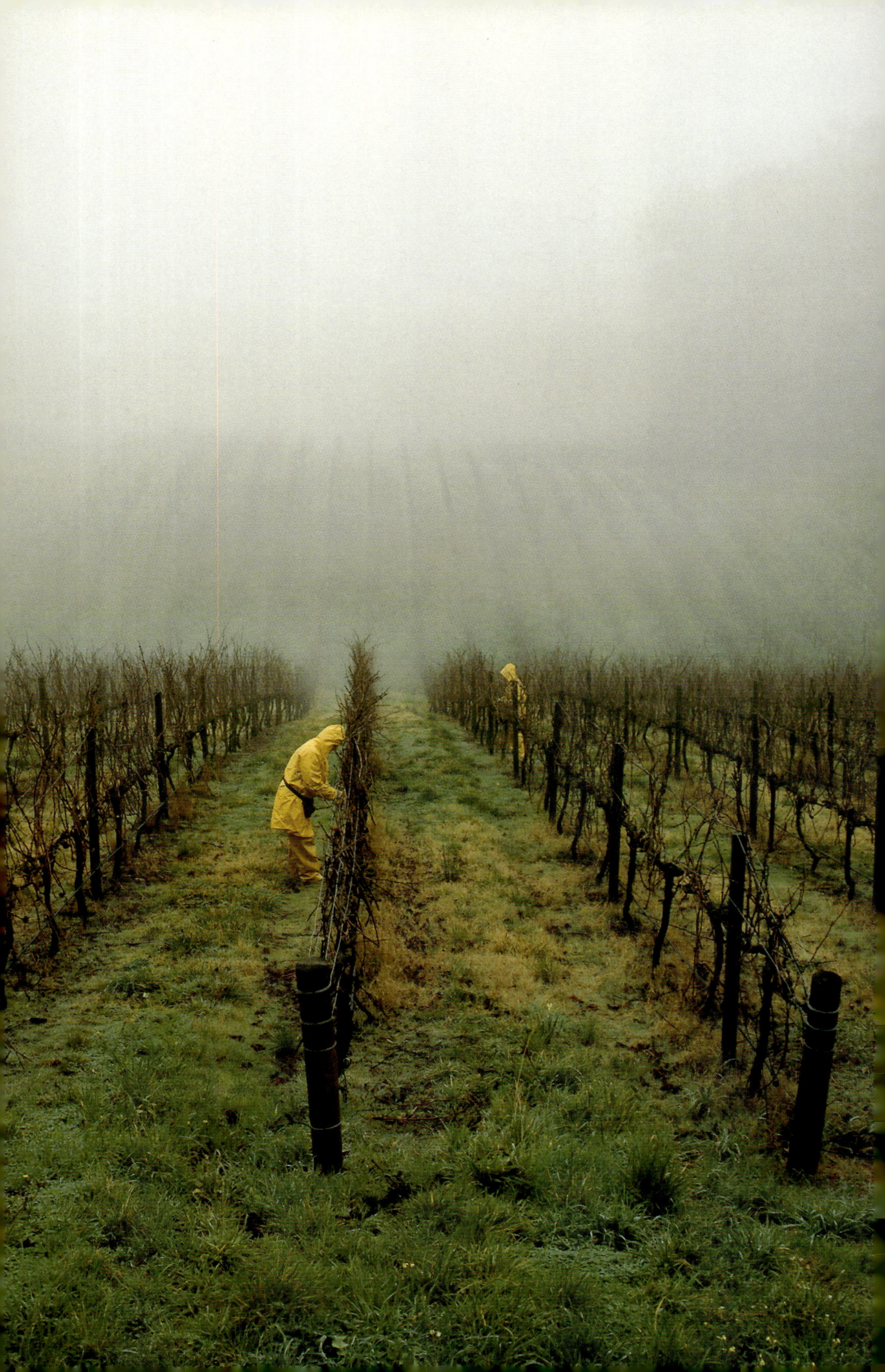

August

Wine Australia, Sydney

Wine Australia — Yarra Valley Masterclasses

Flu, Yarra Valley

Mudgee Wine Show

Still Confined to Barracks, Yarra Valley

Xanadu Merlot Tasting, Margaret River

Clonakilla 1992–2001 Dinner

Seppelt Para Liqueur Tawny 1878–2002

Macedon Wine Show

WINE ODYSSEY

AUGUST 2–5   WINE AUSTRALIA, SYDNEY

After holding the two previous Wine Australias (1998 and 2000) in Melbourne, Wine Australia 2002 has returned to Sydney, although not to the same venue as the inaugural event, staged in 1996. This year it is in the user-friendly environment of Fox Studios, in the grounds of what was once the Sydney Showground. Our target market is the new and occasional consumer; however, we do not wish to miss the opportunity of preaching to the converted, so it is all a fine balancing act.

We have learnt from each preceding Wine Australia, and there is more emphasis than ever on education, ranging from soft to upper level. There is also more food available within the exhibition area than ever before, with the restaurants of Bent Street (the 'eat street' at Fox Studios) providing a major additional dimension.

As well as being chairman of Wine Australia, I am alternately wearing my Coldstream Hills hat, my Winepros hat and my Yarra Valley hat, in the last instance as moderator of Yarra Valley Masterclasses held each day in the Amorim taste theatre.

When you add in the Maurice O'Shea dinner (a black-tie affair for seven hundred people) on the Friday night, and the Bledisloe Cup rugby union test between Australia and New Zealand on the Saturday night (a pulsating last-minute win to Australia), plus a private excursion to what many regard as Sydney's premier restaurant (Aria) on Sunday night, the schedule is a full one.

AUGUST 2–5   WINE AUSTRALIA — YARRA VALLEY MASTERCLASSES

At Wine Australia 2002 the Yarra Valley staged three Masterclasses (some repeated on different days), focusing on chardonnay, pinot noir, cabernet and shiraz. Nine wines were presented on each occasion, and each class had its own theme: 'Chardonnay — Where is it headed?'; 'Pinot Noir — The influence of terroir'; and 'Cabernet and Shiraz — Hot reds in a cool climate'.

I was the moderator for each session, with the winemakers of each of the wines giving background information and answering questions. The winemakers varied from one session to the next, so I was the only person involved in all three presentations and was thus able to stand back a little and look at the overall outcome, which showed just how important terroir is.

I have yet to see a better explanation of terroir than that given by the former owner of Château Cos d'Estournel (in the Bordeaux commune of St Estephe), Bruno Prats: 'The very French notion of terroir looks at all the natural conditions which influence the biology of the vinestock and thus the composition of the grape itself. The terroir is the coming together of the climate, the soil and the landscape. It is the combination of an infinite number of factors: temperatures by night and by day, rainfall distribution, hours of sunlight, slope and drainage, to name but a few. All these factors react with each other to form, in each part of the vineyard, what French wine growers call terroir.'

The terroir, or rather terroirs, of the Yarra Valley are infinitely varied and complex. North and north-east-facing slopes are the most desirable in all parts of the valley, and regardless of orientation, hillsides help deal with springtime waterlogging.

The northern and eastern sides of the valley include the Dixons Creek, Yarra Glen, Diamond Valley, Lilydale and Coldstream sub-regions. The soils throughout are ancient sandstone-derived grey/yellow mixtures of sand, loam and clay, relatively low in pH, and (particularly on hillsides) do not promote over-vigorous growth.

The southern and western sides of the valley include the Wandin, Seville, Yarra Junction and Hoddles Creek sub-regions. The most common soil is an immensely deep vivid red volcanic soil of far more recent origin, necessitating strict canopy and vigour control (the latter partially possible by withholding irrigation). The average altitude is higher, the climate cooler and the rainfall higher.

So it is that the warmer years best suit the southern side, the cooler years the northern side. The early-ripening chardonnay, sauvignon blanc, pinot noir and the temperamental merlot are suited to both sides of the valley, but shiraz and cabernet sauvignon require ultra-careful site selection, impeccable viticulture and a degree of good luck with the weather if they are to fully ripen on the southern side.

AUGUST 8   YARRA VALLEY

Notwithstanding a flu injection earlier in the year, I am sinking fast with a dreaded attack of flu, which often seems to strike in August. The usual effect is to diminish my sense of smell to zero and taste to next to zero. This particular bug seems to have gone direct to my chest rather than first attacking throat and nose, so I have some hope that I may retain some of the senses of taste and smell.

I have long since learnt that I obtain 90 per cent of my knowledge of about 90 per cent of the wines I taste through the bouquet. In other words, in nine out of ten cases, tasting the wine will add only 10 per cent to my total knowledge, and basically will do little more than reinforce the information coming from the bouquet. That 10 per cent will concern itself with structure, and, in particular, the tannin level in the case of red wine. In the remaining 10 per cent of wines, the palate will cause me to significantly re-evaluate the wine, and to go back to the bouquet in some instances. With this 10 per cent, either the fruit flavour will be unexpectedly positive and attractive, or, at the other extreme, faults may materialise: excess tannin, excess acidity, or a wine fault known as mousiness may appear. The latter is due to lack of adequate SO_2 protection and manifests itself on the aftertaste, often five to ten seconds after the wine has been tasted and either swallowed or spat out.

AUGUST 9–10   FLU, YARRA VALLEY

Stuffed full of antibiotics, echinacea, Codral cold tablets and Vitamin C, I spend these two days in bed, which for me is unheard of. Last year, coming back from the Mudgee Wine Show, I caught the flu and had to pull out of the judging of the Hunter Valley Wine Show the following week. I hope history is not going to repeat itself.

AUGUST 11–14   MUDGEE WINE SHOW

With considerable misgivings, I head off to the Mudgee Wine Show, flying to Sydney and then by a small plane to Mudgee. The cocktail of pills and antibiotics seems to be having the appropriate effect, and I can only hope that as the days go by my sense of smell will return.

My hopes turn out to be ill-founded, and I embark on the first class (2002 Semillon) realising that I can smell next to nothing. Much to my surprise, however, I seem to be able to evaluate texture, structure, length and flavour, and although very young semillon is a particularly difficult class to judge, I give what turns out to be Poet's Corner Semillon 18.5 points (gold medal), Miramar 17 points (silver) and Vinifera Wines 16.5 (bronze), the other wines receiving lower points. If my points are significantly astray from the other judges I shall have to withdraw from judging and nominate one of the two associate judges to take my place. Miraculously, we are in near-freakish agreement: unanimous gold medal points for the Poet's Corner, unanimous silver medal points for the Miramar, and likewise bronze points for the Vinifera Wines entry. So I decide that I will press on and hope for the best.

The show continues in much the same fashion over the next two days, my fellow judges, Dr Ray Healy (who has judged the Mudgee Show for many years and is currently chairman of the Hobart Wine Show) and Robert Paul (formerly winemaker at Montrose/Poet's

AUGUST 1

The Yarra Valley in winter; the blue mountains fascinated the early Swiss settlers.

Corner and now with the wine consulting group Wine Net), being in agreement to an extent seldom encountered. The most dramatic instance comes in class 17, for cabernet shiraz blends of any vintage. A small class, but one which caused me to write in the judges' comments, 'Three superb golds, each with its own claim to top spot'. They were in fact Rosemount Estate Mountain Blue of the '98, '99 and 2000 vintages, and we all gave them first-up golds. How could this happen? I honestly don't have the faintest idea. (Postscript: I will henceforth have two injections a year: one in February, one in August.)

There is no doubt that good wines are far easier to judge than bad, and that notwithstanding some challenging vintages between 1998 and 2001, Mudgee's winemakers have responded with great skill, with very few faulty wines in the bottled wine section of the show. In the unbottled section, principally taking in the 2002 vintage, the potential is outstanding: 2002 is the best vintage for shiraz for many years, and will produce some very good cabernets, even if not quite in the class of the shiraz.

The most successful exhibitors are Huntington Estate (nothing new here), Abercorn (with a string of red wine trophies), the Montrose/Poet's Corner group and Thistle Hill.

> Dave Robertson was fifty-four when, on September 2, 2001, he suffered a fatal heart attack, the last in a series of blows that started with the loss of a leg in a motorbike accident in 1976, and continued with abdominal surgery for kidney problems and then emergency heart bypass surgery in 1990.
>
> Typically, he refused to let these problems impede his chosen lifestyle. The compensation money from the accident was used to buy a 45-hectare hobby farm in Mudgee — he began the establishment of Thistle Hill with wife Lesley, while retaining a city home.
>
> The open-heart surgery in 1990 simply led to the family — Lesley plus daughters Lucy and Sally — moving to Thistle Hill to live and work on the vineyard full-time.
>
> Dave continued life as normal, playing golf and tennis, and enjoying good food and wine. In the 2001 spring newsletter which followed his death — and announced the family's decision to continue the business

— they wrote, 'He began to look increasingly like a wine barrel from this point on — rotund, unsteady on the legs and heavily wine-stained.'

I did not attend the funeral, but both the service and the ensuing wake at Thistle Hill were happy, not sad. It was a brilliant spring day, and his daughters spoke in intensely moving terms about their adored father. But it was Lesley who described Dave's last moments, when the ambulance arrived and the paramedics removed Dave's pyjamas to attempt to restart his heart.

Dave, it transpired, had also recently lost a pitched battle with a feral cat he found in the winery. Not wishing to shoot it, he tried instead to get it into a sack, but gave up the attempt after receiving extensive scratches and lacerations. Put shortly, he was a right mess, and Lesley Robertson had no adequate response when the paramedic looked up at her and briskly asked, 'Any medical history?'

In the spring 2001 newsletter the current wines included '1997 Dave's Cabernet Sauvignon', going on to say, 'This wine is dedicated to the memory of its maker, Dave Robertson. He was inherently proud of his Cabernet Sauvignons and believed this would be one of his best. The wine is a deep red colour with aromas of rich plum and oak and a hint of spice. The palate is rewarded with ripe berries, blackcurrant, chocolate and balanced American oak. A deliciously big wine, rather like the man himself …'

At this year's Mudgee Wine Show (August 12–14) Thistle Hill had one of its most successful outcomes, winning two gold, three silver and five bronze medals. Lesley Robertson's joy in finding that Dave's Cabernet was one of the two gold medal wines in the open cabernet sauvignon class was no less than that of the several hundred people at the wine show dinner, who gave her a standing ovation when the certificates were handed out.

AUGUST 18   STILL CONFINED TO BARRACKS, YARRA VALLEY

I am still in the depths of bronchitis flu, and have no option but to withdraw from the Hunter Valley Wine Show, which is to run through until Wednesday this week (August 21). Poignantly, it is Len Evans's last wine show and I am devastated not to be a part of it.

AUGUST 23–24   XANADU MERLOT TASTING, MARGARET RIVER

Partially recovered, I am heading off to Perth late in the afternoon of Friday (August 23), spending the night in Perth and then being flown down (with other journalists) in a chartered plane to Margaret River on Saturday morning. The tasting is scheduled to run from 11 a.m. to 1 p.m., followed by lunch and a trip back to Perth by the same plane in time to connect with the last flight out of Perth to Melbourne, which gets in around midnight.

This is the second time that Xanadu has staged the International Merlot Tasting. Twenty-one wines from around the world are chosen, each representing the best from the country (or state or region) of origin. This year eight wines from Australia, four from France, two from Washington State and two from the Napa Valley (both US), two from New Zealand, one from Chile and one from Italy make up the field.

The formula for the annual benchmark tastings conducted by various Australian wineries was set by Cape Mentelle back in the 1980s, and has been precisely followed ever since.

It is not until all twenty-one wines have been tasted, commented on and ranked that their identities are revealed, and it is then possible to retaste all or any of them knowing their identity.

As is the case with the other wineries following the pattern, such a function carries with it the not inconsiderable risk of the host winery's own wine failing to make any impression. The stronger the field, the better the tasting, but the greater the risk — and Xanadu did not shirk that risk.

The French wines were chosen on the basis of the extravagant points and praise heaped on them by Robert Parker and *The Wine Spectator* (plus their overall reputation). They were Château Trotanoy, Château Pavie, Château La Mondotte and Château Petrus. Given their status and (apparent) success in 1999, one might have expected that my 96 points for each of the Pavie and Petrus, 95 for Trotanoy and 88 for La Mondotte (the last no fault, but simply too massive in extract to engage my affection) would have been par for the course.

The appropriately ornate garden entrance to Xanadu, even if not quite a stately pleasure dome.

In fact the Pavie was 'loathed and hated' by Ray Jordan, who spoke on the flight in which it came up (with enthusiastic nods of support from Tim White), while the Petrus came in for even more scathing criticism from White, who gave the overall summary and had no doubt that the Pavie (considered the best ever made by this highly ranked château) and Petrus were seething with brettanomyces (a yeast spoilage character) and consequently undrinkable.

Technical issues to one side, the main points of difference (and criticism) turned on the amount of oak flavour, of alcohol and of extract. Wrapping these three issues together, should merlot be a medium-bodied wine, with a core of sweet berry fruit and a silky, fine texture, with gently persistent tannins running through the palate and long finish? Or should it be a rich, sumptuous, full-bodied wine with generous fruit matched by equally (if not more) generous oak, and a marked spine of tannin to give this generosity an appropriate framework? Can it be permissible for merlot to cuddle up close to cabernet sauvignon?

I have long since given my vote to the first rather than the second style, but great wines often resist being put into neatly labelled boxes.

As was the case last year, I particularly enjoyed the Xanadu; it shows archetypal varietal character with hints of olive and earth to go with the berry fruit, is admirably balanced and has excellent length. It has also improved out of sight over the past twelve months.

AUGUST 28   CLONAKILLA 1992–2001 DINNER

Tim Kirk, winemaker at his family's Clonakilla winery in Canberra, is putting on a dinner at Melbourne's famed Circa restaurant in St Kilda, the purpose being to present a ten-year vertical tasting (1992–2001) of Clonakilla's icon wine, its Shiraz Viognier.

Until the end of 1996 Tim Kirk was a teacher at Xavier College, in charge of religious education. His winemaking role at Clonakilla was a weekend and holidays affair, marked by dashes from home in Melbourne to the winery on the outskirts of Canberra. The winery was established by his father, Dr John Kirk, who had an equally improbable background. His parents had owned a pub in Ireland, and at a relatively early age he had been put in charge of stock control and ordering new supplies of beer, spirits and wine. By the time he finished at university, he had a PhD in science, and became a research scientist. In 1968 he was offered a job with the CSIRO and moved his family from Ireland to Canberra.

For the first time his boyhood interest in wine had a chance to express itself. He had a keen interest in climate, and has since published several important papers on the subject. He quickly became aware of the similarities between the Canberra climate and that of Bordeaux (and the Rhône Valley), and in 1971 planted an acre each of cabernet sauvignon and riesling.

In the same year Dr Edgar Riek (another CSIRO scientist) planted his first vines on the slopes leading down to Lake George. Viticulture in Canberra was underway.

John Kirk is still actively involved in Clonakilla. 'He does all the paperwork and record-keeping,' says Tim, with a note of profound relief in his voice, 'but he is also still the scientist, and has just planted more riesling, with the vines on a 3-metre grid, each tied to a stake in the German fashion. His idea is to assist air movement around the vines and thus reduce the incidence of disease.'

Tim Kirk singles out two major influences in the development of that style: Dr Bailey Carrodus of the Yarra Valley's Yarra Yering, and a trip to France that allowed him to visit the Rhône Valley and its winemakers.

When I look back over my Clonakilla tasting notes, made over many years, I am struck by the same consistency as is shown at the dinner: the wine has not missed a beat since the disappointing 1991. Indeed, the first flight of five wines (1992 to 1996 inclusive) at the dinner were so similar that had we not been told the order of service, it would have been difficult to decide in which order they had been served — in other words, which was the youngest, which the oldest.

This Peter Pan-like quality comes in large part from the bright, firm, natural acidity of the wines: Kirk has only had to add a touch of acid in one vintage. The recurrent flavours are the classic varietal array of cherry, herb, spice, licorice, bramble and leather, the order of importance varying with the vintage.

The most outstanding wines were the 1994, '97 and the currently available 2001, although there was precious little between those three and the 2000, 1999, '98 and '95. The 2001 has an exuberant bouquet of multi-spice, black cherry, licorice and leather, with impeccable fruit and acid balance, the oak positive but not dominant. The consensus was that it is the best yet.

AUGUST 29   Seppelt Para Liqueur Tawny 1878–2002

I am on the early flight to Sydney, regretting that I did not leave the Clonakilla dinner even earlier. I have at least been able to stay in our unit in town, which has resulted in my getting an extra hour's sleep.

It is the first time a tasting of the hundred-year-old Seppelt Para Liqueur Tawnys has been held for a limited number of journalists and trade. The only other such tasting was staged for me in November 1994, for the purposes of my *Classic Wines of Australia and New Zealand*. The format is the same, although happily the vintages from the twentieth century are different. On the prior occasion we started with the 1994, going backwards in ten-yearly jumps to 1894, then picking up every vintage through to the first, 1878. On this occasion we start with the 2002, and go back in ten-

ABOVE

Yarra Yering winery, our distinguished neighbour.

year jumps to the current release of 1902 (the twenty-fifth hundred-year-old release), then following every vintage back to 1878.

Just as it was before, the tasting is extraordinary: three centuries of a wine which is truly unique, spending one hundred years in barrel before it is first released, and gaining a richness and power which is impossible to adequately describe. The deep brown, olive-rimmed colour, and the oily viscosity of the wine as it is poured, give some visual clues, but the explosion of flavour in the mouth has to be experienced to be believed.

I now have tasting notes of fifty-two vintages of Para Liqueur, and a storehouse of memories which will stay with me as long as I live.

AUGUST 30   MACEDON WINE SHOW

From one end of the wine world to the other in less than a day. The tiny Macedon Wine Show (usually seventy to eighty entries) produces wines from one of Australia's coldest and most windswept wine regions. The wines are almost invariably bracingly high in acidity, the region being best suited to fine sparkling wines and riesling. Like virtually the whole of the eastern half of Australia,

Macedon is begging for rain — the soil and subsoil are painfully dry. There is a surface coating of green grass (thanks largely to 14 mm of rain which fell a few weeks ago, the only rain since January), but the situation is critical. From here south to the Yarra Valley and Mornington Peninsula, some grape growers are actually irrigating to delay premature budburst, a terrible risk for ultra-cool regions which almost invariably encounter spring frosts through September.

The judging of this year's Macedon Wine Show opened predictably enough, with a very strong class of sparkling wines. Seven of the ten entries were awarded silver (six) or gold (one) medal points by Gary Baldwin (consulting oenologist), Andrew Hood (Tasmanian winemaker) and myself.

Mind you, judging sparkling wines is the most difficult task in the Australian wine show system, and we had a few extraneous problems to deal with. In response to the exceedingly brisk ambient temperature of the small judging room, a fire had been lit to warm us up. However, fires smoke, so we had to open the adjacent door and windows to banish the smoke. It was a case of fire to the frying pan, but the quality of the wines shone through.

The winning wine was a pinot chardonnay from the small winery Braewattie, which, if my memory serves me right, had the same success last year. The irony was that John Ellis of Hanging Rock had been partly responsible for making the wine, which edged Hanging Rock Cuvée IX into second place, with the Cuvée VIII a little further back.

The second class brought together gewürztraminers, rieslings, sauvignon blancs and a pinot gris. It turned out to be the strongest table wine class (i.e. non-sparkling), with the 1998 Knight Granite Hills Riesling a first-up unanimous gold medal, going on to win the trophies for Best White Wine and Best Wine of Show.

We expected much more from the largest class of the show — the chardonnays — than it delivered. The majority of the wines hovered just above or just below bronze medal standard, and there is no shame in that, but there were only two wines to stand out: the 2000 Mount Charlie (gold) and 1999 Portree (silver). Both have considerable length, and (properly) show distinct grapefruit/citrus cool-climate flavour, with fruit — rather than oak — the driving force.

If the chardonnays were disappointing, it must be said the pinot noirs were even more so, particularly given the fact that the majority came from the warm 2000 and 2001 vintages. Some of the best-known producers — such as Bindi and Epis — elected not to enter the show, which is entirely their privilege. It also turned out that Rochford had had to withdraw its excellent 2000 Pinot Noir because it no longer fulfilled the qualifying stock requirement.

Perhaps the combined auto-da-fé and wind chill put our palates into a bad mood, but we all agreed that winemaking in the Macedon Ranges wasn't meant to be easy, and that achieving genuine fruit ripeness is particularly difficult in this beautiful but windy region.

The last class — red wines other than pinot noir — produced better results. It was also another instance in which the contract winemaker (Llew Knight of Knight Granite Hills) produced the winning wine, 1999 Candlebark Hill Cabernet Merlot, edging his own 1999 Knight Granite Hills Reserve Shiraz into second place.

Knight Granite Hills and Hanging Rock have both had great results at other shows this year — trophies and golds — with wines which were only given silver medals or less at this show. Rough justice? No, I don't think so; wine judging is an imprecise art, not a science.

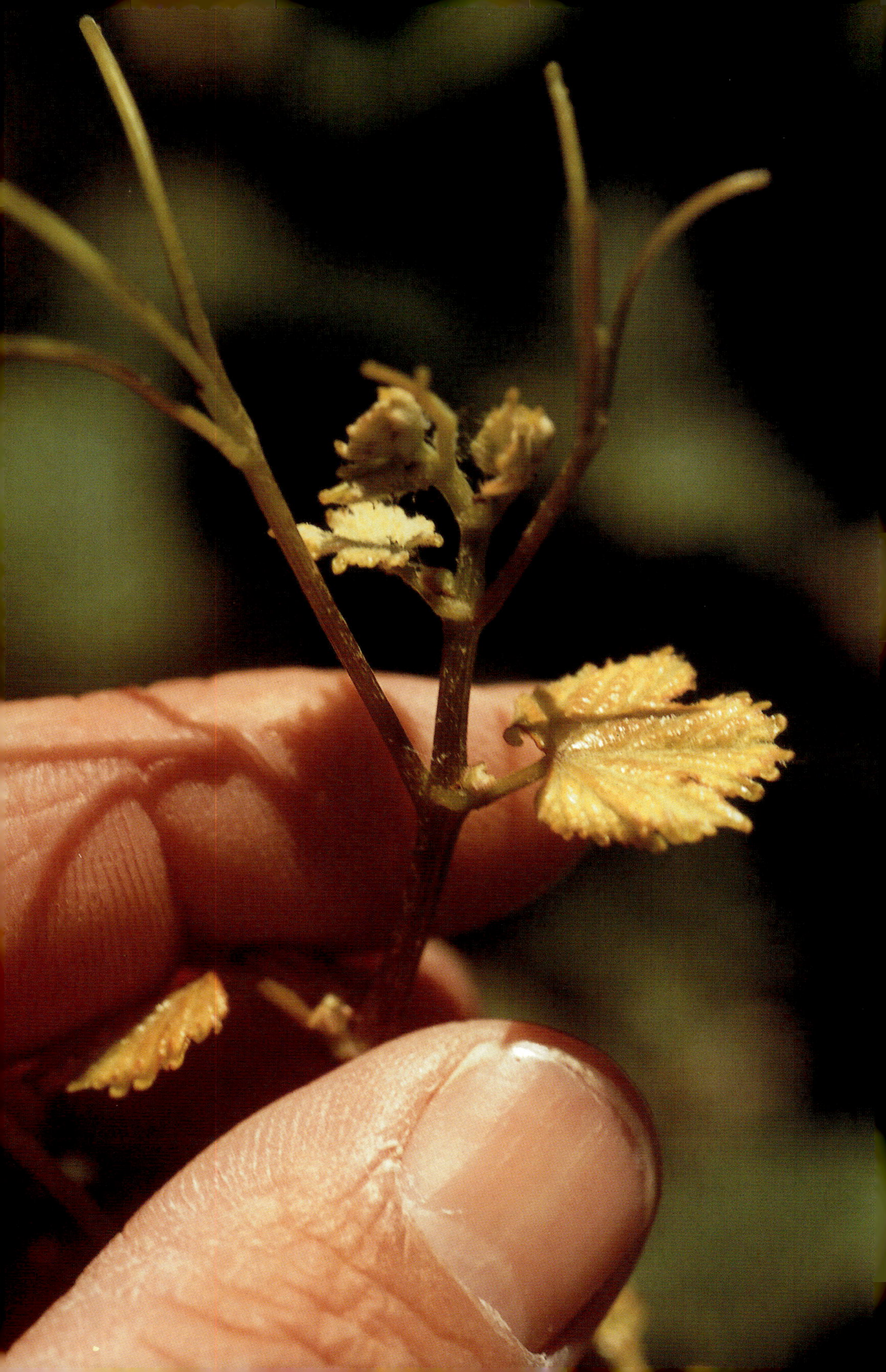

September

Jasper Hill Thank You Lunch

Sommelier of the Year

The Judging

Arthurs Creek Vertical Tasting

Vancouver and The Million Dollar Chardonnay Challenge

University of British Columbia

Vancouver

Okanagan Valley

Opening of Nk'Mip Winery

Opening of Mission Hill Estate

Okanagan Valley: Departure

Yarra Valley

Great Australian Shiraz Challenge

Jacques Reymond

United States Part II

SEPTEMBER 1   JASPER HILL THANK YOU LUNCH

Suzanne and I are off to Cecconi's restaurant at Southbank, on the Yarra River. Ron and Elva Laughton have decided to stage a Thank You Lunch for 250 of their friends and supporters — 160 or so people who have regularly purchased Jasper Hill on the mailing list, retailers, restaurateurs and wine writers. It is a long lunch: the invitation says from 12–5 p.m. and when we leave, shortly after four, at least half the guests are still there, some still energetically dancing. The idea was inspired in part by a family lunch that the owners of Cecconi's staged some time previously for their extended family and friends, which included the Laughtons (who supply Jasper Hill to the restaurant). They (the Laughtons) were so taken by the idea that they decided to do the same — and, for good measure, decided to have precisely the same menu as that of the Cecconi family day.

At an appropriately leisurely pace we move through soft wet polenta topped with baccalà (salt cod) cooked in onions and cream; caprese salad — vine-ripened tomato layered with mozzarella, basil and capers with extra virgin olive oil; risotto with peas and fennel; roasted suckling pig served with braised cabbage and apple plus mixed leaf salad dressed with a garlic and lemon dressing and fried potato with garlic, cayenne and rosemary. At the end comes that quintessential Italian dessert, tiramisù.

We start with 2002 Georgia's Paddock Riesling and 2001 Georgia's Paddock Semillon before moving on to Georgia's Paddock Shiraz, Emily's Paddock Shiraz and Georgia's Paddock Nebbiolo, all from 2001. However, at a side table there is a series of back vintages for tasting, which some apparently regard as an invitation to drink rather than taste.

It has become fashionable among certain wine writing circles to criticise high-alcohol Australian shiraz, and in some circumstances that criticism is justified. My view is that in the case of Jasper Hill it is not; true it is that the wines need fairly rich food to show their best, but the same can be said of Italian wines with hard tannin profiles. In any event, I am more than grateful that it has been prearranged for Suzanne to drive back to the Yarra Valley.

SEPTEMBER 2   Sommelier of the Year

Into Melbourne for the judging of the 2002 Sommelier of the Year competition, which is jointly sponsored by Rosemount and Riedel. My fellow judges this year are Stefano di Pieri of The Grand restaurant at Mildura, Elizabeth Egan of Becco, Anna Aldridge, PR person at large, and Ben Edwards, one-time sommelier, now running an upmarket B&B in a large Victorian-era house called Shandon 1884, who also wears the organiser's hat. The finalists are Melissa Moore of bel mondo, Sydney; Tim Stock of Aria, Sydney; Tony Harper of Anise, Brisbane; Bruce Wallner of Vanitas in Palazzo Versace, Brisbane; and Chris Crawford of Circa The Prince, Melbourne.

The finalists have come from a field of over sixty, and all have had to submit written papers on a wide variety of wine subjects. In previous years the best contestant from each state has been selected, but this year Ben Edwards marked all of the papers without knowing the identity of the contestant and simply picked the top five. Thus the quality of the field is exceptional.

We (the judges) go to have dinner at France Soir, theoretically to discuss tomorrow's happenings. However, Stefano di Pieri is well and truly waylaid, because tonight he has won the coveted award of Best Restaurant of the Year at *The Age Good Food Guide* launch, and Elizabeth Egan, whose Becco restaurant has also been highly successful, is derailed by an errant babysitter.

SEPTEMBER 3   The Judging

In prior years this competition, very much like the Champagne competition run by the Comité Interprofessionnel du Vin de Champagne, the Devaux Sommelier competition and the Negociants Working with Wine competition, has had a fluid judging system which significantly limits the amount of time spent with each contestant. This year Ben Edwards has devised a five-section competition which takes all day to judge, with points for each portion of each section; this introduces a significant degree of numerical objectivity.

First up, the sommeliers have to blind taste six wines and write extensive notes about each of those wines. Then there is a live blind tasting in front of the judges. The contestant has a couple of minutes to assess the wine and then has to describe it and identify it. It is in fact a 1999 generic Bourgogne, and when we — the judges — taste it blind, we are all over the place.

We then proceed to a five-course lunch, with each sommelier choosing an accompanying wine for one course, then serving the wine and discussing the reasons for its choice.

Next each of the contestants is subjected to a mock table situation nicknamed 'The Grill'. Their restaurant's menu and wine list are given to the five judges and we choose three different entrées and three different main courses, asking the contestant in the first instance to recommend a single wine choice for the entrées and another for the main course. This is a very difficult exercise and requires considerable mental agility from the contestants, who basically try to head us away from a single bottle choice and towards wine by the glass or the half-bottle list. It also involves an intimate knowledge of the flavour and texture of each of the dishes.

Finally, each has to write a two-page paper on the following subject: 'The function of a sommelier is to ensure profitability. Discuss.' All the contestants find their way by differing paths of logic to the proposition that the quality of the overall experience in the restaurant and the amount of return business from happy patrons is the best way to ensure profitability.

We mark each section independently, and because of the intense pace of the day have little or no chance of keeping running totals, but when each of us adds up our points and then uses those points to rank the contestants first to fifth, Tim Stock emerges as the unanimous winner of the all-expenses paid trip to Europe.

SEPTEMBER 5   Arthurs Creek Vertical Tasting

By sheer coincidence, I head back to Shandon 1884 for a vertical tasting of Arthurs Creek Cabernet Sauvignon, with twenty-one vintages on show. Earlier in the day I had a Wine Australia board meeting in Melbourne, providing a neat time fit.

SEK Hulme is one of Melbourne's most highly regarded — and experienced, for he is no spring chicken — Senior Counsel, with taxation one of his specialties. (He and I have similar views on the vicious and iniquitous taxation on wine in Australia.)

He also has a wonderfully dry sense of humour, which shows through repeatedly in his account of the history of his vineyard and (superannuated) winery, Arthurs Creek Estate. 'Pedestrian governments,' he says, 'have long since taken away our apostrophe' from the little town of the same name.

It all started in 1974 when Joe, the Italian farm manager of Sek (as he has phonetically always been known) Hulme's property at Arthurs Creek announced 'Miz Yume, we godda have a few graps.'

'With no business plan, no outside advice, no inquiry as to hours of sunlight, no soil analysis, no scientific inquiry of any kind — with nothing but Joe's firm assurance that this paddock reminded him of the vineyard of his uncle, [I] let some grapes be planted,' says Hulme.

A test plot of a number of varieties followed in 1974, but before there were any real results, cabernet sauvignon was chosen, with small commercial plantings in 1976 and 1977, followed by chardonnay in 1981, and yet more cabernet sauvignon in 1997 on another paddock selected by Joe.

The first vintage was made by Tom Lazar at Virgin Hills in 1979. When he ran into financial problems he recommended his neighbour John Flynn, who made the 1980 to 1982 vintages at his tiny Kyneton winery.

When Flynn ran out of space, Sek decided to build his own winery, which in retrospect he says was a decision 'to build the last old-fashioned winery instead of one of the first modern wineries'.

'For a variety of unintended reasons which are embarrassing to recall and tedious to relate,' Hulme admits, he continued to make wines (cabernet sauvignon and chardonnay) but neglected to sell any.

In early 1989 he retained Gary Baldwin (then of Oenotec, now known as Winenet) as consultant. Baldwin's first piece of advice was to close the winery, and after two vintages at nearby Lovegroves of Cottles Bridge (now known as Lovegrove Vineyard and Winery), the winemaking was carried out at Mitchelton until 2000, moving to Yering Station in 2001.

Hulme's attempts to drink the fruits of his labour proving wildly unsuccessful, something had to be done about the relentlessly increasing mountain of stock in the Hayes and Seward warehouse. A forty-year friendship with Joe Sullivan led to the 'revolutionary idea that if you made more wine than the owner could comfortably drink, the thing was to sell it', and to the 1992 appointment of wine distributor Sullivan Wine Agencies to carry out this task.

A committee, made up of Baldwin, Sullivan and Hulme, set about classifying all the wines made between 1979 and 1990; only the 1982, '87, '89 and '90 survived the cut.

The Arthurs Creek label came to the market in 1993, sold directly into Melbourne restaurants and via a mailing list (Arthurs Creek does not have a cellar door and never will). The timing was propitious: the 1992 won the trophy for Best Red Wine in Show at the Southern Victorian Wine Show in 1995; the 1994 won the trophy for Best Cabernet Sauvignon at the Victorian Wines Show, and all vintages from 1992 to 1995 (inclusive) won at least one gold medal.

Woods Wines is now the distributor; telephone 03 9417 1636, elizabethwoods@bigpond.com. The mailing list address is Strathewen Road, Arthurs Creek VIC 3099.

SEPTEMBER 9   Vancouver and The Million Dollar Chardonnay Challenge

I am off to one of the most beautiful cities in the world, Vancouver, as a form of consolation prize in the wake of the cancellation of the Million Dollar Chardonnay of the Century Challenge. The same invitation has been extended to the other senior judges, and all bar one have accepted the invitation.

SEPTEMBER 10   University of British Columbia

Today (like yesterday) the weather is glorious, the temperature around 21°C, the humidity nonexistent, the sun shining in a cloudless and windless blue sky. The forecast for the rest of the week through to Sunday (September 15) is exactly the same.

We're spending the day at the Wine Research Centre of the faculty of Agricultural Sciences at the University of British Columbia. More specifically, our host is Dr Hennie van Vuuren, who holds a dual position as professor and director of food biotechnology, wine being the food in question. He has been involved in research into yeasts for well over a decade, and has produced a genetically modified yeast which carries out both the primary and malolactic fermentation simultaneously. The faculty caters for postgraduate studies only, with eight students currently carrying out research projects for their PhD.

John Avery of the United Kingdom, Bob Campbell MW of New Zealand, Isabelle Bachelard of France, John Salvi of Bordeaux (ex-England) and I are spending the day at the university. (Tony Jordan does not arrive until tomorrow.) Each of us has been asked to bring a Bordeaux-style red, supplemented by bottles supplied by Hennie van Vuuren and some of the students. These are then blind tasted by each of us and each of the students, given points (out of 20) and then ranked by each person first to tenth.

1996 Penfolds Block 46 Kalimna Cabernet Sauvignon comes first, 1982 Penfolds Bin 820 second, 1998 Kingsley Estate (New Zealand) and 1999 De Toren Fusion V (South Africa) equal third, 1998 Tinhorn Creek (Okanagan Valley) fifth, 1990 Pichon Longueville sixth, 2000 Black Hills Nota Bene (Okanagan Valley) seventh, 1993 Château Leoville Barton eighth, 2000 Jackson Triggs Meritage (Ontario) ninth and 1982 Château Cos d'Estournel tenth. The Cos d'Estournel is a very poor bottle, badly oxidised.

After a quick lunch we meet with the board of the International Wine Trust, which was responsible for running the Million Dollar Chardonnay of the Century Challenge, to try to establish reasons for its failure to attract sufficient entries, and to discuss ways forward both with the Challenge and with a range of other possible strategies designed to bring worldwide attention to the University of British Columbia and to the winemakers of the Okanagan Valley. The two and a half hour meeting flies by quickly, with an inevitably wide spread of opinions.

SEPTEMBER 11   VANCOUVER

After a leisurely day seeing the many sights of Vancouver, we are headed to dinner at the waterside home of Sid and Joan Cross. Although we arrive at 6.30 p.m., the evening proceeds at a leisurely pace; after many bottles of champagne and appetisers are disposed of, we proceed to dinner, which starts with a horizontal tasting of all the Meursaults of Domaine des Comtes Lafon of the 1990 vintage. Then follows a lengthy vertical tasting of Caymus Special Select Cabernets from the Napa Valley; we finish with half a dozen Inniskillin Ice Wines, some of considerable age. It is well after midnight before we get back to our hotel, confronted with a 6 a.m. departure for the airport as we head to the Okanagan Valley.

BELOW
Cedar Creek Winery and its vineyards look down on the expanse of the ever-blue Okanagan Lake.

SEPTEMBER 12   OKANAGAN VALLEY

It is just as well that Hennie van Vuuren insisted we arrive at Vancouver airport well over an hour before our departure. Canada Jazz, an offshoot of Air Canada, has introduced an internet booking system with self-check-in tied to the booking. Total confusion and pandemonium prevail before we are allowed to go to the old-style check-in, and then throw ourselves onto the plane.

We quickly learn that the Okanagan Lake is an extremely long one. It has only one crossing (the longest floating bridge in the world), near Kelowna, and the wineries are spread on either side of the lake over very considerable distances. In the end, the only region we do not visit is the extreme north, around Armstrong and Salmon Arm in the Sushwap Lake region, which itself has more than 1000 kilometres of shoreline.

We head first to Cedar Creek Estate winery, owned by the Fitzpatrick family: Senator Ross Fitzpatrick is the proprietor and Gordon Fitzpatrick is the president. There has been a recent change

SEPTEMBER

of winemaker, but in a pattern which becomes all too familiar, the white wines (riesling, pinot gris, pinot blanc and chardonnay) are significantly better than the red wines.

In common with virtually every winery we are to visit, this one has spectacular views out over Lake Okanagan. It draws on three separate vineyards: the first of 19 hectares and surrounding the winery, itself recently upgraded and expanded; then Greata Ranch, south of the winery and on the opposite side of the lake, with 16 hectares; and finally Desert Ridge, in the extreme southern Osoyoos region.

Cedar Creek Vineyards and St Hubertus Estate are virtually neighbours, but they are light years apart in atmosphere. The St Hubertus vineyard dates back to 1920, and is one of the oldest in the Okanagan Valley, although it was not until 1984 that Leo Gerbert acquired the property and started to remove the hybrid varieties and plant vinifera vines in their place, naming the property after the family lodge in Switzerland. His brother Andy owns the adjoining Oak Bay Vineyard; the feel of the vineyards and the Swiss A-framed winery is decidedly rustic, although the white wines — and in particular the Ice Wine — have fair flavour.

ABOVE

The entrance to Quails' Gate, one of the best estate wineries in the Okanagan Valley.

From here we sprint north back to the town of Kelowna in our minivans, then across the lake and south again to Quails' Gate, where we have an excellent lunch in what is one of the most meticulously run vineyards and wineries in the valley — the quality of all the wines reflects great care and commitment.

Back into the minivans, we head further south, to Sumac Ridge Estate, two-thirds of the way down the lake and more or less opposite Naramata, where we are to spend the next few nights. Sumac Ridge was acquired by the Vincor International Group some years ago. It is not altogether obvious to some of us why it enjoys a high reputation, however spectacular the site may be.

From Sumac Ridge we again head south, to Penticton at the southern extremity of the lake; then we turn north and go to Naramata.

We are staying at the Naramata Inn, once a private mansion but now a cross between a guest house and a motel, where eight wineries have an array of wines lined up for tasting. We are due to visit most of these over the next few days, but there are a few (such as Lang Vineyards, Hawthorne Mountain and Jackson Triggs) which are not on our itinerary. After a one and a half hour tasting, there is a semi-formal dinner, whereafter bed beckons in no uncertain fashion.

SEPTEMBER 13   Opening of Nk'Mip Winery

We commence a lengthy drive south to the town of Oliver, which lies between the Osoyoos Lake and Skaha Lake. The day starts cool, but quickly warms up as we reach Gehringer Brothers Estate winery. Walter Gehringer studied at Geisenheim University under Professor Helmut Becker, and was offered the opportunity of bringing in a large number of vinifera crosses bred at Geisenheim. When the Gehringers passed on this offer to the British Columbia Wine Institute, there was no interest; when they then announced that they would bring the varieties in themselves, there was a reversal of policy and varieties such as ehrenfelser, schönburger and auxerrois are now planted at Gehringer and elsewhere.

Here, as one might expect, the white wines are consistently appealing, but it is the Ice Wines which are the most remarkable, including a Riesling Ice Wine, a Minus–9 Ehrenfelser Ice Wine and a Cabernet Franc Ice Wine, the latter still a full pink colour, with a spicy/strawberry palate, showing much less obvious sweetness than its formidable 200 grams per litre of residual sugar.

We move on to lunch at Tinhorn Creek, justly regarded as producing consistently good wines at exceedingly modest prices. We sit on a terrace outside the winery, with the temperature moving past 32°C. California-born and trained winemaker and co-proprietor Sandra Oldfield tells us that, had it been raining, we would have eaten inside in the newly constructed and air-conditioned barrel hall. By the time we finish the delicious lunch, most of us have cause to regret the absence of rain.

Next is Burrowing Owl, one of the hot wineries in the Black Sage Desert region. While it is a relatively recent arrival, with the on-site winery complex still in the course of construction, it is clear that this winery is destined to play a major role in the development of the Okanagan Valley as it is already producing quite outstanding white wines, excellent cabernet franc, very good cabernet sauvignon and remarkably good syrah.

Then yet further south for the official opening of the Nk'Mip, a joint venture between Vincor International and the local Osoyoos band of First Nation Indians, who own the land on which the brand-new winery has been constructed. They also own all the vineyard land; we learn that 25 per cent of all vineyards in British Columbia are planted on land leased from bands (or tribes) of First Nation Indians.

Right through North America, First Nation Indians have the right to catch as many salmon as they wish, when they wish. They are experts in the traditional salmon bake, binding whole sides of large fish to spears which are then driven into the ground at a 40° angle above a fire pit holding a mix of flames and coals. The closer to the ground (and the fire) the spear, the further distant is the fish. Only at the top does it hang directly over the centre of the pit.

The salmon bake has long been a feature of the International Pinot Noir Celebration in Oregon, with dozens of large fish being cooked for hundreds of diners. There, the pits stretch for 20 metres or so. Here, our salmon bake is a small one, but the principle is the same and the outcome tasty and succulent.

However, the opening ceremony and subsequent dinner may well enter the *Guinness Book of Records* for the highest number of speeches, including the highest number of speeches by one individual. It's a long drive back to Naramata in the dead of night, but we gain comfort from the fact that Stefan Buys, our co-host, was once a rally driver.

SEPTEMBER 14   OPENING OF MISSION HILL ESTATE

We depart shortly after 8.30 a.m. to hare back down to south of Oliver for our first visit of the day, to Hester Creek Estate winery. Winemaker Kirby Froese has an interesting background, having worked at Geyser Peak in California, Best's at Great Western, and in Chile. The 400-tonne winery was purchased by capital investors in 1996, but the wines fail to impress. Froese has only just been installed as winemaker, so had no responsibility for the wines we taste; I guess you can't win them all.

BELOW
Burrowing Owl, at the parched southern end of the valley, is totally reliant on irrigation.

SEPTEMBER

From there we go to Domaine Combret, one of the more unusual businesses in the Okanagan Valley, and one that has only recently become a member of the Institute. The business was founded by Robert Combret and family, who emigrated from Provence to Canada in 1992, and established the Domaine with the next year's vintage. We have already tasted a riesling which spent seven years on its lees in tank before being bottled (1994 vintage), and a 1997 chardonnay which spent four years in similar fashion. The word 'interesting' is often used in such instances.

Next port of call is a luridly painted building known as 'The Barn'. It is part of Mission Hill Estate and is used to entertain visitors in the southern part of the Okanagan Valley. It supplies a smorgasbord lunch of the highest quality, the wines on offer including the famous 1992 Chardonnay which won the trophy at the International Wine and Spirit Competition in 1993, and its younger (2000) brother. There is no question that former chief winemaker for Montana, John Simes, knows what he is doing.

Now to Wild Goose Estate winery, at the nonexistent Okanagan Falls, and another seven wines for tasting, followed by the long drive north to Naramata, to hastily change into dinner suits before an even longer drive to Mission Hill for its grand opening.

ABOVE LEFT

The Oosoyoos Indians provide a traditional salmon bake at the opening of Nk'mip Cellars.

ABOVE RIGHT

Early morning tastings at Hester Creek, with newly appointed winemaker Kirby Froese having plenty of work to do.

219

British Columbia's Okanagan Valley is one of the world's most beautiful wine regions, but is a minnow among the whales of the major wine-producing countries. As one of its leading players said to me, 'We've got the place, now all we need is the wine.'

The background statistics are at once illuminating and damned lies. The birth of today's wine industry in the valley is generally regarded as 1990, and while it has 50 wineries, its 2000 hectares produced only 10,000 tonnes in 2000, the same as in 1998, and less than in 1999.

Hardly breakneck growth, even from a small base, yet here I am, one of several hundred dinner-suited (or equivalent) concert and dinner guests at the opening of the A$45 million Mission Hill winery — and last night it was the opening of the opening of the Nk'Mip Cellars.

I cannot leave the Okanagan Valley without writing more about Anthony von Mandl's Mission Hill winery, its opening, and the man himself.

Of Austrian parents, he graduated from the University of British Columbia with a degree in economics, and decided he would set up a small business importing fine wine. To do so he had to deal with the state-owned monopoly which controlled every aspect of wine sales within BC, ferocious rates of duty and a small — albeit thirsty — market.

There were times, he said in a masterly speech at the opening of the winery, when he nearly gave up, tiring of taking three steps forward then two back. His parents persuaded him to continue — and he has ultimately succeeded.

His business expanded to include such staples as Heineken beer, but it was the creation of the Canadian equivalent of Australia's Two Dogs, Mike's Hard Lemonade, which made him a multi-millionaire. Sales across the whole of North America exceed A$120 million a year, and the gross profit margin is something winemakers can only dream of.

He had already commenced Mission Hill in 1991, and in 1992 had lured John Simes from his position as senior winemaker for New Zealand's Montana. In a piece of serendipitous magic, the Mission Hill Chardonnay Simes made that vintage won the International Wine & Spirits Avery Trophy for Best Chardonnay in the competition.

When Tony Mandl (as, so I am told, he was then called) and John Simes were presented with the trophy by John Avery in London's Guild Hall, it put the focus on a region unknown outside Canada, and barely known within it.

Roll the clock ten years forward, and you are standing on the crest of the mountain bordering the west side of the 160-kilometre-long Okanagan Lake. Here stands an amazing array of buildings, many largely decorative, built in a style which I could only describe as a mix of Incan and Greco-Roman.

Underneath is a large winery incorporating what must surely be the most beautiful barrel hall in the world, with soaring concrete arches — I am sorry to say it, but it makes the barrel hall at Yering Station seem pedestrian.

Upstairs one large room is entirely devoted to and takes its name from a gigantic Marc Chagall tapestry, and collections of wine-related antiquities are scattered around. But the two pièces de résistance are the priapic bell tower with four massive bells cast in France and installed by helicopter, and the keystone, which is unveiled as the focal point of the opening. Two sculptors, one Welsh, one English, worked seven days a week for three months on a single 5-tonne block of limestone to create the four-sided representations of pelicans, the bird featured on the von Mandl family coat of arms. The keystone is set in the top of the freestanding arch you pass under to enter the winery complex.

The aim? To create a series of buildings which will be as relevant and awe-inspiring in two hundred years' time as they are today.

SEPTEMBER 15   OKANAGAN VALLEY: DEPARTURE

Our only appointment today is at Gray Monk Cellars, but it's a long drive to the far north — we are late departing and hence late arriving. Instead of an hour for a tasting and brunch, we have only thirty minutes before heading off to the airport, with Stefan Buys convinced we are going to miss the flight. We would probably have made it regardless, but the plane is late, so all is well. The leg is the first of three I take, next flying from Vancouver to Los Angeles,

ABOVE
*Gray Monk —
a colourful farewell.*

thence to Melbourne, arriving safe but well-worn at 8 a.m. on September 17.

SEPTEMBER 17 YARRA VALLEY

As I take the M80 ring road which gets me from Tullamarine Airport to home in a little under an hour (a trip, incidentally, which accounts for something like 80 per cent of the total mileage my car travels each year) I wonder whether I will be able to see the effect of the frosts which caused Domaine Chandon and Tarrawarra to employ helicopters (to disperse frosty air at ground level) during the course of last week. Reassuringly, there is a more or less even sea of tiny green shoots on the early-ripening varieties; the later-ripening varieties are still to go through budburst. When I enquire at the winery, I find that while it was a near-run thing, none of our vineyards was affected; nor are there any reports of damage from our growers.

SEPTEMBER 19 GREAT AUSTRALIAN SHIRAZ CHALLENGE

Having committed myself to judge at the Challenge some considerable time ago, I have had to return home from the United

SEPTEMBER

States for it — and then I head back there early next week. My co-judges are John Duval and Stephen Henschke, Trevor Mast having been waylaid by lawyers at the very last moment to finalise details of the sale of Mount Langi Ghiran. We have a very tough task in front of us: today we have 217 shirazs to taste, with the aim of identifying the top 60 or so, which will then be rejudged tomorrow morning. Judging more than 100 wines of the same type on a given day is an arduous job. Judging more than 200 takes one's powers of concentration and senses of smell and taste to the outer limits of endurance.

With teeth stained black, gums purple and minds spinning we make it to the end. As we pool the points and then proceed to analyse them, we realise that the fates have been on our side, for we have 59 wines to retaste tomorrow, and little, if anything, left outside that group.

After the statutory beer, we head off to the restaurant at Mitchelton Winery, which has opened especially for the event. All the good things we have heard about the young chef prove to be correct. We start with goat's cheese ravioli with artichoke purée, lemon and parsley pistou (a near-relative of pesto, with olive oil and, in this

BELOW

Tahbilk is in many ways a working museum, its past still in evidence.

223

instance, lemon and parsley, ground with a pestle and mortar or in a food processor) matched with a 1982 Tahbilk Riesling — it is a marvellous dish. Next is crisp-skin braised duck legs, deboned, in chive and coriander crêpes with bok choy, tangelos and a reduced orange glaze. This comes with 1968 Tahbilk Reserve Cabernet Sauvignon, 1971 Tahbilk Cabernet Sauvignon and 1976 Château Lafite. 1971 Tahbilk Reserve Shiraz, which Alister Purbrick only recently discovered was in fact made exclusively from the vines planted in 1860, and said to be the oldest in the world, and 1968 Penfolds St Henri were served with cheese, 1975 Château Coutet with crème brûlée, and 1939 Para Liqueur Port with coffee and chocolates.

The Tahbilk reds are, without question, the wines of the night; the two 1971s in particular are outstanding. No lashings of new oak here, nor threatening alcohol, just balanced maturity.

SEPTEMBER 20   GREAT AUSTRALIAN SHIRAZ CHALLENGE

We are greatly relieved at the end of the tasting of the 59 wines sifted out from yesterday, with 10 receiving gold medal points, 29 silver and 11 high bronze medals. There are an additional 88 bronze medal wines selected from the first day's judging.

The Visy Board Trophy for the Best Wine goes to 1999 Tatachilla Foundation Shiraz, with 1999 Ingoldby Reserve Shiraz coming in second. Third place, and the Hahn's Haulage Trophy for Best Shiraz under $25, goes to 1999 Montrose Mudgee Black Shiraz.

In addition to these, 1997 Wynns Coonawarra Michael, 2001 Ballast Stone Estate, 1999 Fox Creek Reserve, 1999 Fullers Barn, 2001 Western Range, 2000 Hanging Rock Heathcote and 2000 Punter's Corner Spartacus Reserve all win golds. The public choice, made before our tasting, was for the Punter's Corner Spartacus Reserve, so for once there was agreement between the judges and the public.

SEPTEMBER 21   JACQUES REYMOND

Suzanne and I have not eaten at Jacques Reymond since the restaurant was redecorated from top to bottom and a new menu was introduced. So that is where we are headed this evening. The menu basically falls into three parts: Carte, Menu Vegetarian (six courses, $80), and Menu Dégustation (six courses, $115). Every single dish on the menu exudes originality, with some combinations that look challenging but in reality are perfection. The most radical menu is the Carte, with thirteen unpriced dishes; you can choose two for $65, three for $90 or four for $115.

We take the easy way out and both have the Menu Dégustation. The dishes (in sequence) are gazpacho, cauliflower cream, tuna tartare with ginger juice; warm salad of white and green asparagus with prawn and scallop; seared swordfish, calamari and black rice risotto with tamarind juice; and frangipani of farmed rabbit and lightly smoked bacon with a light mustard sauce. There is then the only choice, which is for the culmination or 'main' course: five-spice Peking duck and Chinese port, sweet corn fritters and apple chutney, or Flinders Island milk-fed lamb with parmesan gnocchi, natural cooking juices. We decide we will have one of each, Suzanne the lamb, myself the duck, but guessing that we really both want the lamb, Jacques inserts another dish for each of us: the lamb for me and slow-braised oxtail, potato aioli and natural cooking juices for Suzanne.

BELOW

Jacques Reymond — an old friend and a great chef.

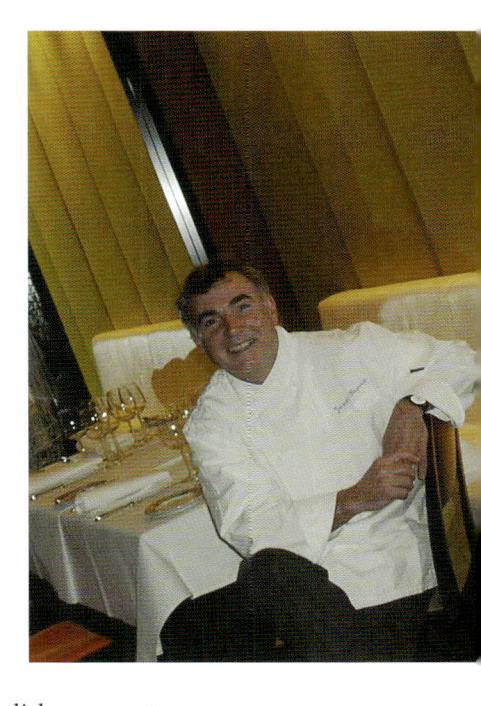

The prawn and warm scallop and asparagus salad, the seared swordfish and the Flinders Island milk-fed lamb are the three greatest dishes I have eaten in Australia. The seafood dishes are at once delicate yet complex, fine yet intensely flavoursome, all the many flavour ingredients melding together, the texture perfection. The milk-fed lamb basically falls within the same category, but is lifted even further by the unbelievably small-boned, meltingly tender and wonderfully flavoured meat.

We choose 1996 Giaconda Chardonnay, by far the best vintage ever made of this outstanding wine, and 1993 Morey St Denis Clos de la Buissière Premier Cru of Domaine Georges Roumier, and both wines do the menu proud.

Jacques Reymond, 78 Williams Road, Prahran, VIC 3181. Telephone (03) 9525 2178, fax (03) 9521 1552.

SEPTEMBER 24   UNITED STATES PART II

I am on board yet another aeroplane, returning to the United States where I will spend the next ten days on an educational tour, starting in San Francisco, moving to Seattle, then Portland, across to New York and ultimately up to Boston. There is a lot of travel involved, but also a lot of activity each day.

I have agreed to make the trip for two reasons. First, I was requested to do so by Kevin McLintock, the managing director of McWilliam's Wines, whom I have known for many years and who was particularly helpful to Coldstream Hills during his time as sales and marketing director of our then distributor, Tucker Seabrook. It is, if you like, part of the 'mates' ethos of Australians. Second, the commercial arrangement lying behind the trip is more likely than not to yield benefits to the Australian wine industry as a whole, not just McWilliam's.

That arrangement is a worldwide joint venture and distribution arrangement between McWilliam's and Gallo; Gallo being by far the largest wine company in the world. The arrangement currently excludes Australasia, but will ultimately extend to all the McWilliam's products; the initial roll-out is of Hanwood Chardonnay and Hanwood Shiraz.

The educational theme is the Australian tradition of blending wines from different regions, its greatest exponents being Colin Preece at Seppelt Great Western, Roger Warren at Hardys, Max Schubert at Penfolds (with Grange, in particular) and Maurice O'Shea at Mount Pleasant in the Hunter Valley. (O'Shea largely contented himself with buying parcels of wine from other Hunter Valley producers, but was not above putting in the odd bit of wine swapped with other makers of the day in other regions.)

So as well as tasting the McWilliam's wines, I present individual region or individual vineyard wines from areas represented in the blends, some produced by other makers. Those wines include Bloodwood Shiraz from Orange, Saltram No 1 Shiraz from the Barossa Valley and Wynns Coonawarra Estate Chardonnay. They accompany Brands of Coonawarra Cabernet Sauvignon, Barwang Chardonnay and Mount Pleasant Chardonnay.

The audiences are made up of a mix of sales and marketing people from the Gallo organisation in each state, their equivalents from the distributor in the state (under US law, alcohol has to be distributed by separate organisations in each state, a hangover from the end of Prohibition), retailers and, at some functions, members of the public.

If nothing else, the trip highlights just how immature the American market still is when it comes to Australian wine, notwithstanding that it is not only Australia's most profitable market, but ranks second only to the United Kingdom and is closing the gap fast. There is great interest in the individual vineyard/region wines, which is certainly not the commercial focus of the joint venture, but does indicate how much scope there is for Australia as a whole.

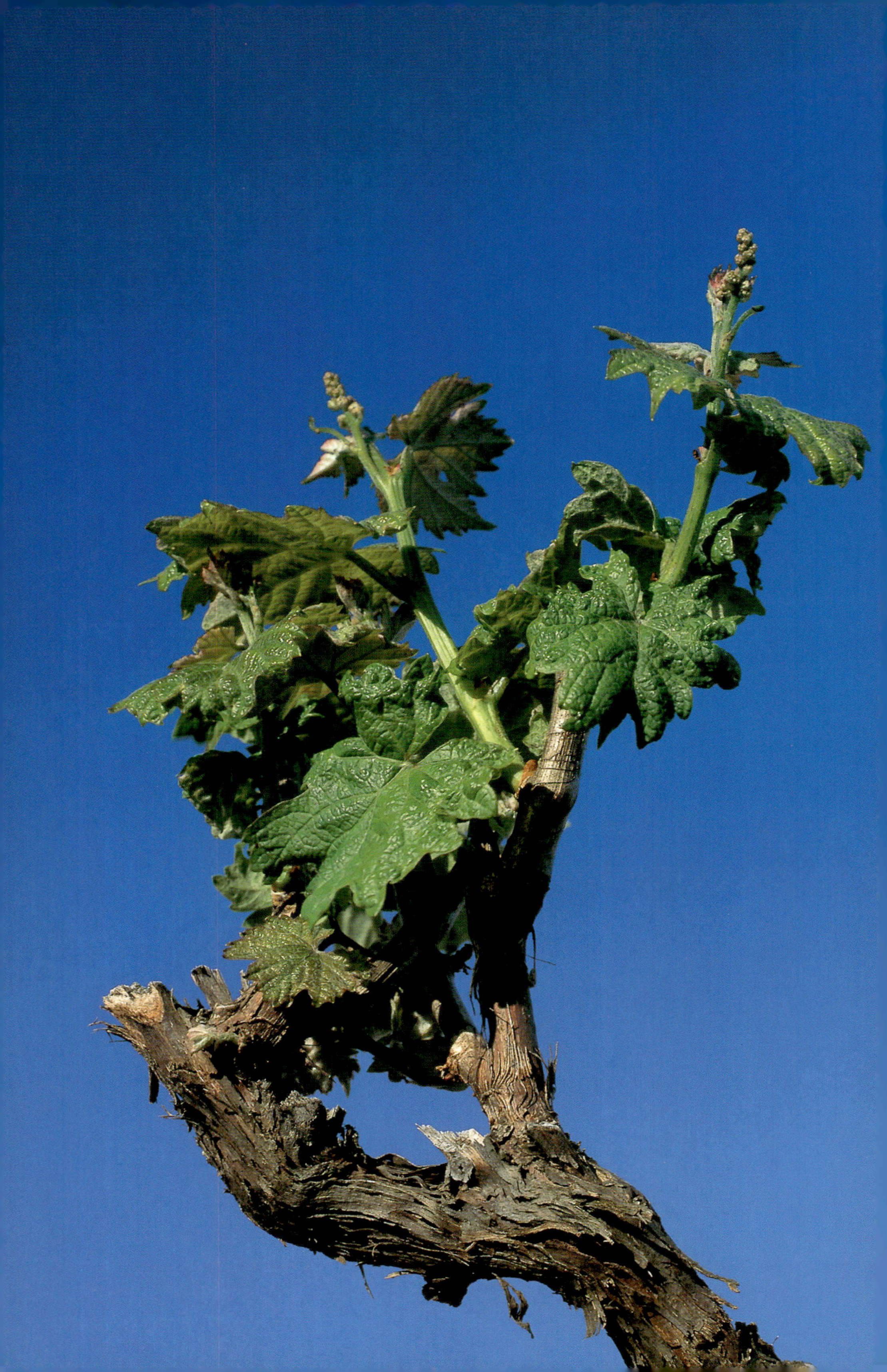

October

The Long Trip Home

Yarra Valley: Budburst

Qantas Western Australian Wine Show

Frankland River, Manjimup, Pemberton

The Top 100 Tasting

La Tâche Monday Table Dinner

Wallabies and Other Visitors

Yarra Valley: Still Green

Hawke's Bay Wine Show, New Zealand

Poronui Ranch, Hawke's Bay

Limestone Coast Wine Show

OCTOBER 4–6   THE LONG TRIP HOME

It is easy to forget just how far the northeast corner of the United States is from Australia, and why New Yorkers, in particular, baulk at making the trip. I leave Boston at 3.30 in the afternoon; the flight time to Los Angeles is six hours, with three hours deducted for the time zone change, so I arrive a little after 6.30 p.m. local time. I then have a five-hour wait at the terminal, where the lounges are spartan to say the least, and depart a little before midnight on the fourteen and a half hour trip to Australia, arriving in Melbourne at 8 a.m. on Sunday, October 6. This all adds up to more than thirty-one hours of travel and transit time, to which you have to add the seven hours since getting up in Boston on the morning of the exit flight, and the twelve hours you need to stay awake on Sunday if you are not to get hooked in a jetlag vice. Thus the total time lapse between getting up in Boston and going to bed in Melbourne is over forty-eight hours.

OCTOBER 6   YARRA VALLEY: BUDBURST

I only have today before I set out again on my all-too-familiar trip to Tullamarine. Budburst has proceeded apace in my absence and the prospects for an average harvest seem good. Bud dissection earlier in the year suggested that there would be one bunch per shoot. (The buds are removed from the vine, frozen, sliced and examined under a microscope.) In fact there is slightly more than one bunch, and there is a large number of shoots, so the decision has been taken to shoot-thin (laboriously, by hand) and remove second bunches on the remaining shoots. (Postscript: the berries and bunches, while evenly sized, turn out to be smaller than usual, and drought further reduces the crop over the whole of eastern Australia, exacerbated by some ill-timed rain in South Australia. Total tonnage will be significantly less than that of 2002.)

While the Yarra Valley is a vivid green, rainfall has been way below average, with virtually no run-off; our dams are largely full simply because of the very low water usage last year. We will get by without undue difficulty, but much of Australia is gripped by very serious drought, so we can count ourselves lucky.

OCTOBER 7   Qantas Western Australian Wine Show

Back on board the familiar confines of a Qantas plane, I head off from Melbourne on the 2.55 p.m. flight to Perth, connecting later that afternoon with a flight down to Albany in the far south-western corner of Western Australia. For the next three days I will be chairing the judging of the Qantas Western Australian Wine Show, which is celebrating its twenty-fifth anniversary, and which is also experiencing the hectic rate of growth prevailing in all wine shows in Australia.

With Zar Brooks and Vanya Cullen as panel leaders, we move through the first two days, judging almost 190 wines per day per panel without undue difficulty, even though that is 30 wines a day more than my preferred maximum. While the judges can handle the number of wines, it limits the scope for discussion with associates, who are there to learn, but who (because of the speed of the process) are often left wondering why their points were so different from those of the judges.

This year there are 925 entries from 220 exhibitors. Last year 147 wineries entered 750 wines, and as recently as 1997 there were only 79 wineries entering 392 wines.

Although there is an argument for the proposition that regional or state shows (as opposed to capital city shows) should allow the entry of unbottled wines, the Qantas Wine Show does not. What is more: all wines entered must be 100 per cent grown and vintaged in Western Australia; any wine can only be entered once; and exhibitors are restricted to a maximum of two wines in any one class. These conditions are as stringent as those encountered in capital city shows, but at this rate of growth, a day of reckoning for the Qantas Wine Show must come well within the next five years, simply because I believe that once the number of entries in a wine show exceeds 1600 wines, quality and other compromises have to be made unless the success of the show is to be judged by the number of entries rather than the integrity of the results.

RIGHT

View from the top of Ferngrove Winery; cover crops every second vine row.

OCTOBER 11   FRANKLAND RIVER, MANJIMUP, PEMBERTON

Before the start of the show, it has been arranged that I will visit the Frankland sub-region, to have lunch at Alkoomi and thereafter go to the new Ferngrove winery, the largest in the region. I am then to be taken around the Pemberton and Manjimup regions, of which I have scant knowledge, having previously visited only very briefly. The Beechcraft Baron plane owned by Ferngrove will ferry me to Perth late in the day. It is as well that all this was organised before Ferngrove won so many trophies at the show!

Ferngrove's operation is a highly sophisticated one, with a business plan far more believable and rational than those of some other newcomers on the Western Australian scene. Much of the production from its extensive vineyards is sold to other leading winemakers on both the west coast and the east coast of Australia; part is sold as juice and tankered out immediately; for other customers, base wine fermented to specification is sold. Ferngrove also has the capacity to act as a custom crush facility for other producers, and is, of course, making wine under its own label. At the present time only a small proportion of the total production is being marketed this way, and most of that is exported. With the extremely experienced Ted Avery as managing director, and with a brand new, expertly designed 5000-tonne winery, it certainly seems to be doing everything correctly.

Patrick Coutts, the Salitage winemaker, is our chauffeur and guide as we wind our way through the forest roads of Pemberton and Manjimup. The countryside is constantly changing, with giant trees — and water — never far away. After almost three hours' driving and several hundred kilometres on the clock, and notwithstanding Patrick Coutts' intimate understanding of the regions, I come away feeling I know even less than when the trip began. However, I am certain that generalisations are completely useless — each region has such a multiplicity of sites and terroirs that those who grow grapes and make wine there have years of trial and error ahead of them.

Another thing is also clear: the best vintages will be the warmer, drier years. Persuading the vines to stop growing, and to properly ripen the grapes (brown seeds, not green), will never be easy.

After being flown back to Perth with fellow judge Zar Brooks, the pilot insists on driving me to my hotel, the Hyatt. I ask him whether he is employed by Ferngrove or flies for others as well, and he politely says, 'Well, actually, I am the managing director and I just enjoy the chance to fly.' Murray Burton — it is he — is as charming as he is intelligent and laughs off my acute embarrassment.

BELOW
Starting on the tasting for this year's Top 100 for the Weekend Australian.

OCTOBER 13–19   THE TOP 100 TASTING

Back at home, today (Sunday) I commence the tasting of the 1000-plus wines submitted for this year's Top 100 selection, published each year as a special lift-out section of *The Weekend Australian*. My plan is to taste 160 wines each day, fortified by large bottles of soda water, and cheese and green olives. Peter Mitchell, who normally works at the cellar door on weekends, is my steward. He has laboriously catalogued, sorted and cross-referenced the 2000 bottles (two bottles of each wine are submitted, in part to deal with cork taint problems, and in part to get a second bottle for photography if the wine is selected in the Top 100.) Paula, my personal assistant, then enters the wines into our database, cross-referencing any prior tasting notes. It is a process which takes weeks of work — every bit as long as the tasting itself.

The wines are sorted by variety and then subdivided by price: white wines under $20 in one section, over $20 in another; the divide for red wines is $25. I taste white wines in the morning and red wines in the afternoon, with the wines sorted by variety within the timeframe of the day. Peter Mitchell has a photographic memory and is incredibly organised, finding the second bottle so quickly when taint or other problems arise that I barely notice the interruption.

The day starts each morning around 9 a.m., with a 45-minute break for lunch, and continues until 4 p.m. or a little after. Lunchtime and late in the day give me a chance to catch up with all the other things happening in my office, and also provide a break from the intense mental concentration required.

OCTOBER 14   LA TÂCHE MONDAY TABLE DINNER

I have refused to accept any other invitation or interruption during the week, but the La Tâche dinner is irresistible. I am an extremely irregular member of the Monday Table, a group of a dozen Melbourne wine lovers who meet once a month for dinner, each producing a bottle of wine within the scene set for the dinner. We take it in turns to organise the meal at a leading restaurant and look after the arrangements to ensure that the right wines turn up, but there have been a few famous instances when Murphy has prevailed. Mercifully, no such problems occur tonight.

The dinner is held in the small private dining room at Circa, one of Melbourne's best restaurants. We start with two mystery champagnes, accompanied by brioche filled with enoki and oyster mushroom. The champagnes turn out to be 1985 Salon and 1985 Bollinger RD, the exercise being to contrast the Salon Blanc de Blancs against the high pinot percentage of the Bollinger RD.

Wild barramundi, Moreton Bay bugs and champagne sauce accompany the two mystery white burgundies: 1996 Le Montrachet of Laguiche and 1973 Le Montrachet of Baron Thenard, the former tight and classy, with decades to go, the latter totally oxidised. Perhaps Murphy is taking a small hand in tonight's dinner after all.

La Tâche 1998, '96, '93 and '90 are served with roasted saddle of venison with celeriac purée and sauce poivrade (a demi-glaze with pepper). With this flight, and the following two, we know the vintages represented, but not the order in which they are served. Next come the 1985, '78, '70 and '69, with duck breast with chorizo ravioli and a Madeira sauce, and finally we have the '43 and '42 with roasted stuffed rabbit saddle with wilted cos and mustard velouté (a thick, creamy sauce based on roux — melted butter and flour — with mustard the predominant added flavour, doubtless plus stock added to achieve the desired thickness).

By common consensus, the 1978 is the greatest of many great wines (how could you not give it 100 points?). There is a split between the 1942 and '43 next, some preferring the '42, others the '43, and then the 1990.

The most confusing vintages are the 1969 and '70: the former should have been richer, riper and stronger, the latter lighter and less ripe. In fact, the wines are the other way around, and only one person comes up with the right answer.

But this is not really about guessing vintages; it is rather a dinner to honour one of the very greatest red wines of the world. The common link is the sublime intensity and length of the wines, intensity achieved so effortlessly that it is easy to look through and past it. The tasting also demonstrates that just when you think these wines might have reached a peak, such as with the 1990, they go on for another fifty years without batting an eyelid. The retail value of the wines, incidentally, is well in excess of $1000 a bottle; the '85 is currently being offered by a leading retailer at $1500.

OCTOBER 15   WALLABIES AND OTHER VISITORS

Creatures which attack grapevines you have planted and nurtured give rise to similar emotions as would an actual or potential threat to your children. Ever since 1986, the annual depredations of a handful of wallabies living in the hillside forest above the house have brought my blood to boiling point. They are particularly devastating in spring, eating the new shoots and their unborn grapes, ending that year's potential crops. If they return often enough, the vine will eventually give up.

Wallabies are protected so I cannot chronicle here my all-too-few successful attempts to protect my vines. Kangaroos, on the other hand, much prefer the grass growing between the rows and seldom touch the vines. There are far more resident kangaroos around the house and they give Suzanne and me great pleasure as we watch them box each other, or observe joeys hopping in and out of their mothers' pouches — sometimes at such a seemingly advanced age you cannot imagine how they can fit, diving in head first, legs poking out at the top, before magically turning around so head appears in place of legs seconds later.

We also have feral deer living permanently in the hillside forest, which appear only occasionally on the road from the house down to the winery. They are just as destructive of vines as wallabies, but, for whatever reason, seldom move into the vineyard.

BELOW
Wallaby drinking from the goldfish pond at the house; kangaroos are more welcome.

OCTOBER 19   YARRA VALLEY: STILL GREEN

The Top 100 tasting having finished ahead of schedule yesterday, I have a day to think about other things. The Yarra Valley continues to look as if it is part of the Irish countryside, so vivid are the grass and the growing tips of the vines, but there has still been little or no run-off into the dams. Melbourne's water storage is not much more than 50 per cent full, and water restrictions seem inevitable in the coming summer. But the Yarra Valley is lucky; much of Australia continues in severe drought, and bushfires have recently destroyed houses in many parts of New South Wales and Queensland, including the Hunter Valley.

OCTOBER

OCTOBER 20–24 HAWKE'S BAY WINE SHOW, NEW ZEALAND

On yet another Qantas plane to Auckland, thence south to Napier for the Hawke's Bay Wine Show. I arrive to find the cruelty of nature once again exposed: the vignerons of Hawke's Bay have lost virtually all their chardonnay to frost, the worst in thirty years, and this only two years after substantial damage was caused to the 2001 vintage. There is little frost protection in place, largely because frosts are (theoretically) so rare that the cost of protection is not justified. The most sadly ironic sight is at a vineyard where a giant wind machine has been installed: like a huge windmill, its blades are driven at high speed and, in theory, break up the cold air. In this instance the cold air was so deep, there was no warmer air to take its place. The only vines the machine protected are a dozen or so at the immediate rear of the large diesel motor which drives it — they were warmed by the exhaust fumes — and their luxuriant growth is in stark contrast to the bare vines stretching into the distance.

The Hawke's Bay Mercedes Benz Wine Show is a new kid on the block, this year's show being only the second. It is also innovative, dividing the

BELOW

The Martinborough Vineyard of Craggy Range (my host during the show).

wines into Bordeaux styles and Burgundy styles, and having a dedicated panel for each style. It then has an overseas judge to head each panel, the remainder of the judges and associates being New Zealanders.

Andrew Caillard MW, of Langton's Fine Wine Auctions, headed the Burgundy-style panel, and judged the chardonnays, pinot noirs, shirazs, pinot gris and aromatic white wines (the last, predominantly rieslings and gewürztraminers, not really fitting in either of the main two categories). His panel's real work came with the 54 chardonnays — this was by far the largest class in the show.

The Bordeaux-style panel came under my jurisdiction and covered the cabernet sauvignon, merlot, Bordeaux blend and other Bordeaux varietal classes (four in all) plus the sauvignon blanc and/or semillon class. Given that the greatest strength of Hawke's Bay lies with its Bordeaux-style reds, I would be hard pressed to deny that I came out on the right side.

The Bordeaux blend class was by far the largest (35 wines). There were a number of strong silver medals, but the 2000 Matariki Wines Quintology stood out like a beacon, winning the gold medal and the trophy. It is a five-variety blend (cabernet sauvignon, merlot, cabernet franc, syrah and malbec), both bouquet and palate flooded with sweet cassis fruit, and elicited unanimous first-up golds from all three judges.

Owned by former All Black John O'Connor and wife Rosemary, the 45-hectare vineyard is run on a low-yield basis aimed (successfully) at maximising intense fruit flavours; in the winery, the aim is to preserve that which the vineyard gives. It was (and is) a striking contrast to the approach of many of the other winemakers, with whose wines over-extraction seems to be leading to toughness and hard tannins. (Matariki's 2000 Reserve Syrah also won the trophy in its class.)

The striking and powerful 2000 Mills Reef Elspeth Malbec took gold and top place in the Other Bordeaux Varietal class, Mills Reef completing an impressive double when its 2002 Reserve Gewürztraminer won gold and the trophy in the Aromatic White Wine class.

Finally, two outstanding sauvignon blancs stood toe to toe (they happened to be next to each other in the 28-strong class) for the trophy, both winning gold medals. In the end, the complex, partially barrel-fermented 2002 Kemblefield The Distinction Sauvignon Blanc justly emerged the winner over the Delegat's Hawke's Bay Sauvignon Blanc, an elegant, passionfruit/tropical-accented wine of impeccable length.

None of this, it must be said, holds a candle to the one and a half days of trout fishing at Poronui Ranch which follows the judging. New Zealand's Hawke's Bay has it all.

OCTOBER 23–24   PORONUI RANCH, HAWKE'S BAY

A chance question about trout fishing in the lead-up to the show, and an immediate and enthusiastic response from my end, means that this morning I am being collected by helicopter from the forecourt of the Craggy Range Winery, to be taken directly to the Mohaka River with my guide, Grant Petheridge. Poronui Ranch is owned by a wealthy American businessman, Mark Blake, who purchased the 6500-hectare property some years ago. It then boasted a simple fishing hut; he has since built an exclusive luxury complex for hunters and fly-fishers alike. It is in exceedingly remote mountainous country, and all manner of game abounds, with four types of deer, plus mountain goats and even merino sheep (which have run wild for a hundred years); all are considered fair game. When it comes to the fish, however, it is strictly catch and release.

Mark Blake is not only a dedicated fly-fisher; he has also had a lifelong interest in wine, and has acquired a Hawke's Bay vineyard so that he can produce his own wines under the Blake Family label. When he heard I was interested in fly fishing, he sent me a FedEx parcel during my last American trip; I had no idea it was coming, but the brochures and background material prepared me for what I am about to see.

The weather is perfect: clear blue skies and only the occasional breath of wind, which barely penetrates the ravines in which we fish. Helicopter is the only way in and out of this part of the river, unless one comes downstream by raft. We have two fly-fishing rods, one is a powerful 2.6-metre Sage rod (mine) and the other a lightweight 2.2-metre rod, and there are two radically different ways to fish the river with no trout rising. The first, with the big rod, is to fish across stream with a small nymph and an indicator on the line; the other is to fish directly upstream with the small rod, fishing to previously located brown trout quietly feeding in the shallow ripple, often no more than 30 cm deep, at the water's edge.

Like all guides, Grant has the eyes of an eagle and can see the brown trout long before I do. With considerable guidance, some luck and the occasional piece of skill, I manage to catch four 1.6-kilo trout, one 1.8-kilo and four 2.3-kilo trout, including a rainbow, all on the first day. It is by far the greatest day's trout-fishing of my life, and I am more than happy to return to the lodge when the helicopter arrives to pick us up from a tiny shingle beach on the side of the stream at around four o'clock.

Grant, Eve (a marvellous Irish woman who runs the ranch) and I have a wine tasting in the massive underground wine cellar in a separate part of the ranch, where wine dinners for up to twenty people are held on demand. Later this evening we have dinner in the main dining room; this demonstrates that Eve, as well as having many other talents, is a very accomplished chef.

We return to the river around 9.30 a.m. the next morning, this time much further downstream, in water which carries far more rainbows than brown trout, the aim being to catch the rainbows. The river has other ideas and I end up catching another 1.6-kilo and

BELOW

The wild reaches of the Mohaka River are accessible only by helicopter.

BELOW RIGHT

One of the many brown trout (2 kilos or so) about to be returned to the river.

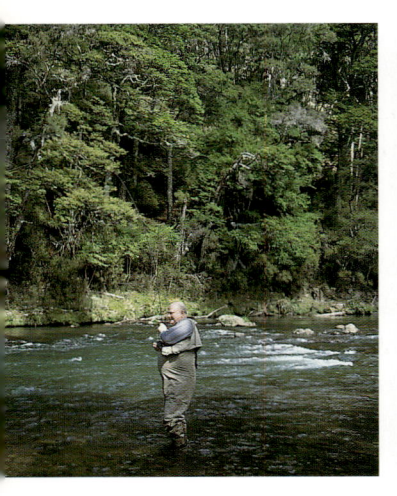

Patron saint at Mount Gambier; guarding the vineyard.

2.3-kilo brown trout before hooking into what turns out to be a 2.7-kilo brown trout on the light rod, landing the fish after an exhilarating twenty-minute fight. At 12.30 p.m. the helicopter arrives and whisks me to Napier Airport — still in waders and full fishing gear — where I carry out a Superman-like change into street clothes and board the flight to Auckland forty-five minutes later. With the three-hour time change, I am back home in the Yarra Valley at 7 p.m. that evening.

OCTOBER 28–NOVEMBER 1   LIMESTONE COAST WINE SHOW

Late in the afternoon I am once more in a plane, this time a much smaller one heading to Mount Gambier. Over the next two days we will judge the second Limestone Coast Wine Show; if it turns out to be as enjoyable as last year's show I shall be more than happy.

> The 2002 Limestone Coast Wine Show had a formidable standard to live up to — the show committee had pulled out all stops to make the first show one to remember, and one to aspire to be invited back to judge. Well, the second show didn't just live up to the first — it exceeded it; how many rabbits the show committee can pull out of the hat in the years to come remains to be seen. Perhaps nothing is impossible.

The social highlights included a six-course dinner with a spectacular array of specially chosen wines, with a Limestone Coast wine paired with an international classic counterpart for each dish. Only local ingredients were used for the dinner, starting with three canapés: sugar-cured salmon, Naracoorte yabbie tails and rare Limestone Coast lamb fillet.

The first entrée was a galantine of local corn-fed chicken (deboned, cooked, pressed and served in cold slices) and Millicent farmed rabbit; the second entrée was a fillet of Robe barramundi. The main course was yearling Limestone Coast beef; followed by cheese (with 1982 Château Leoville Las Cases and 1982 Wynns John Riddoch Cabernet Sauvignon); and finally, lime and lemon tart with local double cream and fresh raspberries.

A remarkable culinary achievement, even if held at a normal venue. But what about a limestone cave over 10 metres underground in the middle of a vineyard in the middle of nowhere? The cave was discovered a hundred years ago, then sealed over and forgotten for eighty-five years. It has a seriously small entrance, requiring you to bend over double for the first stages of descent. Cooking is impossible here — it was done in a tent in the vineyard, courtesy of a mobile generator.

The Show itself produced some outstanding trophy wines. The 2002 Leconfield Riesling, with its exceptional length and citrussy/minerally acid finish, added to its Adelaide trophy with the Best Aromatic White Wine trophy. It was pipped at the post by the 2001 Jacob's Creek Premium Chardonnay (artfully weaving barrel fermentation, lees contact and malolactic fermentation in a complex but subtle web) for the Best White Wine of Show.

The complex, rich, intense, layered fruit of Majella's 2000 The Mallea won the trophy for Best Blended Red Wine, but I'm not sure I didn't prefer the 2000 Majella Shiraz, the top gold medal out of the 37 wines in the 2000 and older shiraz class. This had all the richness, depth and texture to its sweet dark berry, plum and licorice fruit one could wish for, yet was wonderfully elegant.

Orlando's 1998 Lawson's Padthaway Shiraz won the trophies for Best Individual Vineyard Wine and Best Shiraz: it is still a youthful purple, and has a depth of fruit flavour which will ensure a cellar life of thirty years or more.

The star of the show was the yet-to-be-released 2000 Jamiesons Run Reserve Cabernet Sauvignon: Best Cabernet, Best Red Wine and Best Wine of Show. Winemaker Andrew Hales said he had tried to produce a wine of elegance rather than opulent power, with the Bordeaux model somewhere in the back of his mind, and it was for precisely this that we singled it out for the three top red wine trophies.

And as a fitting finale, 1991 Lindemans Limestone Ridge Shiraz Cabernet won the trophy for Best Museum Wine, drawing my comment: 'As close to perfection as an imperfect world will allow.'

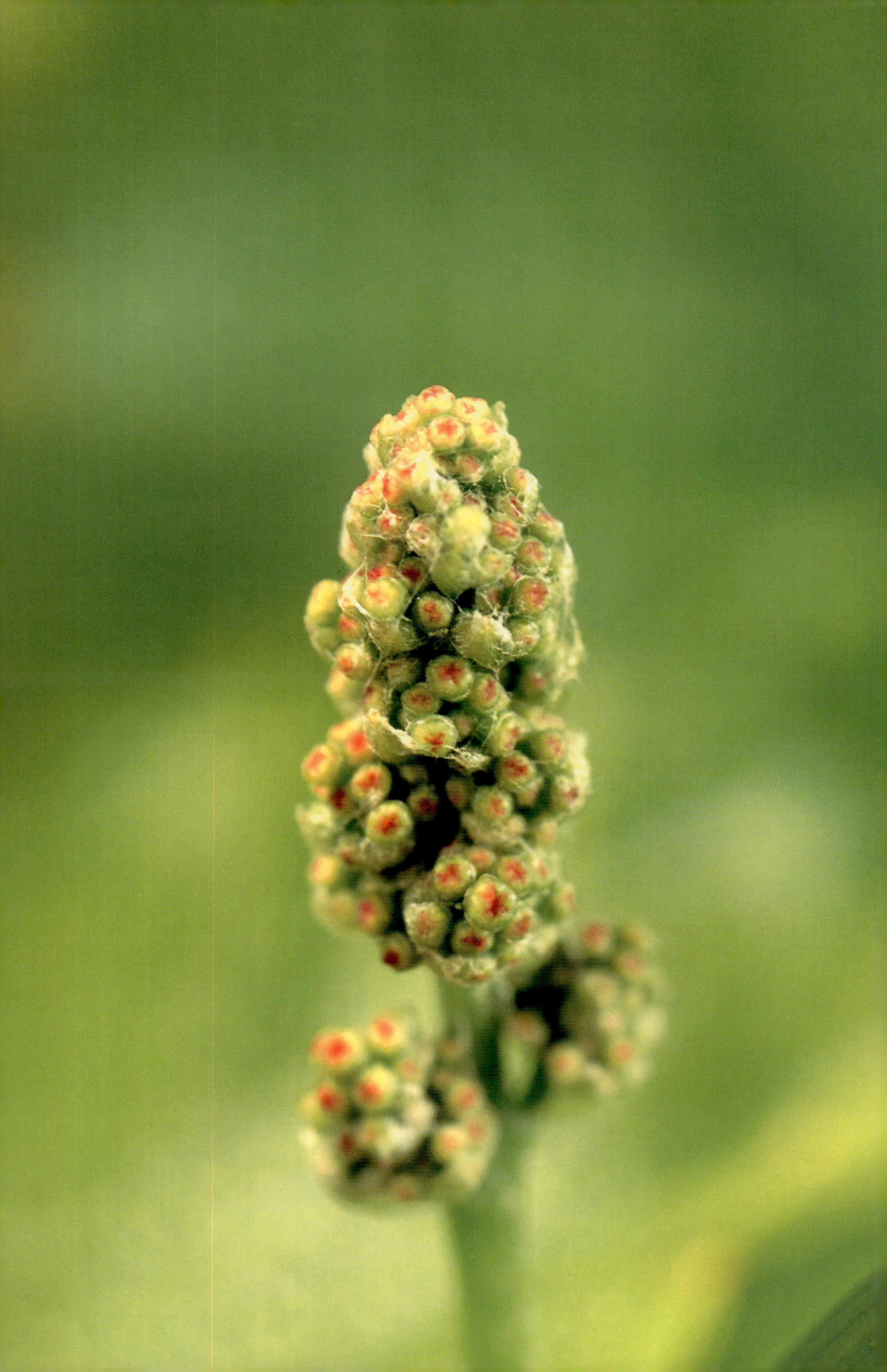

November

Outlook Conference, Adelaide

Yarra Valley: Wildlife

Qantas Western Australian Wine Show Dinner, Perth

Melbourne: St Vincents Institute of Medical Research

Yarra Valley: Hosting Harvey Steiman

Vintage Cellars National Wine Show, Canberra

Len Evans Tutorials, Hunter Valley

Yarra Valley: More Wine Tasting

Yarra Valley: 2002 Pinot Noir

Negociants Fellowship, Sydney

NOVEMBER 4 OUTLOOK CONFERENCE, ADELAIDE

The annual Wine Outlook Conference has established itself as a major event in the Australian wine calendar. The industry assembles speakers both from within the ranks of the Australian Wine and Brandy Corporation and Winemakers Federation and from overseas. It examines the factors currently affecting the production and the sales sides of the industry, the latter focusing (inevitably) on exports.

If you believe in the strategy of buying straw hats in winter, now (or next spring) is the time to be planting new vineyards, with a 50/50 or 60/40 split between white (primarily chardonnay) and red (shiraz, cabernet sauvignon and merlot) grapes. You should also be looking to plant in a cool rather than warm climate.

But if one of Australia's largest winemakers has bulk wine from the 2002 vintage held in all manner of emergency storage, from shipping containers to beer tanks (the company is not Beringer Blass, incidentally) to custom crush facilities; if grape prices have fallen over each of the past two years, and will fall again next vintage; and if all the projections point to a continuation of the oversupply of grapes in 2003 and 2004, why should anyone in their right mind be planting new vineyards now?

The answers were provided at the Wine Outlook Conference.

On the supply side, the key paper was prepared by Lawrie Stanford, the Australian Wine and Brandy Corporation's chief analyst. As a preamble, he pointed to the lag time of three to five years between planting and the resulting wine coming onto the market.

Next, there has been a dramatic decrease in new plantings, magnified by the accelerated removal of existing vines producing lesser, unwanted varieties: from a high of 14,000 net hectares (net being the difference between new plantings minus removals in a given period) planted in 1998 (16 per cent of bearing hectares at that time) to 1000 net hectares in 2001 (less than 1 per cent of bearing hectares).

The 2002 vintage was a strange one: yields were very low in cool-climate regions, but well above average in the warm engine rooms of Sunraysia, the Riverland and the Riverina. Overall, yields were up — the national harvest of 1.59 million tonnes was up 11 per cent over 2001.

If yields return to normal levels in 2003, the crush will show little or no change from 2002. But the El Niño-driven drought, and the probability of it continuing through to vintage, suggests that yields may be below normal. Moreover, the cool overcast conditions of December 2001 seem to have affected bunch size, if not bunch numbers.

While it may be said that the cure is worse than the illness, a somewhat reduced crush (in the region of 6–10 per cent) in 2003 would help the depletion of the national wine stock, which is at an all-time high. 2004 will see a continuation of the oversupply of red wine (even today there is a shortage rather than an oversupply, of chardonnay) but by 2005 demand and supply will come back into balance, and by 2006 supply will be insufficient to meet demand unless a lot of straw-hat buyers emerge next spring.

NOVEMBER 5   YARRA VALLEY: WILDLIFE

The rain continues to be conspicuous by its absence and we still have had little or no run-off into our dams. All the long-range forecasts point to a continuation of the drought. Incredibly, or perhaps typically, the valley is still green, although it is skin deep.

One of our resident echidnas returns today. It stands on its hind legs, resting its paws on the edge of the bird bath in the fern garden, its long, beak-like snout near the water as it has a long drink. Standing up this way, it is between 40 and 50 cm in height — so different from how we normally see it, wobbling along the ground, snuffling at the undergrowth and turning itself into a tight little ball whenever alarmed. Birdlife around the house has increased quite dramatically; barely a week goes by without the sound of a new and unidentified bird.

One with which we are very familiar, although the flock of four or six seldom stays long, is the huge black cockatoo known as a gang gang. Like the white sulphur-crested cockatoo, these are extremely destructive, their powerful beaks scything through young branches, seemingly just to show off. Their food source is the gumnuts on certain gum trees, and they keep up a constant low-pitched, almost growling chatter as they feed. Their flight pattern as they depart is

ABOVE
Poplars have long been planted as windbreaks in Coonawarra.

unique: they flap their wings far more slowly and in a metronomically regular beat than any other bird as they commence their flight, and keep up the same beat until they reach their next destination. Gliding, however, is not part of the flight repertoire; they would simply drop out of the sky.

NOVEMBER 6   QANTAS WESTERN AUSTRALIAN WINE SHOW DINNER, PERTH

I am returning to Perth to speak at two events covering the top 50 wines from the Qantas Western Australian Wine Show. The first event is a tasting of the top 50 wines, running throughout the late afternoon and early evening; the second is a dinner featuring the gold medal winners. It is part of the job of the chairman of the Show, although I can ill afford the time.

NOVEMBER 7   MELBOURNE: ST VINCENTS INSTITUTE OF MEDICAL RESEARCH

Tonight I am the guest speaker at a dinner held in the Melbourne Casino complex by the St Vincents Institute of Medical Research, known as a 'Hero's Dinner'. The idea is to have speakers from various fields of activity who are well known, and who talk about their role in their field and how they came to be there. It is a fundraising dinner, albeit in a somewhat indirect fashion. The Institute is heavily dependent on private funding, and this is one means to both publicise the work it is carrying out and, through that publicity, attract donations. It has a worldwide reputation for its research, but there is an ever-pressing need for funding.

NOVEMBER 8 YARRA VALLEY: HOSTING HARVEY STEIMAN

Harvey Steiman, editor at large for *The Wine Spectator*, is nearing the end of a two-week trip around Australia, and joins Suzanne and me at home for an informal dinner and tasting of the Coldstream Hills current release wines. Harvey Steiman knows Australia and Australian wines very well, and also has a profound knowledge of fine food, and his in-depth articles on Australia in *The Wine Spectator* are very important to the industry. Less well known is his considerable knowledge of classical music.

He is far from the typical American, and over the years he has won the respect of many people in the Australian wine industry, myself included.

LEFT

My office from the outside; when I'm not on a plane, it's home base.

NOVEMBER 10–14 V<small>INTAGE</small> C<small>ELLARS</small> N<small>ATIONAL</small> W<small>INE</small> S<small>HOW</small>, C<small>ANBERRA</small>

I arrive in Canberra in the early evening to find that Qantas has failed to load my Styropak of wines for the judges' dinner during the Show. They are two bottles of 1989 Clos Pignan (1989 is the year chosen as the theme by the chairman of judges, Tim James) and a bottle of 1949 Moulin Touchais. I have signed a breakage disclaimer, but am left to wonder what attitude Qantas will take if the wine 'disappears'. Luckily, it is found and arrives on the next flight, so all is well.

In the meantime I have dinner with one of the two overseas judges, Darrell Corti, of Sacramento, California, who has been a close friend since the late 1980s, when he bobbed up as an American judge at the second (and last) Qantas Cup Challenge between Australia and the United States. Immensely erudite and with a fabulous knowledge of the wines of the world, including a special fascination for Madeira, he quickly became a close friend of Len Evans, Ian MacKenzie and myself (the Australian judges at the Cup).

Since that time he has judged on a number of occasions at the National Wine Show, and at other capital city shows in Australia. But it is fair to say that he enjoys the National Wine Show most, and equally fair to say that the other Australian judges who have known him from prior events are of the same view.

He runs a family business (started by his parents many years ago) which is very like that once run by Melbourne wine identity Doug Crittenden. Both businesses have (or had) a strong high-end grocery component, but an even more important fine wine division. In Australia, at least, the technical term is 'licensed grocer', so both Darrell and Doug laughingly refer to themselves as grocers.

Tim Atkin, of the United Kingdom, is the other overseas judge, and another person very well known and much respected by Australians. He caused a major stir earlier in the year by criticising Australian wine and suggesting that at least some of the largest producers had taken their eye off the ball; that Australian wines no longer represented the outstanding value they once did; and that the industry needed to get its act together. His comments (he is the editor of *Harpers* magazine) came as a complete surprise, simply because he has been such a staunch supporter of Australian wine over the years. The element of surprise doubtless led to an overreaction, but both sides are now relaxed.

The Show itself is without the least shadow of doubt the best run and most enjoyable of its kind in the country. The week is made even more memorable by two utterly exceptional meals held at a relatively new restaurant, Anise, situated in the West Row, Melbourne Building, Canberra City, telephone 02 6257 0700, fax 02 6257 9854. Justin (spelt without an 'e', which is confusing) and her partner Jeff were together at several restaurants in Canberra before establishing their own place, but seem to have risen to another level at Anise. Not only is it the best restaurant in Canberra; it is one of the best in Australia.

The judges' dinner commences with a magnum of 1989 Krug, which requires no particular food match, although the hors d'oeuvres are delicious. The first bracket of five off-dry rieslings from Alsace and Germany is a different proposition; Jeff presents seared Atlantic salmon fillet with Siamese watercress and tamarind dressing. The magic lies not in the salmon (perfectly cooked though it is) but in the tamarind dressing, which gives an extremely complex semi-sweet flavour which precisely matches that of the wines, tying in the salmon.

Rillettes of rabbit with pickled dwarf peaches follows, with full-bodied white wines and a couple of pinot noirs; then roasted rack of milk-fed lamb served with a Persian fetta and olive tart comes with the many red wines.

The sauternes come with caramelised apple tartlet and vanilla bean ice-cream, which may sound run of the mill but in reality is another triumph.

After the conclusion of the trophy judging on Thursday morning, we all decide to return to Anise for a farewell lunch before departing to the four corners of the globe.

NOVEMBER 17–22   LEN EVANS TUTORIALS, HUNTER VALLEY

I am on my way to the Hunter Valley, having flown down from Ballina earlier in the day; the night previously my son Angus married his partner of many years, Michelle, at Byron Bay on the north coast of New South Wales. I am filled with pride, remembering how Angus spoke — so movingly and with such radiant happiness.

My arrival at Loggerheads, the extraordinary house Len and Trish Evans have built in the Hunter Valley, gives me an added measure of happiness. Len Evans, awarded an OBE and an OA for his lifetime of service to the wine industry, has been very ill with severe cardiac problems over the past days, weeks and months, although the history goes right back to bypass surgery decades ago. I had feared he would be unable to run the week-long tutorials, but he in fact looks much better than he did when I last saw him.

The twelve students, selected from well over a hundred applicants, arrive during the morning and we all meet at lunchtime. Some are winemakers, some work in the retail/wholesale wine trade, and some are sommeliers. Each has been selected on the basis that he or she has the potential to become a first-class wine judge in the

BELOW
One of the courtyard wings at Loggerheads, Len and Trish Evans's cleverly named house.

context of the Australian wine show system. The winner gets a trip to Europe with all-important letters of introduction from Len Evans and the various sponsors of the Tutorials, ten in all, who have each contributed $5000 towards the cost.

The contestants are Paul Bowyer, Aaron Brasher, Tom Carson, James Chatto, Samantha Connew, Cameron Douglas, Sally Harper, Melissa Moore, Phillip Rich, Edward Tomlinson, Matt Wenk and Martin Williams. After lunch at The Lodge, the luxury establishment owned by a consortium of business people headed by Len Evans, we move to Rothbury for a three-hour blind tasting of chardonnays, with over half the total time allotted to discussion of the wines, the session running from 2 p.m. to 5 p.m. The thirty chardonnays come from Australia, France, New Zealand and California, the youngest from 2001, the oldest from 1995, and are arranged in random order.

Australian classics include 1995 Leeuwin Estate, 1999 Yattarna, 2000 Giaconda, 2000 Petaluma Tiers, 2000 Tyrrell's Vat 47 and 1995 Lakes Folly, while the French burgundies include 1999 Chevalier-Montrachet, 2000 Criots-Bâtard-Montrachet and 1998 Bâtard-Montrachet.

It is a very challenging tasting, even for the judges, who are Len Evans, Ian McKenzie, Iain Riggs and myself (with Brian Croser arriving tomorrow). It is further complicated by one wine being

ABOVE LEFT
The courtyard tile patterns were all created and laid by the Evanses' friends.

ABOVE
Len Evans AO, OBE; father of the Australian wine industry.

slightly corked, another badly corked. Some of the students are thoroughly confused by the diversity of the tasting, but some come through with flying colours.

Dinner this evening is at The Lodge, with the menu specially designed to accompany the various blind tasting exercises and Options games. The Options game, devised forty years ago by Len Evans, allows for five questions to be asked about an unknown wine, each question having three possible answers, one of which must be correct (in the case of Bordeaux, the options can extend to four on certain questions).

To say the exercises are not easy is to put it mildly. The first exercise turns on five white burgundies; we are told that each comes from a different region or commune in Burgundy, and that the wines come from consecutive vintages. The exercise is to identify the commune and vintage for each wine. They turn out to be (in order of presentation): 1998 Corton-Charlemagne Bonneau du Martray, 1997 Meursault Poruzots, 1996 Macon, 1995 Puligny-Montrachet les Folatières and 1999 Chassagne-Montrachet les Chenevottes.

The next exercise is to identify five wines which all come from the same country, the same area and the same winemaker, and, having done that, to identify the vintages. An easier task than the first, but by no means simple. The wines are revealed to be 1999, '97, '95, '91 and '90 Jaboulet La Chapelle, from the Rhône Valley.

The third exercise has four regional wines of one vintage; the students have to identify the vintage, then the region and the producer (or château) for each. Here the wines are 1978 Bordeauxs from Château la Mission Haut Brion, Château Pichon Lalande, Château Lafleur and Château Ausone.

The exercises run through the entrée and main course, and we now move to the Options wines. The first wine is ultimately revealed to be 1998 Jaboulet La Chapelle; the second an exceedingly rare 1989 Grapillons de Latour, made from the second harvest in that extraordinary vintage, the second harvest being of the little green bunches which would normally be left on the vine, but which ripened because of the warm dry conditions. Since very few people in the world are even aware of the existence of the wine (it has never been sold commercially, and was never made before 1989), correct answers are as much a matter of luck as anything else. The final wine is 1974 Simi Cabernet Sauvignon from the Alexander Valley in the United States, surprisingly youthful and sweet.

The meal concludes with a bracket of three varieties of Madeira; we have to specify the styles and the approximate ages. They turn out to be 1898 Sercial, 1934 Malmsey and 1898 Verdelho.

NOVEMBER 19

Today we begin the full-day format which will also apply over the next two days, with a varietal judging tasting in the morning, two Masterclasses in the afternoon and an exercise and Options dinner in the evening. An enormous amount of ground is covered in the process.

We open with the judging and discussion of thirty shiraz wines from around the world, with a number of Northern Rhône Valley wines (including 1995 Guigal Côte-Rotie Brune et Blonde, the special syrah cuvée of '97 Château Fonsalette, '91 Chapoutier Le Sizeranne and the top of the range '98 Delas Côte-Rotie Seigneur Maugiron), plus wines from Italy, Chile, California and, of course, Australia. Here the big names are 1996 Grange, '93 Brokenwood Graveyard, '93 Henschke Hill of Grace, 2000 Torbreck The Factor, 1990 Wynns Coonawarra Michael, '98 Clonakilla Shiraz Viognier and 2001 Jasper Hill Georgia's Paddock. Throwing in the two Tuscan wines (Fontodi and Isole e Olena), the variation in weight, ripeness, oak and style vary enormously. The Grange receives unanimous gold medals from the judges and strong support from the students, the Chapoutier receives unanimous gold medals from the judges, and the Brokenwood Graveyard receives gold medals from the students and judges alike.

After lunch David Ridge presents a Barolo Masterclass, with wines from each of the five most important communes — La Morra, Barolo, Castiglione Falletto, Monforte d'Alba and Serralunga. The wines all come from top producers, the majority from the outstanding 1997 and 1998 vintages, but including other classic

ABOVE
The kangaroos appear on cue every afternoon on the paddock in front of Loggerheads for the numerous international visitors.

vintages, such as 1990 and 1996. The differing characters from the communes come through very strongly, but so do the varying approaches of the traditional makers and the modernists. It is one of the most interesting tastings I have been to in years, in no small measure due to my (relative) ignorance of Barolo.

The last Masterclass of the day is presented by Ian McKenzie, with ten of the greatest of all champagnes: 1995 Taittinger Comtes de Champagne Blanc de Blancs, '90 Billecart-Salmon Grand Cuvée Brut, '93 Dom Perignon, '89 Pommery Louise, '96 Perrier-Jouet La Belle Epoque, '93 Pol Roger Sir Winston Churchill, '95 Veuve Clicquot La Grande Dame, '96 Roederer Cristal, '95 Bollinger Grand Année and '88 Krug Vintage. The wines are diligently tasted by judges and students alike, but there is not too much spitting evident.

The dinner this evening has the same devilish mix of wines and exercises as last night, the link being their extremely high quality.

NOVEMBER 20

The three-hour morning session on our third morning is a judging of thirty cabernet sauvignons and cabernet blends. Once again it is an eclectic selection, roaming through California, Chile, Italy, New Zealand (Waiheke Island and Hawke's Bay), Bordeaux and Australia. The wines range from French classics such as 1979 Château Mouton Rothschild, '83 Château Latour and '95 Château Ducru Beaucaillou to a rare 1966 Inglenook Cabernet Sauvignon, a '95 Opus One and a '97 Spottswoode, all from the Napa Valley.

The Australians include Wynns John Riddoch, Howard Park, Wendouree, Petaluma, Cullen, Coldstream Hills (which I don't recognise but which receives top marks from the students — perhaps they do) and the Jimmy Watson Trophy-winning 1998 Blass Black Label (unfortunately, a flawed bottle due to cork problems).

After lunch Brian Croser presents an extremely interesting Riesling Masterclass. The wines are 2002 Grosset Polish Hill, '02 Petaluma Hanlin Hill, 1998 Orlando Steingarten, '99 Domaine Weinbach Cuvée St Catherine Grand Cru Schlossberg, '97 Josmeyer Grand Cru Hengst, '96 Marcel Deiss Grand Cru de Altenberg, '91 Trimbach Clos St Hune, '99 JJ Prum Graacher Himmelreich Kabinett, 2001 Egon Muller Scharzhofberger Kabinett, '01 Dr Loosen Wehlener Sonnenuhr Kabinett and 1989 Argyle (from Oregon).

Croser makes the point that riesling does have a credible claim to be the most noble grape variety of all, if only because it requires the least winemaking expertise to express its varietal character and place of origin. It succeeds only in continental climates, in which the cold nights towards the end of the summer/early autumn cause the vine to respond by ripening the seeds in the grapes notwithstanding relatively low sugar levels. It is for this reason that some of the great German rieslings (particularly from the Mosel Valley) have alcohol levels below 10°. Somewhat controversially, he is also of the view that a certain amount of botrytis in dry rieslings enhances varietal character, rather than modifying it.

At 3.30 p.m. we start what is certain to be the most overwhelming of all of the Masterclasses, with Gary Steel presenting a scintillating array of white burgundies from the great 2000 white wine vintage and red burgundies from the equally great red wine 1999 vintage. For good measure, seven of the nine white burgundies are Grand Crus, and five of the ten red burgundies are Grand Crus.

The white burgundies are Laroche Chablis Les Clos, la Vougeraie Vougeot Clos Blanc de Vougeot, la Vougeraie Corton-Charlemagne, Bouchard Père et Fils Meursault-Perrières, Louis Carillon Bienvenues-Bâtard-Montrachet, Blain-Gagnard Criots-Bâtard-Montrachet, Blain-Gagnard Bâtard-Montrachet, Bouchard Père et Fils Chevalier-Montrachet and Bouchard Père et Fils Montrachet.

The red burgundies are Matrot Volnay-Santenots, Comte Armand Pommard Clos des Epeneaux, Bouchard Père et Fils Beaune-Greves, Bouchard Père et Fils Le Corton, Henri Gouges Nuits-St-Georges Les Pruliers, Bouchard Père et Fils Richebourg, Mongeard-Mugneret Clos de Vougeot, Comte de Vogüe Musigny Vieilles Vignes, la Vougeraie Bonnes-Mares and Armand Rousseau Le Chambertin.

And so to dinner, and yet more tantalising wines and devilish questions.

NOVEMBER 21

This morning's judging is of thirty pinot noirs, from Burgundy, Australia, Oregon and New Zealand. The vintages span 1994–2001 and once again include many of the icon wines from the New World, as well as Grand Crus (and others) from Burgundy. The five most highly rated wines (by the judges) are the 1998 Rousseau Le Chambertin, a whisker in front of the 1994 Bannockburn Serre, intense, long and multi-dimensional; then a surprise packet in the form of the 1997 Domaine Dujac Charmes Chambertin, fine, silky and savoury, with excellent mouthfeel and length; the 2001 Ata Rangi (with some dissension on my part because of its massive size and extract); 1998 Gibbston Valley Reserve, rich and complex, big in the mouth, with layered flavours; and 2000 Bass Phillip Reserve, powerfully fragrant, with the oaky/stalky aromas more than balanced by the intense and lingering palate.

I present the first Masterclass in the afternoon, this time on Bordeaux. The wines, all from the 1999 vintage, are Château Trotanoy, Château Cheval Blanc, Château Cos d'Estournel, Château Latour, Château Leoville Las Cases, Château Margaux and Château Haut Brion.

I approach the wines from a number of different perspectives: historical, geological, viticultural, right bank/left bank, investment, winemaking, vintage, the influence of American wine critic Robert Parker, and then finally the sensory perspective as we taste the wines. My aim is to put the wines into a broad context of time and place.

The second Masterclass of the afternoon is on sweet white wines and is presented by Iain Riggs. Here the wines are again incredibly varied. They are 1970 Marc Bredif Vouvray Demi-Sec, '93 Diznoko Tokaji Aszu 5 Puttonyos, '88 Château Coutet Barsac, '76 Château d'Yquem, '00 De Bortoli Noble One, '97 Hugel Gewürztraminer SGN, '96 Egon Müller Scharzhofberger Spätlese, '97 JJ Prum Wehlener Sonnenuhr Auslese, '89 JL Wolf Burklin Rupp Beerenauslese and '99 Gunderloch Nackenheim Rothenberg Trockenbeerenauslese.

Both this afternoon's Masterclasses and this evening's dinner are being conducted in the absence of Len Evans. He has double-booked himself for the tutorials, having forgotten that he is also meant to be Master of Ceremonies at the black-tie dinner in the Great Hall of Parliament following last week's Vintage Cellars' National Wine Show. No amount of talking can persuade him to change his mind, and the only way he can be back for the Friday morning combined Masterclass and exercise is to be driven from the Hunter Valley to Canberra and back, a five-hour trip each way. This will get him back into the Hunter at 3 a.m. on Friday morning after presiding at the dinner. It's hardly the type of engagement someone in the best of health would contemplate, let alone someone with the cardiac and other related problems Len is facing.

I am standing in as chairman of the dinner, finding myself in the enjoyable position of not having to worry about the exercises or Options wines.

NOVEMBER 22

Somehow or other Len Evans makes it back home, and after a slightly delayed start we embark on the centrepiece of the four days: a Domaine de la Romanée-Conti (DRC for short) Masterclass presented by Len Evans. It has six Grand Cru vineyards, two of them monopoles or exclusivities: La Tâche and Romanée-Conti. Evans discusses the characteristics of each of the vineyards, putting them into two groups: on the feminine side, Romanée-St Vivant, Grands Echézeaux and Echézeaux, and, on the masculine side, Romanée-Conti, Richebourg and La Tâche. It is a division he made many years ago (and he would fry in hell before conceding that there was or is any element of political incorrectness in it) and is one which DRC co-owner Aubert de Villaine agrees with, with one major exception: in some vintages he believes La Tâche should be grouped on the feminine side, and Grands Echézeaux on the masculine side.

The first part of the exercise is to identify the six vineyards; once their identity is known, the task is to assign the vintages. Not knowing the vintage makes the vineyard exercise exceptionally difficult, and I am not too sure that knowledge of the vineyard helps overmuch in identifying the vintages. Nonetheless, the overall winner (or dux) of the week, Tom Carson of Yering Station, gets eight out of twelve correct, more than anyone else. (In fact, the marks for this exercise were only a small fraction of the total assessment.)

Five of the students come within a hair's breadth of each other: they are Aaron Brasher, Tom Carson, James Chatto, Phillip Rich and Martin Williams. It is the old story: how do you in all conscience say that one, rather than the others, deserves the trip to France? There is no easy answer to that, but it's also true that none of the students will ever again taste so many great wines in the space of a week, no matter how long they live or where they work. It is perhaps for this reason that there is no shortage of judges willing to pay their own way to the event, donate their time and (in some instances) either donate outright some of the wines, or make them available at far less than their true value. I, for one, shall return for as long as I am asked.

NOVEMBER 25   YARRA VALLEY: MORE WINE TASTING

I am spending the day tasting 190 wines which have stacked up since the end of the Top 100 tastings, with the knowledge that there is about the same number again which I will have to tackle in the next two weeks. And just around the corner is the major deluge of wines which will arrive in January and February for the *2004 Wine Companion*.

NOVEMBER 26 YARRA VALLEY: 2002 PINOT NOIR

Today Andrew Fleming and I have a near-to-final look at the component parts of the varietal pinot noir from 2002. Only one component remains in question now; indeed, it comes down to the issue of how much of this component should be included in the final blend of a dozen different wines. As we do the tasting, the 2002 varietal chardonnay is on its way to Seppelt Great Western for bottling, the blend having been previously decided, with a make of around 11,000 cases, compared with 18,000 cases of pinot noir.

As well as deciding the components for the pinot noir, the annual logistical battle looms as we endeavour to filter the wine. For reasons which are far from clear, the light-bodied, low-tannin pinot noir is acknowledged by all and sundry as by far the most difficult of all red wines to filter. If we were sufficiently certain that the bacteriological background of the wine (and, in particular, brettanomyces) was safe, we might be tempted to bypass filtration altogether. However, in that case, we would need to fairly heavily fine the wine with egg whites (which bind with microscopic suspended sediments, causing them to precipitate to the bottom of the vessel) to reach acceptable clarity, and prior experience tells us this has a far more drastic effect on the flavour of the wine than filtration does.

NOVEMBER 27 NEGOCIANTS FELLOWSHIP, SYDNEY

I am in Sydney for the day and night to chair the judging of the Negociants Working With Wine Fellowship finalists, who come from all around Australia. Negociants is the export/import arm of Yalumba, and this is the fifth year it has run the Fellowship course. Three hundred people applied, and over one hundred attended the tastings/masterclasses that were held around Australia, with the assistance of some of Negociants' overseas suppliers. This year Egon

Müller (of the famous Scharzhofberger winery in Mosel-Saar-Ruwer) and Etienne Hugel (of Hugel et Fils in Alsace) came to Australia to conduct Riesling Masterclasses. Those attending the classes are Negociants' employees on the one hand and members of the broader wine trade on the other, the latter not being Negociants' employees; and the eleven finalists come from both groups.

My fellow judges are fine food purveyor Simon Johnson, Sally Evans (then of Winepros), Greg Trott (of Wirra Wirra) and David Lemire (of Yalumba). It's never an easy task, but in the end Adam O'Neill of Brisbane is the Negociants winner and Langdon Farrelly of Perth is the wine trade winner. Both will head off to Europe to visit all of Negociants' winery principals in Italy, Germany and France. These wineries are all highly distinguished, and offer the degree of hospitality reserved for their most important clients.

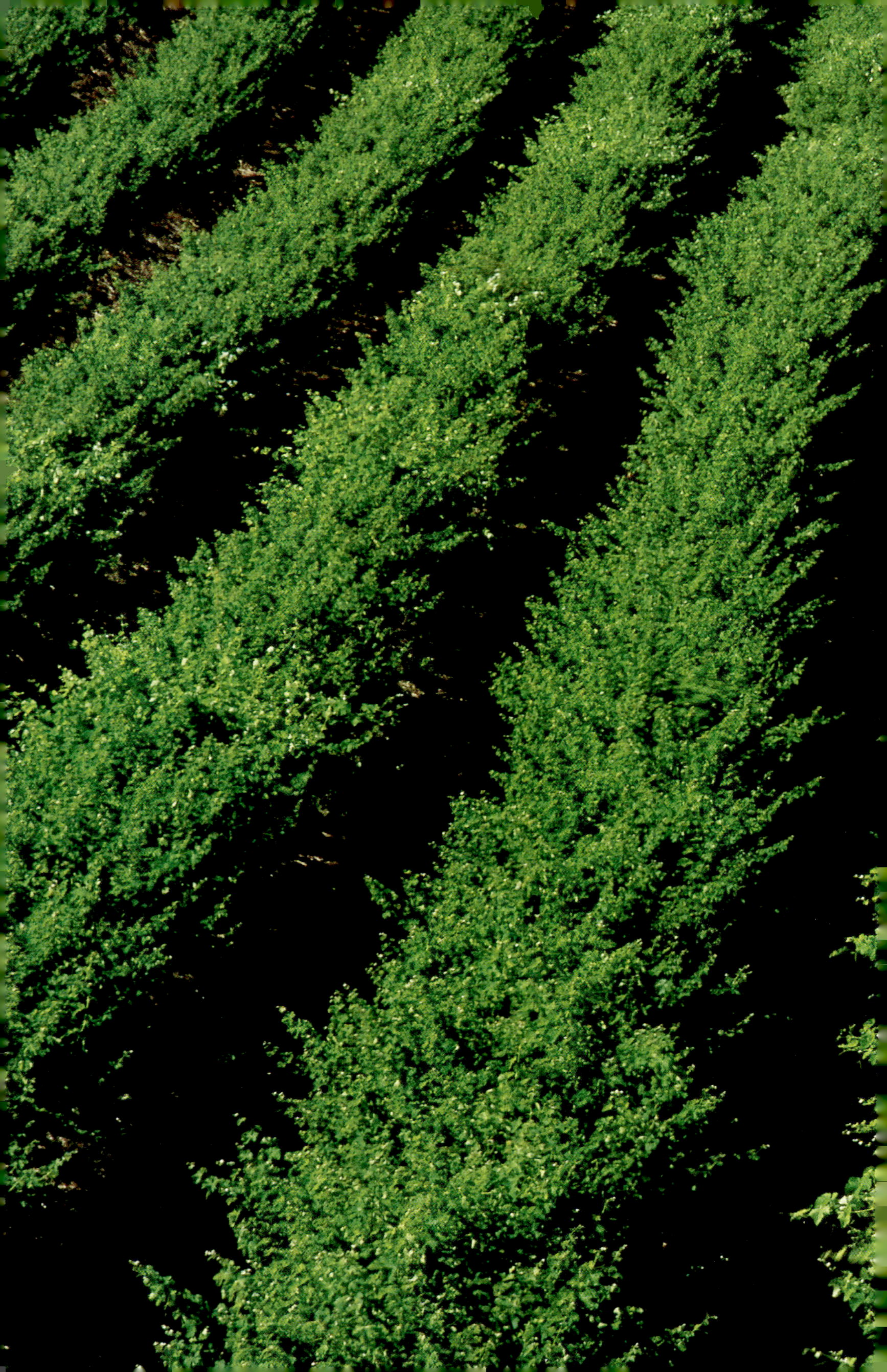

December

Playing Host, Yarra Valley

Launch of *Liquid Gold*

Tasting, Yarra Valley

Fire and Drought

Kangaroos

Sirromet, Gold Coast, Queensland

Albert River Winery

Sirromet Holden Racetrack

Seven Scenes Vineyard, Granite Belt

Ballandean Estate

Robert Channon Wines

Yarra Valley: The Drought Bites

Christmas Day

Yarra Valley: The Holiday Period

Year's End

DECEMBER 2–3   PLAYING HOST, YARRA VALLEY

Michael and Janice Fridjhon, with their seven-month-old son, are spending two days with us. Michael Fridjhon is one of the leading figures in South African wine, and he and Janice are old friends. It is a good excuse to drink some fine wine and generally lounge about for two days.

DECEMBER 8   LAUNCH OF *LIQUID GOLD*

The Victorian launch of Nicholas Faith's *Liquid Gold*, subtitled 'The Story of Australian Wine and Its Makers', is held at Domaine Chandon. Faith is a journalist whose career has covered both finance and wine, and, for good measure, both print media and television. His all-time classic wine book to date is *The Wine Masters*, a history of the Bordeaux wine industry triggered by the scandal in the mid-1970s leading to the suicide of one of the Cruse family. Written in a thoroughly user-friendly, rollicking style, *Liquid Gold* makes compulsive reading, and is particularly interesting in its coverage of recent as well as ancient history.

DECEMBER 10   TASTING, YARRA VALLEY

Another 160 wines to taste, including wines from a number of new wineries. The pace is showing no sign of slackening, and it seems likely that the *2004 Wine Companion* will break last year's record of 183 new wineries.

DECEMBER 12   FIRE AND DROUGHT

We have had only one or two days of really hot weather so far; the heat accumulation to now is far less than it was in either 2000 or 2001. While we have not had more than token run-off into the dams, we have had two periods of rain over the past two weeks which have replenished surface soil moisture. Contrast this with the fires surrounding Sydney, cutting the freeway to the Hunter Valley, and threatening houses and vineyards in the area. And this is only December, with the hottest months (January and February) still to come.

DECEMBER 14   KANGAROOS

Our resident band of kangaroos especially enjoys weekends, because there is usually no tractor traffic. They can absolutely be relied on to appear out of the forest in the hills immediately behind the house at 5.45 p.m.

The dominant male comes first, to check that all is in order, then the mothers with young in pouch or at heel come with some of the others of unknown sex (I suspect these are principally female). They are only interested in the grass, and have no designs whatsoever on the vines. This seems to be simply an issue of food availability; at Taltarni, for example, kangaroos caused total havoc when the vineyard was being established in the 1970s, forcing the erection of a massive perimeter fence. Grass on the other side of the Great Dividing Range is far less dependable than it is here. The kangaroos spend the night grazing, returning to the forest early the following morning, sometimes hastened by the arrival of the vineyard workers.

The other night, driving up to the house, I came across what can only be described as a kangaroo child bride, a small female with her first offspring by her side, no higher than my knee. Normally, the offspring would jump back into the mother's pouch, but (without undue haste) she decided to move off the road and down a steep bank to the start of the vines. The adolescent followed somewhat unsteadily in her tracks, but once rejoined both were quite happy to start grazing as if they were quite alone.

For me the weekends are precious, particularly when (as now) I am working on three books, with a fourth due to start sometime early in the new year, and my annual commitment to update the Australian section of Hugh Johnson's *Pocket Wine Book* to be done over the Christmas/New Year period. The slowing of the pace of activity in December is superficial.

RIGHT
Kangaroos immediately outside our house.

DECEMBER 16   TASTING, YARRA VALLEY

Yet another tasting and even more new wineries than in the last tasting. The mountain of tasting notes which I have to transcribe is growing remorselessly.

DECEMBER 18   SIRROMET, GOLD COAST, QUEENSLAND

No, I'm not here on holidays; quite apart from anything else, this is the rainy season (drought permitting). But I do feel like a Surfers Paradise Old Boy as we drive from Coolangatta airport through Surfers Paradise to Conrad Jupiters, where I am staying. Over thirty years ago a client (and friend) became quite heavily involved in real estate in Surfers Paradise. He had the vision, but like others before and since, turned buying at the top of the market and selling at the bottom into an art form. If only …

I am in fact here at the behest of Sirromet, by far the largest and most serious winery in Queensland. It is owned by the Morris family, with father Terry and mother Lurleen at the head.

While it is strategically placed on the Gold Coast Hinterland, and has some vines surrounding it, its 1000-tonne crush (plus or minus this year depending on the final vagaries of the drought) will come predominantly from the Granite Belt, where Sirromet has 56 hectares of estate vineyards, and to a lesser degree from the South Burnett Valley.

Terry Morris has not become one of Queensland's more wealthy men by accident; his business acumen shows through in his choice of Adam Chapman as winemaker. Adam was one of Australia's early Flying Winemakers, making wine all over France, but has also spent seven years making wine in the Granite Belt region at Ballandean Estate. However, it has to be said that Chapman has also found the ideal employer: someone with a very large chequebook, who has absolutely no desire to become involved in the technicalities of winemaking, but who is busy counting the bales of hay harvested that day on some of the land surrounding the winery as we come in to land by Sirromet helicopter.

As a winery presently capable of crushing 1500 tonnes (100,000 cases or so) Sirromet is impressive enough, but it has been built so that the crush can extend to 5000 tonnes without undue difficulty. The technical aspects of the design, not to mention the state-of-the-art equipment, are as good as anything one might find in the most trendy or important wine regions of Australia.

We have lunch at the Sirromet restaurant, which is almost as surprising as the winery itself. One would expect to find a menu such

LEFT

Peter Mitchell acts as my steward, organising the wine tastings for the 2003 Wine Companion.

as the one we have today in a smart Sydney or Melbourne brasserie restaurant, not in the country. I chose ravioli with grilled calf's sweetbreads in a saffron and Malaysian curry broth, and have every reason to be pleased with my choice. When I meet the executive chef, Erik van Alphen, I ask him whether the menu goes a little over the top and whether dishes such as the one I chose are ignored. The answer on both scores is no.

The winery and restaurant complex is sufficiently large for us to require a golf buggy for our circumnavigations, which we do before embarking on a barrel tasting of wines from the 2002 vintage. We are joined by Alain Rousseau, a French winemaker who worked for a number of years as chief winemaker at Moorilla Estate in Tasmania; I am dying to ask him why he came from one of the coolest parts of Australia to one of the warmest. I ask, and the answer is the challenge it provided. Be that as it may, and acknowledging that the Sirromet wines cover three price points, $15, $20 and over $20, I am impressed — to put it mildly — by the seriousness with which the making of the top end wines is being approached.

DECEMBER 19   ALBERT RIVER WINERY

Another helicopter ride, this time over Tamborine Mountain to Albert River Winery, the creation of David and Jeanette Bladin. While the winery is only forty-five minutes' drive from the coast, the climate here is substantially modified by Mount Tamborine and the associated ranges, with a lowering of the rainfall and some definite moderation in temperature, coupled with breezes which start to blow every day from around 11.30 a.m. Thus the variety predominantly planted around the Auchenflower House, which is the nerve centre of the operation, is shiraz, which is not picked until the end of March. The vineyard shows absolutely no sign of disease, and it is intended that more and more of the grapes used will be estate-grown. At the moment a significant portion comes from the 40-hectare Inglewood Vineyard, situated further inland, south of the Granite Belt.

The story of Tamborine House (in which the Bladins live) is extraordinary enough: it was the house and the property which gave rise to the name 'Mount Tamborine', not vice versa. But all this fades into insignificance against the achievement of rescuing Auchenflower House from being sold for scrap timber. This involved cutting it down, in a specialised operation, into pieces which were transportable, organising the four semitrailers with special load dispensation to move the pieces, and then painstakingly re-erecting this vast house — which was home to three Queensland premiers in the nineteenth and early twentieth centuries — in its original location in Brisbane. It had in fact been moved from its original site in 1970, and it was for this reason that the National Trust had no interest in preventing its demolition, but equally had no objection to the Bladins buying the house. They prefer not to talk about the total cost, but they do say that the house was bought for $20,000, and the pieces moved at a cost of $60,000 before the real job of re-erection began.

The Bladins encountered labyrinthine rules, regulations and permit requirements, finding out in many instances only at the last moment that they weren't allowed to do this or that. However, the restoration, costing many, many times the initial outlay, has been superbly done. As you look at the vast room which used to be the ballroom, and now has within it the main tasting area, the second-largest collection of corkscrews in the world and other such things, it is impossible to see where and how the building was cut down and then re-erected.

DECEMBER 19   SIRROMET HOLDEN RACETRACK

I am here to be taken onto the racetrack by Paul Morris, who drives the Sirromet Holden V8 Supercar in race meetings around Australia. This is quite apart from seeing the three hangars of veteran cars, covering Holdens from the first made to the present time, Holden racing cars from the beginning to the present time, and a magnificent collection of vintage racing cars of all types, including Bugattis. The fourth hangar is given over to the building of the race cars which will be used in 2004. All that General Motors provides are the sub-frame, the engine block (a special Chevrolet engine block from the United States) and the door panels (which are stripped of

ABOVE
Sirromet Winery's striking architecture.

everything except the outer shell). The car is then built piece by piece with hand-crafted parts — the finished car has nothing whatsoever to do with any Holden car to be found on the road.

As I prepare for the drive, it becomes clear that there is no way I am going to fit in the fireproof racing suit: both its girth and its length are too small. The next problem is the helmet. The first two helmets tried don't even get halfway on — one gouges bits of skin out of my forehead as I try to force it down, before realising that to do so I will have to disassemble my ears. After a protracted search, an AMG helmet is found, which does the job perfectly. However, then comes the most difficult task of all: getting into the car. After minutes of struggle I am literally fed in feet first through the side reinforcing struts, supported by various onlookers, only to find that there is no way my helmeted head is going to get under the roll bars. The helmet is removed and, with more pushing and shoving as if I am a recalcitrant racehorse at the gates, I am finally in the car.

There is no possibility of the helmet going back on, because there is only 5 cm between the top of my head and various of the roll bars and cross-support tubing which turn the driving area into a crash-proof cube. The solution lies with the multi-pointed safety harness, tightened to the point where I suspect all circulation is likely to stop if I move against it. My only thought throughout this whole process is how lucky I am that no one nearby has a video camera — my getting into the car would make the top of the charts for 'Australia's Funniest Home Video Show'.

With an explosive roar we are off, driving at death-defying speeds, alternately fiercely accelerating and then even more fiercely braking, the noise indescribable even through ear plugs. I have seen it often enough on television through race cams, but you have no idea of the brute force and lightning speed of gear changes, braking, and so forth until you're in the car. As I get out, someone asks me what it was like; my answer is, 'Like a big dipper thrill ride taking place on a flat surface.'

This evening we are having dinner at Terry Morris's house, which has a water frontage to the Nerang River. Part of the dinner is two mud crabs which were caught in pots laid directly in front of the house. The whole extended Morris family live in houses more or less adjacent, within a very large area that is entered by a common security gate, and over dinner I learn much from Paul Morris about the way the races between Holden and Ford are conducted.

DECEMBER 20   SEVEN SCENES VINEYARD, GRANITE BELT

After last-minute weather checks the night before to decide whether we are going to the Granite Belt by helicopter as planned (45–60

LEFT

Some of the stones at Sirromet's Seven Scenes Vineyard in the Granite Belt weren't worth moving.

minutes), or by road (three hours), our decision to use the helicopter seems to be the right one, for the morning breaks bright and clear with only a small amount of cloud cover.

Seven Scenes is the largest Sirromet estate vineyard and is in typical rugged Granite Belt country. The total area is over 300 hectares, but only 100 hectares are planted, with two 8-hectare blocks by far the largest, the remainder broken up into 41 blocks. This after massive granite boulders were blown up and removed by bulldozer before planting could commence. The name of the vineyard is well chosen: it does indeed display seven very different scenes or vistas from its hilly contours and valleys. Like much of Queensland, the Granite Belt is in the grip of its worst-ever drought, but while the vineyard is suffering, it is in better condition than one might imagine. The irony is that two of the four periods of rain to yield more than 25 mm since the start of the year have also brought hail, with overall losses likely to be in excess of 20 per cent of the grapes.

DECEMBER 20   BALLANDEAN ESTATE

We are having lunch at Ballandean Estate with Angelo Puglisi. It is a meeting of old friends, for Adam Chapman worked as winemaker at Ballandean Estate between 1991 and 1997, leaving it to join Sirromet, and I have known Angelo for even longer, going back to my days of judging the Small Winemakers Show in Stanthorpe and to the common distribution of Coldstream Hills and Ballandean Estate by Tucker Seabrook. Before lunch we have a remarkable retrospective tasting, going back to the mid-1980s (the 1985 Semillon is one of the stars, with all the character and complexity the Hunter might give a wine of similar age), and then try the legendary 1991 and '93 Late Harvest Sylvaners.

DECEMBER 20   ROBERT CHANNON WINES

Once more into the helicopter and across to Robert Channon Wines, all on its own, due east of Stanthorpe. Robert Channon is an English lawyer who was for many years a partner with one of the leading

Australian law firms, Freehills. If Sirromet doesn't prove the point that there are winemakers in Queensland who are deadly serious about the quality of their wines, and who legitimately aspire to produce wines every bit as good as those to be found 'down south' (Queensland-speak for the other states), then Robert Channon puts the final nail into the coffin, as it were.

Between 1998 and now he has established just under 8 hectares of verdelho, chardonnay, merlot, shiraz and cabernet sauvignon. They are entirely covered with a permanent netting enclosure, which more than doubles the establishment cost per acre. The purpose of the netting is to protect against excessive wind, hail, birds and even kangaroos, but it seems to be having an additional benefit — it is reducing the amount of effective sunlight and slowing the vine growth and ripening process to a certain degree.

You would not find a more immaculately tended vineyard anywhere in Australia, and in a very short space of time the quality of the fruit coming from the vineyard has been vividly demonstrated. Having highly talented South African winemaker Mark Ravenscroft is doubtless also a factor, but in the twelve months since opening the cellar door, Robert Channon Wines has won five trophies, five gold medals, four silver medals and a number of other awards for its wines. Its 2001 and 2002 Verdelhos are the best examples of this variety I have ever tasted.

DECEMBER 21   YARRA VALLEY: THE DROUGHT BITES

I have only been away since Wednesday morning (December 18), but in those three days the valley has turned from green to golden brown in response to continuous temperatures above 30°C. I cannot ever remember such a rapid transformation; I knew the green was only skin deep, but I had no idea the skin was so thin. Some years the valley remains green for the whole twelve months; more often, it turns brown in February, reverting to green when the season breaks and the first rains arrive in April. Losing the green in December is not unprecedented (2000 was such a year), but the speed of the transformation is another story.

RIGHT

The Healesville Sanctuary tells us the lace monitor may be up to fifty years old; it moved on after a month's residence.

However, the outlook for the coming week is temperatures in the low 20s, so in terms of the overall weather for the first three months of the growing season (September to now) the weather has been good.

DECEMBER 22   Yarra Valley

There are times when our house starts to feel like a wildlife sanctuary. The flat roof is home to a lace monitor, a type of goanna; we have been told it is probably fifty years old. It keeps the ceiling free of mice and rats, and shares its house with the possums which Suzanne feeds each night with fruit scraps.

The monitor, our Burmese cat Saras, resident kookaburras and grey currawongs all present threats to the small nesting birds around the house. A blackbird recently constructed a beautiful nest under the eave of our main door in a native vine; I can see part of its incredibly indirect and complicated return to the nest with food for its day-old chicks. It is obviously determined not to lead predators to an easy meal. It is a minor miracle that the eggs have hatched; every time either of us so much as approaches the door from the inside, off the bird whirrs in a flash; ditto on our return.

The distrust of the blackbird is as misplaced as the trust of a quail which took up residence in the garden on the other side of the door, with a rapidly diminishing brood of chicks. She and her two remaining offspring — she had four originally — disappeared one night, my only consolation being the absence of quail feathers in the garden, our house or Saras's mouth.

A grey shrike has a different approach, taking over the wooden box attached to a rafter above the verandah and emblazoned with the name 'Possum Hilton' by Suzanne, who intended it for a small ring-tailed possum and its family. The new use as a nest became obvious when a kookaburra began to sit patiently on the verandah railing, ignoring scraps of meat and staring upwards at the box.

The wedgetailed eagles which live in the hills behind our house cause a great commotion among all the birds — particularly the magpies — on the rare occasions when they come down to what might be called combat level, but it seems to me that they are in the all bark, no bite category.

Crimson rosellas, red-browed finches (which I have always called firetails), bronzewings and turtle doves all contest the various dishes and hanging feeders containing birdseed, so busy squabbling with each other that I doubt they see the eagles. The blackbirds and grey shrikes sometimes forget that they are insectivores and peck at the birdseed if the (rare) opportunity arises.

Wombats, wallabies, kangaroos, feral deer and echidnas are all house visitors — the kangaroos the most common — and all have found the rocky water cascade outside the bathroom. While wary as yet, I suspect they will come to regard it as their own in the hot dry summer days and evenings ahead.

BELOW

Christmas lunch.

DECEMBER 25   CHRISTMAS DAY

I finally found time yesterday to drive into Melbourne and do my Christmas shopping, primarily for Suzanne. Heroically, she has done the remainder for the many relatives who migrate to our house for Christmas Day, some staying overnight for Boxing Day, a few longer still.

Suzanne's sister Robyn, husband Tom, their daughter Ali (completing a PhD at Melbourne University) and son Nick (an apprentice chef when he isn't surfing) live in Melbourne. They are always present for Christmas, the children sometimes with partners. Suzanne's brother Andrew (a pilot) and Swiss-born wife Bea (Beatrice) live in Cairns, but always come down with their exceptionally beautiful daughters Nina and Isabelle, who, with homespun Australian humour, are known as 'the ugly sisters'. Their beauty — to which they are, miraculously, seemingly oblivious — is matched by their intelligence.

My thirty-three-year-old daughter Caroline (an editor at Nine MSN) and her husband Will (a senior executive with SBS) both live in Sydney and have to juggle competing demands from Will's family in that city, Caroline's mother Liz who lives in Tewantin, Queensland, and us here in the Yarra Valley.

My thirty-one-year-old son Angus (who, like Ali, is reaching the end of a PhD degree, at Southern Cross University's Lismore campus) and his wife Michelle are likewise subjected to a three-way tug of war.

Regardless of who or how many attend, a long lunch is a feature of the day, after a protracted unwrapping of Christmas presents under a highly decorated Christmas tree, ever-changing from one year to the next. Suzanne is a highly skilled cook and, partly through her position as founder of the 120-plus producers of the Yarra Valley Food Group, only ever uses the best and freshest products.

A whole leg of ham on the bone, cold smoked salmon from Mohr (alas, the last, for Mohr has decided the business is too competitive), free-range Yarra Valley chicken, platter upon platter of vegetables, and bread from Babka, a specialist bakery in Melbourne, make up the bulk of the food on the table. Oh, and yes, there is plenty of champagne before the meal, and unlimited white and red wine during, particularly for those staying the night. Some elect to take a long afternoon walk around the vineyard and its surrounds, others to sleep. My lips are sealed as to the identity of the respective sleepers and walkers.

DECEMBER 27–30   YARRA VALLEY: THE HOLIDAY PERIOD

I treasure these days, and the week or more either side; not having to get into the car and drive to the airport brings an enormous sense of relief. It is as if I am on holiday, even though it is a productive time in terms of wine writing. The telephone seldom rings, the fax is silent and the emails are never urgent.

It also enables me to indulge in watching sport on television, or even to spend Boxing Day at the Melbourne Cricket Ground. I try to keep these vices hidden, but I am happy to regard two flies crawling up a wall as a sporting contest of interest, provided I am sure the flies have their mind on the job. Being Sydney-born and bred, I understand all codes of football (these days even footie, as Australian Rules is called) and have loved cricket since I was a small boy.

DECEMBER 31   YEAR'S END

Today is Suzanne's and my wedding anniversary. She chose the date for the wedding eighteen years ago so I would not forget it. I don't, but from time to time I do lose track of the years.

Suzanne has been my partner in many ways. We worked equally hard to establish Coldstream Hills back in 1985, to nurture it through to its status as a small public company in early 1988, and sustain it as it struggled in the 1989–92 recession.

The property we acquired in 1985 had the house in which we now live, but no vines, so establishing the original 5 hectares of vineyard in the Amphitheatre and on what we today call House Block Chardonnay was a priority. But we also set about major changes both inside and outside the house, and Suzanne was the catalyst for these. When we purchased it, the fawn brick of its walls (both exterior and interior) and interior curves, most unrelated to the external shell, were features we felt we could do without. There were vast expanses of concrete under the front of the house (which came in very useful) but even larger expanses at the rear and further up the hill.

WINE ODYSSEY

ABOVE
View to the house in 1985; no vines.

Once the concrete ended, there were piles of broken bricks and rubble left over from the construction of the house around ten years earlier. The house itself stood out like a beacon high up the hillside; indeed, in 1983 we had taken Caroline and Angus on a drive up and down 'the big dipper', the dead-end of the southern extremity of Maddens Lane from which you access the house by another steep dirt road. We were hoping to share in the breathtaking views we knew the house must have, but were disappointed. Little did we guess that in two years' time the place would become our home.

With the aid of our next-door neighbour and treasured builder, Les Skate, the interior of the house was transformed: most of the curves went, the fawn brick interior wall facings were concrete bagged and an entirely new kitchen was installed, all under the exacting supervision (and design) of Suzanne. The basic shape of the house is a half-moon on a cantilevered slab facing out to the expanses of the Yarra Valley and its encircling hills. Only one front room did not have floor-to-ceiling glass then — the kitchen, one of the most-used rooms in any house. It now does.

We also began planting trees and shrubs, and creating a garden at the front of the house where there was none previously. The shady rear was planted with tree ferns and smaller ferns, tan bark covered unwanted concrete, and a circular concrete courtyard was transformed by Suzanne, with planter boxes around the perimeter and paving bricks laid in a circular pattern.

The biggest change was to render the outside of the house with a proprietary mix of coloured material, in our case dark green. Once again, it was Suzanne who noticed a building on the Maroondah Highway which hadn't changed colour for years and tracked down the supplier. Over fifteen years later, the finish is much the same as the day it went on.

By utilising the concrete area underneath the house — a de facto four-car garage — and filling in the spaces between the supporting columns for the concrete slab on which the house sits, I was able to create an instant and large cellar. The double skin of bricks, with insulation between the two, creates a stable temperature environment.

Three years ago, it became appropriate for me to set up my own office separate from the winery. Once again, it was Suzanne's lateral thinking and design ability which led to the utilisation of the remaining section of the downstairs concrete slab, more floor-to-ceiling plate glass and coir matting on the floor. In the twinkling of an eye, and at minimal cost, an office was established which easily

LEFT

Galvanised weldmesh racks in my cellar.

accommodates Paula, Beth, myself and all appurtenances. To look at it, you would assume it was part of the original design.

It was facilitated by the prior extension of the upstairs concrete verandah which runs along most of the length of the house. Sitting on that verandah in summer evenings is, and always will be, a special experience. The Maroondah Highway is over 5 kilometres away and there is no traffic noise from that source. We are around the corner of the hill and higher than the winery, while there is only bush behind us. We can see the Warramate and Yarra Yering wineries and houses in front of us — they are the closest neighbours other than the largely hidden Coldstream Hills cellar door — but they are sufficiently far away and down the valley that we cannot hear (or see) movement there. So it is that the solitude is absolute: we have only the calls of birds, the chirping of crickets, and (it must be admitted) the summer buzz of mosquitoes to punctuate the silence. As the darkness falls, the bark of a distant dog and the disgruntled bellow of a steer might come echoing up the hillside, but we auto-filter them out.

Until the eucalypts we planted grew tall, we could see the outline of Melbourne's Collins Place and Rialto Towers — in which I worked as a lawyer between 1985 and 1988 — to our extreme left (or west). As I sat in my office in town, I knew that if I had a telescope I would be able to see our home and vineyard. We look straight out to the north over the broadest part of the valley to Dixons Creek and the hills behind, while to the east the hills are both larger and closer, with Mount St Leonards the highest.

In the seeming peace and quiet, it is easy to forget the frenetic rate of growth and change in the Australian wine industry since 1985, the year we arrived here. In 1984–85, Australia imported 13.1 million litres of wine, and exported only 8.7 million litres. In 2001–02, the country imported 14.4 million litres, a negligible increase over the intervening seventeen years. But exports had soared to 77.6 million litres by 1991–92 and to 417.2 million litres by 2001–02. The increase in value has been equally dramatic: from $20.5 million in 1984–85 to $2 billion in 2001–02 (and $2.4 billion in the twelve months to March 2003).

Grapevine plantings were initially slow to react; it was not until 1995 that the 72.9 million hectares exceeded the 69.7 million hectares of 1980. But in the ensuing seven years to 2002, plantings have soared to 158.5 million hectares.

In 1985, Australia barely registered in the world scene as a producer, and its exports were so tiny it did not appear in any of the official international statistics. Today, Australia is fifth in the world in terms of wine production, and probably third behind France and Italy in the export stakes (in both instances by value rather than volume).

These enormous changes have inevitably been reflected in the growth of the Yarra Valley. It was a major viticultural region in the last forty years of the nineteenth century, its vignerons largely Swiss, but also including Dame Nellie Melba's father, David Mitchell. The Swiss connection came through Charles La Trobe's wife, who was born and raised in Neuchatel. The de Castella, de Pury and Deschamps families were leaders: the de Castellas as growers and viticultural consultants (and ultimately gave birth to Robert de Castella); while Baron Guillaume de Pury built the three-storey Yeringberg winery still used by his grandson Guill de Pury and his family. But by 1920, the last vines of Yeringberg and David Mitchell (who had purchased St Huberts, founded by Hubert de Castella, and who had also planted a substantial vineyard at Coldstream on the slopes leading down to the present-day airfield) were uprooted, and winemaking ceased for half a century. The cause was not, as many people assumed, the vine louse phylloxera which devastated both Europe and much of the rest of Victoria, but simple economics. In de Castella's scornful words, 'the Yarra Valley fell to the cow', as a proposed state-funded cooperative winery became a dairy instead.

Federation ended protective state tariffs, and by the early 1900s viticulture had been profoundly changed by the establishment of high-yielding irrigated vineyards along the Murray River, and by 1913 at Griffith on the Murrumbidgee River. Market tastes, both in Australia and the United Kingdom, were for the cheap sherries and ports which these regions produced so readily. On the other side, the market for fine, cool-climate table wines, which had been so successful in the nineteenth century, disappeared.

WINE ODYSSEY

In the second half of the 1960s and early '70s (just as I was establishing Brokenwood in the Hunter Valley), vineyards returned to the Yarra Valley. Establishment dates are tricky things (is it the year the property was purchased, or the vines planted, of the first crop, or the first wine made, or the first wine released?) and are also the cause of much dissent and angst between those contending for pride of place, but between 1963 and 1971, Wantirna Estate, St Huberts, Kellybrook, Fergussons, Chateau Yarrinya (now De Bortoli), Yarra Yering, Yeringberg, Warramate and Mount Mary were all taking shape.

By 1985 there were 16 wineries; today the figure is 89. In the last twelve months alone, 17 new wineries have opened for business, so by 2004 the number will exceed 100. At first blush, exciting stuff, particularly given the international reputation the Yarra Valley has obtained for the quality of its wine, food and tourism.

More large-scale accommodation and convention-type facilities are badly needed. Because of its proximity to Melbourne (one hour from the CBD, 20–30 minutes from the wealthy eastern suburbs) tourism here has revolved around day trips, so the options for dinner are very limited. There is plenty of bed and breakfast accommodation, and small restaurants scattered around the many

BELOW
View from the house in 1985, before the vines.

284

ABOVE
View from the house in later years, with vines.

little towns and settlements within the greater Yarra Valley are numerous. Most, however, are decidedly rustic, and are seldom found by tourists.

The similarities with the Napa Valley or the Hunter Valley in the 1960s and '70s are all too clear. Change will continue to come rapidly, and the planning authorities within the Shire of Yarra Ranges are going to need both a crystal ball and the wisdom of Solomon if they are to get the balance right. The Napa Valley has long since gone over the top, and is suffering from self-asphyxiation as it struggles to deal with the never-ending stream of tourists jamming roads, restaurants and accommodation alike. Nor can the once unspoilt Hunter Valley claim any particular virtue, when developments such as that on the corner of McDonalds and Broke Roads — known by locals as 'Little Kosovo' — are allowed.

There are in-built checks in the Yarra Valley planning scheme which should allow the right balance to be struck. But the sheer physical beauty of the Yarra Valley and its proximity to such a large city as Melbourne make it at once a unique jewel and a very tempting target. It is something which Suzanne, who is centrally involved in promoting the natural produce of the valley (as opposed to just grapes), is as aware of as am I. Living up here in our hillside house with its panoramic views means we see every change, big or small, in the landscape.

Our view is an ever-changing display of light, colour and shape; we can see the sun shining in one part of the valley and rain drenching another part at precisely the same time. One of the most beautiful displays comes in those late afternoons when there is cloud cover over the valley but the setting sun in the west breaks free of the clouds and sends its rays up the valley, creating an incandescent light one might expect from a giant movie set.

Then there are the variations of the passing seasons. The spring growth of the vines is lime green, the small shoots giving the rows a military precision unequalled at any other time of the year — except, perhaps, in winter. Summer sees the vines at their luxuriant best, and as summer progresses, their deep green increasingly contrasts with the golden grass of the grazing properties which still abound in the area.

Autumn has my vote as the most beautiful time of year, particularly early in the morning. Fairyfloss skeins of mist rise off the many dams, entwining themselves around tall tees and buildings and filling the hollows, then lifting as a veil before the approach of the rising sun. Sometimes the entire valley is filled with fog, but we are always above it, much like an aeroplane above clouds. As it finally lifts, we will be briefly immersed, but then the sun breaks through, leaving diamond droplets on trees, vines and spider webs. Some years there is a vivid display of yellows, golds and reds by the vines, especially if there is plenty of moisture in the ground. In the drought years, the end comes quickly: the leaves go straight from green to brown, dropping off before they have a chance to change colour.

Winter has its own special qualities. If it's raining and cold (which it is supposed to be) there is not much solace beyond the large fireplace in our combined living and dining room. But rose-coloured dawns, suffusing fog and sky alike, can bring contentment on the coldest of days. Flowers, too, bloom in unexpected ways and places, and the sense of urgency which is part and parcel of the vigneron's life during the other three seasons is much reduced.